Beyond the Fence

A Culinary View of Historic Lexington

**Published by Central Baptist Hospital Foundation Cancer Program
Lexington, KY**

To obtain additional copies of *Beyond the Fence: A Culinary View of Historic Lexington* or for more information about the Central Baptist Hospital Cancer Program please contact:

Central Baptist Hospital / Beyond the Fence
1740 Nicholasville Road
Lexington, KY 40503
859-260-6105
859-260-6117 (fax)
e-mail: cbhbeyondthefencecookbook@bhsi.com
www.beyondthefencecookbook.com

ISBN: 978-0-9843148-0-5

First Printing   8,000 copies   2010
Second Printing   10,000 copies   2010

Photographs, except where specifically-credited, copyright © Marc Manning

Cover Image: Three Chimneys Farm
Back Cover Image: Elmendorf Farm
Title Page Image: WinStar Farm

WIMMER
COOKBOOKS

A CONSOLIDATED GRAPHICS COMPANY

800.548.2537 wimmerco.com

Preface

"The Bluegrass Region of Kentucky, land set apart
by geographers, historians, and the folkways of its inhabitants...
is likewise a state of mind...and a satisfactory way of life."

Kentucky's Historian Laureate for Life, Dr. Thomas D. Clark (1903-2005)

Millions of visitors from around the world visit the Bluegrass Region of Central Kentucky, journey through tree-canopied landscapes and marvel at manicured pastures bordered by miles of historic rock and modern plank fencing, safeguards of the area's signature industry, the horse. Surrounded by treasured icons of its heritage, Lexington, Kentucky's second largest city, is the geographic, economic, and cultural center of the Bluegrass. The area's historic districts, framed by aged ornamental iron and elaborately-embellished entryways, showcase classic architecture and distinctive landmarks, cherished symbols of rich Bluegrass tradition.

This exceptional landscape, widely known and admired as nature's finest parkland, is a blend of natural and cultural splendor. An exceptional contribution to Bluegrass renown is the warm hospitality extended by its residents... at the core of that hospitality is the tradition of preparing and sharing good food.

Beyond the Fence: A Culinary View of Historic Lexington affords a seasonal tour beyond the classic stone, plank, and iron fences of the Bluegrass. Pressed between historical vignettes and exquisite images, this book presents tested recipes offered by the Region's finest culinarians and restaurateurs, features foods and menus that blend Bluegrass heritage and modern techniques, and offers glimpses inside some of the area's most enduring gathering places.

Fayette County's Lexington is a city upholding a unique sense of community born of a respect for the legacy of those who came before and an appreciation for those who create its contemporary culture. With a desire to support citizens in need, the Central Baptist Hospital Cancer Program organized this worthwhile community project. The subject is exceptional, the cause is imminently worthy, and the honor is ours in presenting *Beyond the Fence: A Culinary View of Historic Lexington*.

Beyond The Fence Committee

Foreword

Central Baptist Hospital in Lexington, Kentucky, has provided healthcare to the people of Central Kentucky since 1954. What began as a 173-bed community hospital is now a 383-bed major regional referral center. The most preferred hospital in Lexington, Central Baptist Hospital offers the latest medical advances in an environment of compassion. Like the community of Lexington, Central Baptist prides itself on a rich history built on a foundation of faith and family, stewardship for the gifts with which we have been entrusted, and a progressive vision.

As a part of Baptist Healthcare System of Kentucky, Central Baptist has remained a community based, not-for-profit hospital. The Cancer Care Center was established at Central Baptist Hospital in 1990. Today, nearly one out of every ten individuals diagnosed with cancer in the state of Kentucky are diagnosed and/or treated at Central Baptist. Each year, over 10,000 cancer survivors use the services of Central Baptist Hospital Cancer Care Center in their fight against cancer.

The physicians and staff of Central Baptist Hospital aggressively pursue both knowledge and opportunities to serve individuals and families who face cancer. Their commitment to excellence and service remains at the heart of our cancer program. Our services include programs for wellness, cancer prevention, screening and early diagnosis, genetics, nutrition, patient navigation, clinical research, minimally invasive surgery, the most advanced targeted radiation and chemotherapy treatments, home health, palliative care, patient education, support, and survivorship. Our leadership goal is to anticipate, recognize and meet the needs of those we serve with a state-of-the-art solution.

The publication of this cookbook, *Beyond the Fence: A Culinary View of Historic Lexington*, is an endeavor to provide funding in order for the Central Baptist Cancer Care Center to continue the tradition of exceptional, compassionate service for those touched by cancer. All funds raised through the proceeds of this cookbook will support the mission of the Cancer Care Center. We thank you for helping us in our efforts.

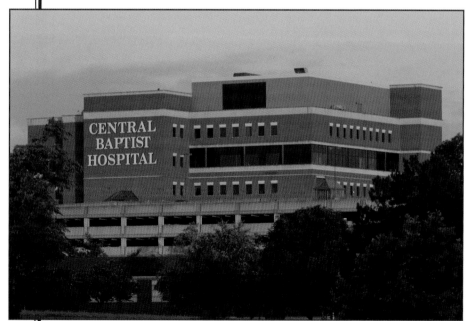

Working Together....

Beyond the Fence:
A Culinary View of Historic Lexington

*Our sincere gratitude is given to the following individuals and
organizations that have generously supported the efforts of this project.*

Winners Circle
$50,000

Central Baptist Hospital Auxiliary

Finish Line
$10,000-$19,999

Brett Construction Company
In Honor of Bill and Eunice Hall

Central Baptist Hospital

Central Baptist Hospital Foundation

Central Baptist Hospital Medical Staff

Jarboe Construction Company
Ben Jarboe — Jim Tudor

Top of the Stretch
$1,000-$9,999

Dr. and Mrs. Alan Beckman

Dr. Hope Cottrill

Crothall Healthcare
Val Emery

Dr. and Mrs. Elvis Donaldson

Dr. and Mrs. Russsell Eldridge

Marta and John Hayne

Patty and James Mason

Meridian Partners, LLC
*Robert Locker — Mark Shepherd
Hameed Koury — Owen Barnes*

RTB, LLC
*Robert and Dewey Locker
Reagan and Kelly Taylor*

Edward A. Receski

Kay and Rodney Ross

Mrs. Betty Gifford Simms

Dr. and Mrs. Peter Tate

Mr. and Mrs. Timothy E.N. Terry

Starting Gate
$0-$999

Central Baptist Hospital Radiation Oncology / Cyberknife

Paula and Anthony J. Tillman

Introduction

The Commonwealth of Kentucky is blessed with distinct physiographic regions. The Bluegrass Region encompasses the central portion of the state, with seven counties of the Inner Bluegrass known as the heart and Lexington the heartbeat. Extending north to the Ohio River and south into the center of the Commonwealth, this emerald plateau is bordered by the Ohio River on the north and west and the Knobs, a twisted series of sugar-loaf mountains, on the east and south.

The Commonwealth's second largest city in its earlier cultural history was christened the 'Athens of the West,' and in modern marketing is branded the 'Horse Capital of the World.' How did this expanse of lush canebrake and crystal springs fiercely protected by bands of inhospitable natives mature into the "Athens of the West," heart of the Bluegrass?

✦ History and Heritage ✦

"But Lexington will ever be,
The Loveliest and the Best;
A Paradise thou'rt still to me,
Sweet Athens of the West."

William McConnell and his fellow frontiersmen established a campsite in the area of McConnell Springs in the year 1775. Hearing news of the first shot fired in the Revolutionary War, they christened the frontier town 'Lexington.' Fayette County later assumed its present boundaries and was named in honor of the Revolutionary War hero, General Marquis de Lafayette. Although threats and peril existed on the frontier, settlers were lured by generous Virginia land grants and the natural offerings of the Inner Bluegrass... deep fertile soil, abundant supply of clear water, and expansive plateaus suitable for pasturing livestock.

Lexington grew rapidly and due to the influence of culture and higher learning was known as the Athens of the West. Transylvania University, established in 1780, became the first college west of the Allegheny Mountains, established the first medical school, an early law school, and educated many of history's notable citizens. By the second decade of the nineteenth century, Lexington had become one of the largest and most cultured cities west of the Alleghenies, ...educationally, politically, professionally, and artistically. The Agricultural and Mechanical College, offering classes in 1865 on Henry Clay's Fayette County estate, evolved into the University of Kentucky, one of the Commonwealth's land grant universities.

Envision a city surrounded by one of nature's finest parklands of magnificent farms and natural splendor. Fayette County encompasses 283 square miles strategically located at the intersection of Interstates 64 and 75, with a population in excess of 282,000 citizens. Governed by the Lexington-Fayette Urban County

Government, modern Lexington's diversified economy includes universities, industry, restaurants, retail, arts and cultural organizations. Bluegrass icons including historic homes, public house museums, and public parks illustrate Lexington and Fayette County's architectural distinction. Sports venues, Keeneland Race Course, The Kentucky Horse Park, Red Mile, and scores of attractions contribute to a strong tourist market and a satisfying way of life.

⚜ Land, Limestone, and Bluegrass ⚜

*"The Bluegrass of Kentucky is one of the rural areas in the United States
where the community value of the land often is the equal of its intrinsic value."*

The Kentucky, Thomas Clark

From the earliest days, the natural wealth of the Inner Bluegrass Region determined land usage and lured settlers to the new frontier. Hunters observed large herds of grazing mammals and flocks of fowl, indicating a rich environment for livestock culture. Declaring the region a 'second paradise,' surveyors and explorers established towns near clear limestone springs, and entrepreneurs located mills along flowing creeks and rivers in order to power grain operations.

Kentucky's topography and climate contributed to mixed farming on the English scale—grain farming and orchard culture, as well as lavish livestock production...mules, cattle, goats, swine, and chickens. The area's long growing season, adequate rainfall, and generally moderate winter contributed to the Bluegrass reputation as a 'land flowing with milk and honey.'

Natural foundation for a profitable livestock industry is the Region's bedrock, deep deposits of limestone that impart to soil and water calcium-rich properties, contributing to animals' strong bones and efficient growth. Early settlers noted that a quick-growing perennial grass thrived on this base and flourished in the warm sun and humid conditions. Its introduction to the area has been the subject of much conjecture, but as the native canebrake and timber were cleared, bluegrass replaced wilderness with expanses of emerald pastures. *Poa pratensis* is a robust, protein-rich grass of which there are fifty or more varieties. Known as June grass in the eastern United States, its delicate blue flowers appearing in early spring inspired the name for the Bluegrass Region. Prime pastures and natural limestone water sources led early horsemen to introduce blooded livestock from the colonies and Europe, creating what has become the world's largest equine nursery.

Throughout the history of the Bluegrass, farmers have exhibited a strong economic and cultural influence, beginning with Henry Clay, nineteenth-century Kentucky statesman and progressive Fayette County land owner, who along with his contemporaries, syndicated the area's first Thoroughbreds and imported livestock from Europe. Upholding the heritage and traditions of the Region are generations of Kentucky farm families, and individuals of diverse ethnicities and cultures. The influence of equine enthusiasts seeking an interest in the Horse Capital of the World — natives of Europe, Dubai, Ireland, Canada and scores of foreign countries — has strengthened the reputation of the Bluegrass as a great melting pot of tradition and innovation.

In the Lexington area the world's most celebrated horses are bred, foaled, registered, trained, bought and sold, raced, retired, and immortalized. In addition, a strong general economy of cattle, grain, fruit and vegetable farms contribute to a well-diversified agricultural economy. Fayette County ranks among the leaders of Kentucky's 120 counties in farm production, generating in excess of $500 million in annual agricultural sales (2007) and creating thousands of jobs. Capitalizing on the lure of Central Kentucky's horse country, in recent years agritourism has infused as much as $1 billion into the local economy.

♣ Inside the Fence ♣

The horse farm with its manicured landscape has become the area's signature industry and internationally-recognized symbol of Kentucky. Complementing impressive farm entrances, world-class barns and homes, signature color schemes, and a panoramic parkland of manicured paddocks is the fence, one of the most essential elements of the equine environment. Humble split-rail, historic dry stack stone, miles of oak plank, woven wire, and elaborate wrought iron outlining Lexington's historic districts…the fence has evolved throughout history into a hallmark of the Bluegrass Region.

Framing the Bluegrass, the fence protects the Region's signature industry, the horse. Dr. Thomas Clark noted that from the very beginning of Kentucky's settlement the horse was an extremely durable pioneer, vital to resisting Indian raids, breaking new ground, and providing transportation throughout the frontier. In fact, as settlers established Harrods Town, Boonesboro, and Bryan's Station, Lexington's 1789 horse population numbered 9,607, compared to 9,000 people.

In the years following the Revolutionary War, England's great Thoroughbreds, Herod, Matchem, and Eclipse were imported, providing basic bloodlines, and infusing running ability as well as foundation genetics that contributed to the improvement of other equine breeds. The English Thoroughbred, Messenger, was brought to America in 1788 as the foundation sire to be mated with native and Thoroughbred stock, producing the Standardbred or trotter. Third of the light breeds of horse found on Bluegrass farms is the American Saddlebred, a Bluegrass product. The American Thoroughbred, Denmark, foaled in 1830 and matched with Standardbreds and horses of refined gait, provided foundation genetics for the stylish and intelligent three-and five-gaited equine, noted for performance in the show ring.

As early as 1800 the new nation recognized Kentucky for the quality of its equine population, and by 1840 the Commonwealth had earned a sterling reputation in horse breeding. After Civil War battles and raids decimated the Inner Bluegrass horse population, crops and animal herds were rebuilt quickly and reached dimensions unseen in earlier decades. After 1875, Kentucky farmers began breeding horses for a national market, horse barns replaced hemp and grain fields, and the Inner Bluegrass Region began to assume its position as Horse Capital of the World, a distinction it holds today.

Bluegrass Hospitality

"The Blue Grass region of Kentucky is celebrated for the
fertility of its soil, its flocks and blooded stocks, and last, but far from least,
for the hospitality of the people, and their table luxuries."

Out of Kentucky Kitchens, Marion Flexner

Embedded in the fabric that is the rich tapestry of the Bluegrass run the threads of history, heritage, of hospitality and traditions….deep and rich, connecting the past with contemporary lifestyle. History records the presence of silver tea services in pioneer log houses…some of those are treasured in modern area homes as cherished antiques.

The Bluegrass Region is renowned for hospitality, perhaps one of its more notable traditions…visitors are always welcome! The pioneer city was gateway to westward expansion, the center of a growing nation where travel and trade routes brought many influences, cultures, and traditions together. From the early 1800s Lexingtonians welcomed all visitors and exhibited a style of cultured living comparable to the fine cities in the East.

A commemorative writing by Kentucky's Historian Laureate, Thomas Clark: "Men and women of culture laid the foundation of the youthful city. Talented artists and architects planned its gracious homes. Women of charm and men of force and understanding lived in them. Fashions in houses changed with the generations, wealth flowed into the city, and with wealth came expanding public institutions, endowment of libraries, invention, art, poetry and music…the great fertility of the Bluegrass coupled with the industriousness of the pioneers brought about a prosperity and culture still existing in Lexington today."

As illustrated by the great variety of international restaurants in Lexington, the centerpiece of Bluegrass hospitality, its food, has for the past few centuries been influenced by societies around the world. Many traditional dishes were imported by the diverse culture of early settlers who came to the Land of Tomorrow-Kentucke. Since Lexington was a hub for western expansion, other recipes and traditions were brought by traders, planters, and international dignitaries who traveled through the area.

The description of typical Kentucky food would likely resemble the burgoo that originated here. As Marion Flexner, food columnist and author reflected, "All sources combine to create a vast culinary knowledge…a unique blend of many old-world cultures seasoned with native ingenuity, a cross section of American cookery at its best." An illustration: Alice Longworth, daughter of President Theodore Roosevelt, visited Lexington in 1907, and was served champagne and Queen Elizabeth salad, but the official menu also included country ham, beaten biscuits, and barbecued mutton.

Imagine providing the luxurious banquets that were customary in nineteenth century Kentucky without electricity, refrigeration, and a readily-available supply of water. The ingenuity of Bluegrass cooks was legendary. Without refrigeration, fresh eggs were stored in brine or heavy lime water for winter use, and kept for as long as five months. Vanilla, imported from France, and spices and sugar were costly and available on an infrequent basis; sugar arrived once a year via flatboat from New Orleans. Inventive cooks substituted fermented cider, sorghum, and homemade fruit and berry syrups as sweetening.

The area's natural salt licks provided a supply of the precious mineral, so vitally important for preserving meat and game. Salt also provided an indispensable ingredient for fermenting cabbage into sauerkraut, an important source of Vitamin C for the pioneers. Brining and pickling vegetables ..green beans, beets, corn, cucumbers…as well as fermenting fruit and berry vinegars extended the seasonal food source. Smoking added flavor to cured and dried meats. Drying vegetables and fruits provided a winter supply of beans, peas…and seeds for next year's gardens. Green beans strung on slender canes or string and allowed to air dry were known as shucky beans or 'leather britches.' The beans are rehydrated and cooked slowly. Illustrating the traditional and contemporary influences co-existing on local menus are recipes for country green beans cooked slowly with ham hock, and the continental tender-crisp haricots verts…both staples on Bluegrass tables.

⚜ Horse Capital of the World ⚜

Within the Bluegrass, modern culture and economy are blended by the common denominator…love of the horse. The title of Horse Capital of the World is celebrated throughout Lexington and Fayette County on business stationery and street signage. The names of great Thoroughbreds—Citation, Man O' War, Secretariat, John Henry, Big Brown, and Smarty Jones appear throughout the region. Mounted police patrol city streets on horseback, top-hatted drivers enthrall visitors with local lore during carriage rides through Gratz Park, life-sized, artistically-embellished fiberglass horses embellish city intersections. City parks at every corridor honor the horse in bronze statue and the limestone water that has flowed through the bedrock of the region in magnificent fountains. The Fayette County agriculture registry lists farms named in honor of famous equines: Spendthrift, Dixiana, Domino Stud, Hamburg Place, Man O' War, and Fair Play.

Solid as the limestone beneath the Bluegrass is the philosophy of giving back, based on a heritage of caring for those in need and desire to improve quality of life. As early Lexington citizens banded together in the mid 1830s to care for Lexington's cholera epidemic orphans, contemporary citizens participate through hundreds of charitable organizations dedicated to educational needs, human services, and other worthy causes. Equally impressive are the numbers of organizations dedicated to the well being of the horse… the University of Kentucky's Gluck Equine Research Center and a multitude of farms and organizations dedicated to the Thoroughbred in distress or retirement.

Celebrating all that is unique and notable about Lexington and Fayette County, *Beyond the Fence* illustrates the past and present with images and vignettes detailing the area's unique culture, rich history, and traditional icons. Peppered with a measure of timeless recipes, notable neighbors, seasoned characters, and illustrious citizens, the result is a view—beyond the fence—of the incomparable Bluegrass.

TABLE OF CONTENTS

SPRING

MENU

Henry Clay Mint Julep

Citrus Marinated Shrimp with Louis Sauce

Limestone Bibb Lettuce Salad
Fruit and Poppy Seed Dressing

Grilled Bourbon Beef Tenderloin
Henry Bain Sauce

Southern Cheese Grits

Roasted Asparagus with Sesame Seeds

Special Occasion Rolls

Ice Box Lemon Pie

Spring Meet Mint Tea

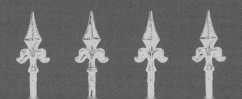

SPRING

"You don't just go to the Derby, you become a part of Derby history."

Kentucky's four distinct seasons afford an opportunity to enjoy the colorful landscapes and seasonal fare of one of nature's most spectacular parklands. As Winter's drab days bow to the lion and lamb of Spring, the Commonwealth awakens in bud and branch. Sleeping fruit orchards burst into brilliant bloom, native Redbud and Dogwood trees punctuate the countryside with welcome splendor, and the blue grass that characterizes the region crowns limestone-enriched pastures with azure haze. Winter's lackluster turf inches into shades of green as the Bluegrass tapestry is magically reborn.

The fresh days of Spring bring a new round of invitations and events, as if all nature and natives are throwing off the coat of winter chill. The Kentucky Horse Park prepares for signature equestrian events of the Rolex Kentucky Three-Day Event. Keeneland's picturesque landscape extends blossoms of white and pink Dogwood, welcoming buyers and racers back to the Commonwealth. April's race meet leads fans and Thoroughbred hopefuls on to Derby Day, the first Saturday in May.

The Kentucky Derby, as the first jewel in the Triple Crown of Thoroughbred horseracing, is followed by the Preakness and Belmont. Louisville's Churchill Downs hosts the Run for the Roses, the oldest consecutively-run horse race in the United States, named for the handmade blanket of red roses presented in the Winner's Circle. The best three-year-old fillies in the world compete in the Kentucky Oaks, an equally historic race that has been run on the Friday before Derby Day since its founding in 1875.

The weeks leading to the first Saturday in May bring visitors from around the world to Kentucky. Coined 'Derby Fever,' the annual rite showcases house parties and events welcoming friends, princes, kings, ambassadors, celebrities, and leaders of the Thoroughbred world to enjoy festive food and entertainment.

Featuring the best offerings of a Kentucky Spring, Derby menus may provide creative twists, but are usually based on the traditional…ham and biscuits, tender shoots of asparagus and early strawberries, Benedictine spread, and fresh green Bibb lettuce. Bread Pudding and bourbon-flavored desserts complete the repast, with a frosty Mint Julep topping the list of required libation.

One Lexington tour boasts: "Louisville has the Race, But Lexington has the Reason." The Horse Capital of the World provides the competitors…bred, born and prepared for the classic 1¼-mile race. On recent Derby days, Lexington's Keeneland has offered a popular venue for celebrating traditional food, race simulcasting, and the parade of Derby attire, planned from year to year by ladies and gentlemen alike… and topped by just the right hat.

Bluegrass Boundaries

During a Kentucky Spring, the signature four-board plank fences appear to monogram Bluegrass pastures, anticipating the arrival of new foals and a fresh new season. 'Plank,' 'four-board,' 'wood' are terms associated with the signature fence of the Region. Nineteenth century horsemen chose the plank fence to replace wooden split rail, providing a more secure boundary for livestock and involving much less labor than construction of the historic rock fence.

The four-board fence is said to have originated because a horse's eyesight is poor and the horizontal boards are readily seen, particularly at night. As early as 1872, the plank fence had become a Bluegrass icon and remains so today. Along area roadways, the sturdy wood fence is often constructed behind rock or stone fences. In the interior of the farm, double-fenced paddocks provide an alleyway for leading stallions into the barn and for protecting the spirited animals from each other.

Mint Julep

" A mint julep is not a product of a formula. It is a ceremony
and must be performed by a gentleman possessing a true sense of the artistic,
a deep reverence for the ingredients and a proper appreciation of the occasion."

~ Lt. Gen. S.B. Buckner, Jr., 1937

In 1792 Kentucky, a 'julap' might have been taken by adults and children upon arising, considered a healthful way to combat fevers brought by night air and hot climates. Early English concoctions were nonalcoholic, medicinal syrups, but by mid-eighteenth century many contained spirits.

An early connoisseur of fine bourbon, nineteenth-century Kentucky statesman and Senator Henry Clay is credited with introducing the julep to Washington Society at the Willard Hotel, and it has been a Kentucky Derby fixture since.

As with most traditions, recipes vary regarding whether the mint should be bruised or muddled, the sweetener simple syrup or granular sugar, the bourbon stirred or slowly swirled, served in a silver julep cup or a commemorative glass. Common denominators however, are crushed or snow ice, a straw, and mint sprig garnish, preferably Kentucky Colonel Spearmint….and the admonition that the libation be sipped slowly.

As Henry Clay vociferously defended the proper Mint Julep recipe during his tenure in Washington,

the controversy was later illustrated by humorist, Irvin S. Cobb in his 1936 Recipe Book *"…well, down our way we've always had a theory that the Civil War was not brought on by Secession or Slavery or the State's Rights issue. These matters contributed to the quarrel, but there is a deeper reason. It was brought on by some Yankee coming down south and putting nutmeg in a julep. So our folks just up and left the Union flat."*

Lemon Champagne Punch

4   (6 ounce) cans frozen concentrated lemonade, partially thawed

4   (6 ounce) cans frozen pineapple juice, partially thawed

1½   quarts cold water

2   quarts ginger ale, chilled

1   quart sparkling water

1   (750 ml) bottle dry champagne, chilled

Mix lemonade, pineapple juice and water. Chill until serving time. Prior to serving, add ginger ale and sparkling water, stirring, in a large punch bowl. Pour chilled champagne over all and serve.

Serves 50

Spring Meet Mint Tea

1   quart boiling water

2   quart-size tea bags

¾   cup packed fresh mint leaves

1   cup sugar

¼   cup plus 2 tablespoons fresh lemon juice

1   quart cold water

Garnish: fresh mint sprigs

Pour boiling water over tea bags and ¾ cup mint leaves in a teapot or saucepan; cover and steep 5 to 10 minutes. Remove and discard tea bags and mint. Add sugar and lemon juice, stirring until sugar dissolves. Stir in cold water. Serve over ice. Garnish with mint sprigs.

Makes 2 quarts

Henry Clay's 19th Century Mint Julep Recipe

The mint leaves, fresh and tender, should be pressed against a coin-silver goblet with the back of a silver spoon. Only bruise the leaves gently and then remove them from the goblet. Half fill with cracked ice. Mellow bourbon, aged in oaken barrels, is poured from the jigger and allowed to slide slowly through the cracked ice.

In another receptacle, granulated sugar is slowly mixed into chilled limestone water to make a silvery mixture as smooth as some rare Egyptian oil, then poured on top of the ice. While beads of moisture gather on the burnished exterior of the silver goblet, garnish the brim of the goblet with the choicest sprigs of mint.

Courtesy Ashland: The Henry Clay Estate

Ashland: The Henry Clay Estate

*"At home in Lexington, he was revered
as a leading lawyer and gentleman farmer."*

Lexington's Henry Clay wrote in 1849, "… I occupy as good a farm as any that he (Moses) would have found, if he had reached it; and it has been acquired not by hereditary descent, but by my own labor."

A one-room law office stands today on Lexington's Mill Street, once home to the Great Compromiser and Sage of the West. From here the 'Kentucky gentleman' launched a career that brought him fame and fortune in national politics. Henry Clay (1777-1852), early nineteenth-century statesman, famous orator, U.S. Senator, Speaker of the House, Secretary of State, and three-time Presidential candidate was also an innovative Lexington, Kentucky farmer. Along with his wife, Lucretia, who managed the farm, Henry Clay introduced innovative farming practices and European breeds of livestock to Kentucky during the nineteenth century.

According to Ashland: "the Clay Estate occupied as many as 600 acres, where he raised fine thoroughbred horses… The landscape engineer who designed Washington, D.C. planned the landscaping at Ashland, purportedly using every Kentucky indigenous tree and shrub, including majestic Ash trees…thus, 'Ashland.' At home in the Bluegrass, Henry Clay was revered as a leading lawyer and gentleman farmer."

Today the original Ashland estate has been replaced by communities at Richmond and Sycamore Road, including Ashland Park and Shriner's Hospital. Ashland, The Henry Clay Estate listed on the National Register of Historic Places, has been open to the public as a museum house

since 1950. The 18-room mansion, constructed in sections by Clay, his son, and granddaughter, is available for public tours. The Ginkgo Tree Café shares the shade of historic trees with the formal garden and outbuildings. Safeguarded by handsome decorative iron gates, Ashland's garden has been expertly cared for by the Garden Club of Lexington, Inc. since 1950.

Cinnamon Puffs

PHIL DUNN, *Chef*

⅓	cup unsalted butter, softened	¼	teaspoon salt
1	cup sugar, divided	¼	teaspoon ground nutmeg
1	large egg	½	cup milk
1½	cups all-purpose flour	1	teaspoon ground cinnamon
1½	teaspoons baking powder	1	cup butter, melted

Preheat oven to 350 degrees. Place butter, ½ cup sugar and egg in food processor. Mix until smooth. Add flour, baking powder, salt, nutmeg and milk. Process until smooth, scraping sides often. Fill greased mini muffin pans ⅔ full. Bake 20 to 25 minutes until golden brown. Combine remaining sugar and cinnamon. Dip baked puffs in melted butter and roll in cinnamon sugar.

Makes 30 puffs

Veggie Frittata

1	large red bell pepper, chopped	7	large eggs, lightly beaten
1	cup sliced fresh mushrooms	½	cup mayonnaise
1½	cups (6 ounces) shredded Swiss cheese, divided	¾	teaspoon salt
		2	tablespoons chopped fresh basil
¼	pound asparagus, cut into 1-inch pieces	½	teaspoon black pepper

Preheat oven to 375 degrees. Layer bell pepper, mushrooms and half of cheese in a lightly greased 9½-inch, deep dish pie plate. Top with asparagus and remaining cheese. Combine eggs, mayonnaise, salt, basil and black pepper; pour evenly over cheese. Bake 35 minutes or until a knife inserted in center comes out clean. Let stand 5 minutes before serving. Serve warm.

Serves 6-8

Governor's Derby Breakfast

After partying late into the evening, many revelers rise early on Derby Day to accept the Governor's invitation to breakfast. Since the 1930s, the Commonwealth's chief executive has hosted the Governor's Derby Breakfast on the state capitol grounds, entertaining thousands with a traditional breakfast and gala festivities. A typical grocery list: 2,080 pounds of country ham, 15,000 biscuits, 10,000 servings of juice, 25,000 eggs, 1,200 pounds of sausage, 60 bushels of apples, 15,000 cups of coffee and 15,000 servings of cheese grits. Uniquely Kentucky!

Lexington Cemetery

More than a gateway, the monumental stone entrance to Lexington Cemetery is flanked by handsome iron pedestrian gates, and inscribed "Lexington Cemetery, Organized 1849." Termed Lexington's "garden of history," the final resting place of some of the city's most notable citizens also provides a majestic sanctuary for visitors. Prompted by the cholera epidemics of the mid-nineteenth century, a group of prominent Lexingtonians purchased Boswell's Woods, a forty-acre tract of land on the city's edge. As the pioneer "first hill" and early churches' private cemeteries were filled, the need for a more modern burial ground was realized, thus the founders promoted the idea of a welcoming garden cemetery.

Since 1849, more than 60,000 people have been interred in the park-like gardens, including Henry Clay; Adolph Rupp, Kentucky's acclaimed basketball coach; David A. Sayre, cemetery incorporator; and seven Civil War generals representing both sides of the conflict.

Sprinkled with thousands of tulips in the spring, the natural beauty of this land only increases through the seasons as 170 acres of pristine Bluegrass, secluded with ponds and gardens, become a picturesque sanctuary. The Lexington Cemetery is a natural haven for animals, 100 recorded species of birds, and is anchored by more than 200 species of trees.

This nationally-known arboretum is adorned by hundreds of artistic and historical shrines. Most noted is the staggering 120-foot monument dedicated to Henry Clay. The impressive Corinthian-columned statue made from native Kentucky limestone, was erected in 1857 five years after Clay's death, at a cost of $50,000, a sum that translates to more than $1 million dollars in today's currency.

Stuffed Berry French Toast

1	stick butter	1	teaspoon ground cinnamon
1	loaf Texas toast	⅛	teaspoon almond extract
6	large eggs, beaten	1	(8 ounce) package cream cheese
1½	cups whole milk	1	jar red raspberry preserves
¾	teaspoon vanilla extract		Garnish: powdered sugar

In a large bowl beat together eggs, milk, vanilla, cinnamon and almond extract. Dip bread into egg mixture, coating both sides. In an electric skillet, cook bread for 2 to 3 minutes on both sides in a small amount of butter until golden brown.

Place one piece of cooked toast on cookie sheet and spread with 1 tablespoon cream cheese. Place another piece of cooked toast on cookie sheet and spread with 1 to 2 teaspoons raspberry preserves. Stack the 2 pieces of toast together so that the cream cheese and preserves are in the middle. As French toast is being prepared, can hold in a 200 degree warm oven for 10 to 15 minutes until entire batch is made.

Cut diagonally and sprinkle with powdered sugar to garnish. Serve warm.

Blackberry or blueberry preserves may be used in place of red raspberry preserves.

Serves 4-6

Keeneland's Track Kitchen... Bluegrass Breakfast Secret

Only in the Horse Capital of the World do early risers have an opportunity to watch horses conduct their dawn workouts, and then enjoy breakfast at the Track Kitchen with jockeys, trainers, owners, and businessmen. Keeneland is one of the few tracks that allows visitors in the barn and paddock areas...and then offers them breakfast. Open from 6:00-11:00 a.m. seven days a week, year round, Turf Catering's Track Kitchen buffet features a hearty breakfast of bacon, eggs, sausage, biscuits, country gravy, potatoes, grits, and cereal. And that earthy barn aroma may just be from the boots of the exercise rider sitting at the next table!

Rolex Kentucky Three-Day Event
RK3DE

For more than 25 years, the Horse Park has hosted the Rolex Kentucky Three Day Event, which crowns world champions in eight equestrian disciplines, including dressage, cross country, and jumping. The world's best horses and riders compete annually for prize money, a Rolex timepiece, the classic Kentucky Julep Cup, and an opportunity to compete in the $350,000 Rolex Grand Slam of Eventing. Organized by Equestrian Events, Inc., the event draws 100,000 spectators and is telecast around the globe. Every Spring the Kentucky Horse Park is transformed into an international fair featuring equine and food vendors and world-class athletes.

Citrus-Marinated Shrimp with Louis Sauce

2	cups fresh orange juice		1	lime, sliced
2	cups grapefruit juice		1	grapefruit, sliced
2	cups pineapple juice		1	teaspoon dried, crushed red pepper
½	cup fresh lemon juice		4	pounds large fresh shrimp, peeled, deveined and cooked (thawed frozen shrimp may be used)
½	cup fresh lime juice			
1	lemon, sliced			Lettuce leaves
1	orange, sliced			Louis Sauce

Combine juices, fruit slices and red pepper in a large shallow dish or heavy duty zip top plastic bag. Add shrimp, cover or seal and chill at least 4 hours. Drain off liquid. Serve shrimp over lettuce leaves with Louis Sauce.

LOUIS SAUCE

1	(12 ounce) jar chili sauce		1	tablespoon prepared horseradish
2	cups mayonnaise		1½	teaspoons Greek seasoning
2	tablespoons grated onion		1½	teaspoons Worcestershire sauce
2	tablespoons grated lemon rind		¼	teaspoon ground red pepper
3	tablespoons lemon juice		½	teaspoon hot sauce

Mix all ingredients together. Cover and chill until ready to serve.

Executive Mansion Heritage Cheese Wafers

MARGARET LANE, *Former Executive Director Kentucky Governor's Mansion*

1	cup butter (do not substitute)	1	large egg, beaten
2	cups all-purpose flour	75	pecan halves
½	pound sharp Cheddar cheese, grated		Salt

Preheat oven to 350 degrees. Mix butter, flour and cheese with fork until blended. Roll dough out on floured surface to ¼-inch thickness and cut with 1-inch round cookie cutter. Place on cookie sheet and brush tops with beaten egg. Place pecan half on each. Bake 10 minutes. After removing from oven, sprinkle each with a dash of salt and cool on wire rack.

Cheese wafers are perfect accompaniments to salads, soups or served as a savory appetizer.

Makes 75 wafers

Benedictine Spread

1	medium cucumber, peeled and seeded	Pinch of cayenne pepper or dash of Tabasco sauce
1	medium onion	
2	(8 ounce) packages cream cheese, softened	2-3 drops of green food coloring to achieve a light green color
1	teaspoon salt	Mayonnaise (to thin)

Finely chop cucumber and onion in food processor. Drain well and discard liquid. Place cream cheese, cucumber and onion in processor and blend until spreadable. Add remaining ingredients, using only enough mayonnaise to thin. Place in jars. Serve chilled on crackers or as a sandwich filling.

Memorable Menus: Golden Horseshoe

1953 Menu

Complete dinner for $3.75

Seafood Cocktail

Pan Fried Country Ham Steak, Red Gravy

Hominy, Greens, Fried Apples

Green Salad

Cornbread

Chess Pie

"May we suggest a Mint Julep, a dinner wine and Benedictine and Brandy for a perfect dinner."

Menu: Jerome and Virginia Redfearn

Bluegrass Beer Cheese

½	teaspoon garlic chips	1	tablespoon Worcestershire sauce
½	teaspoon dry mustard		Dashes of Tabasco sauce, to taste
½	teaspoon salt	3	(8 ounce) packages Cracker Barrel cheese spread, softened
2	ounces warm beer		

Soak garlic chips in water for 1 hour; drain. Mix dry mustard, salt, beer, Worcestershire sauce and Tabasco sauce into softened cheese spread until blended. Store in refrigerator. Serve with crackers or as a dip for raw vegetables.

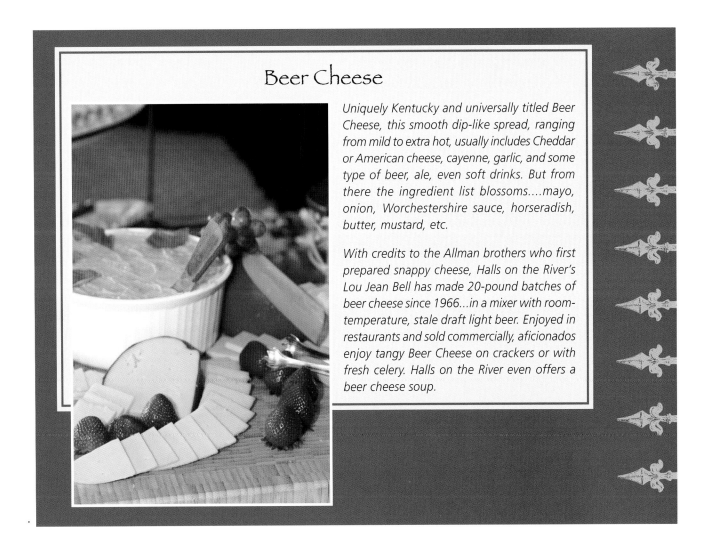

Beer Cheese

Uniquely Kentucky and universally titled Beer Cheese, this smooth dip-like spread, ranging from mild to extra hot, usually includes Cheddar or American cheese, cayenne, garlic, and some type of beer, ale, even soft drinks. But from there the ingredient list blossoms....mayo, onion, Worchestershire sauce, horseradish, butter, mustard, etc.

With credits to the Allman brothers who first prepared snappy cheese, Halls on the River's Lou Jean Bell has made 20-pound batches of beer cheese since 1966...in a mixer with room-temperature, stale draft light beer. Enjoyed in restaurants and sold commercially, aficionados enjoy tangy Beer Cheese on crackers or with fresh celery. Halls on the River even offers a beer cheese soup.

Capers and Cream Cheese Spread

¼ pound butter, softened

1 (8 ounce) package cream cheese, softened

1 tablespoon chopped green pepper

1 tablespoon chopped onion

2 teaspoons chopped capers

¼ teaspoon dry mustard

¼ teaspoon ground pepper

Mix all ingredients together and refrigerate until ready to serve. Allow to sit at room temperature for 30 minutes prior to serving. Serve with party rye bread or crackers.

Serves 15-20

Creamy Dreamy Spinach, Onion and Bacon Dip

1 pound bacon, cooked and crumbled

1 (10 ounce) package frozen chopped spinach, thawed and squeezed dry

1 (10 ounce) package frozen chopped onion, thawed and squeezed dry

3 (8 ounce) packages cream cheese, softened

1 (5 ounce) package shredded Parmesan cheese

1 cup shredded mozzarella cheese

½ cup mayonnaise

Preheat oven to 350 degrees. Combine all ingredients in a medium bowl. Spoon mixture into a 2-quart baking dish. Bake 30 minutes or until hot and bubbly. Serve with tortilla chips or wheat thin crackers.

Serves 15-20

Monticule

Sweet Cinnamon Chips with Strawberry Salsa

CINNAMON CHIPS

10 (10 inch) white flour tortillas | 1 cup cinnamon sugar

Preheat oven to 350 degrees. Place tortillas on baking sheets and spray the tortillas with non-stick cooking spray. Immediately sprinkle with cinnamon sugar. Cut each tortilla into 8 triangles. Bake 8 to 10 minutes. Serve warm.

SALSA

2 kiwi, peeled and diced

2 Golden Delicious apples, peeled and diced

1 pound fresh strawberries, cut into pieces

2 tablespoons sugar

3 tablespoons strawberry jelly

1 tablespoon brown sugar

Mix all salsa ingredients together and chill for at least 2 hours. Best if chilled longer. Serve with cinnamon chips.

Serves 8-10

Monticule

In 1989 Dr. Gary Knapp purchased a 200-acre farm on Fayette County's Harp-Innis Pike and christened it Monticule, a French term meaning large hill or small mountain. Today Monticule Farm encompasses 630 acres of prime Bluegrass pastures, bordered by white plank fences and embellished with flowering trees and shrubs.

Anchored by the farm's deep, rich soil and rolling landscape, 9,000 tree seedlings thrive in the on-farm tree nursery, providing evergreens and native species for a landscape plan that takes advantage of the natural ebb and flow of the land, creating a graceful pattern of beautiful vistas.

Monticule's barns were designed utilizing a classic format as seen at Calumet and Dixiana Farms, but incorporating modern technology. In addition to producing many other stakes winners, Monticule was the breeder of 2008 Derby and Preakness winner, Big Brown, who received an Eclipse Award as American Champion Three-Year-Old Horse of the Year.

Kentucky Horse Park

THE PLACE TO GET CLOSE TO HORSES

Framed by miles of white plank fencing and anchored by life-sized statues of two Thoroughbred greats, Man O' War and Secretariat, the 1,200-acre Kentucky Horse Park hosts almost 900,000 visitors and 15,000 competition horses in 75 annual events. The Park, located in Fayette County on Newtown Pike, is the showcase for Kentucky's horse industry.

Brainchild of noted Bluegrass horseman, John R. Gaines, the thirty-year-old Kentucky Horse Park is an authentic working farm, home to more than 50 breeds of horses. The Hall of Champions has housed some of the area's great Thoroughbreds in its stalls...Bold Forbes, Cigar, and John Henry who held court there for 22 years. Within sight of the Hall of Champions, the Park's Museum, in addition to showcasing world-class exhibits, displays the famed Calumet Farm trophy collection.

Sharing the grounds with horse-related museums, galleries, and theaters, the Park's National Horse Center complex hosts the headquarters of more than 30 equine organizations representing various breeds of horses, equine associations, practitioners, and artists. Aspiring jockeys and horsemen enroll in the North American Racing Academy, which is headquartered at the Kentucky Horse Park. Southern Lights, an off-season million-light extravaganza, attracts more than 25,000 cars to the Park from Thanksgiving to New Year's Day.

Gazpacho Soup

4	cups peeled and diced cucumbers	1	(46 ounce) can tomato juice
3	fresh tomatoes, peeled	2	tablespoons wine vinegar
1¼	cups finely chopped celery	4	tablespoons olive oil
1	cup finely chopped green onions	2	tablespoons Worcestershire sauce
1	cup finely chopped pimentos	1	teaspoon salt
1	cup finely chopped green bell peppers	1	teaspoon black pepper
2	cloves garlic, finely chopped		

To peel the tomatoes, first cut a shallow X on the bottom of the tomatoes. Prepare a bowl of ice water; set aside. Place a pot of water on the stove and bring to a boil. Drop the tomatoes into the boiling water; remove after 30 seconds or when the skin begins to peel. Quickly remove the tomatoes and place in the bowl of ice water for 5 minutes. Remove the tomatoes from the ice water and peel. Chop into bite size pieces.

Combine all ingredients in a gallon jar. Cover with lid and shake well. Keep refrigerated until ready to serve. Shake well before serving.

Serves 8

Joe Bologna's Restaurant & Pizzeria

Highlighted by 41 stained glass windows and original nineteenth-century hardwood floors, Joe Bologna's may not seem like the typical pizza place... because it's not. Built in 1891 for the Maxwell Street Presbyterian Church, this building has served as a synagogue, school, and now a locally-famous restaurant. Listed on the National Register of Historic Places, this house of worship was converted into Joe Bologna's Restaurant & Pizzeria in 1973, serving homemade garlic bread sticks, pizza, and pasta to locals and area visitors. Conveniently located on Maxwell Street, the alternative atmosphere and handmade specialties remain a recipe for success more than thirty-five years later.

Fiesta Chicken Soup

6	corn tortillas	1	(14½ ounce) can chicken broth
1	small onion, chopped	4	cups cooked, chopped chicken
2	garlic cloves, minced	2	tablespoons fresh cilantro
1	tablespoon vegetable oil	1	(8 ounce) container sour cream
1	(31 ounce) can refried beans	2	cups shredded Monterey Jack or Cheddar cheese
2	(14½ ounce) cans petite diced tomatoes		
1	(14½ ounce) can diced tomatoes with mild green chilies		

Preheat oven to 350 degrees. Cut tortillas into thin strips. Place on a lightly greased baking sheet and bake 15 minutes. Stir every 5 minutes. Cool.

Sauté onion and garlic in hot vegetable oil in Dutch oven over medium-high heat for 5 minutes or until tender. Add refried beans, tomatoes, broth and chicken, stirring until smooth. Bring mixture to a boil. Reduce heat and simmer 15 minutes. Stir in chopped cilantro. Ladle into individual bowls and dollop with sour cream. Top with cheese and baked tortilla strips. Serve immediately.

Makes 14 cups

Country Pinto Beans

1	pound dried pinto beans	1	teaspoon salt
2	quarts water	½	teaspoon ground black pepper
1	tablespoon bacon grease		

Clean and rinse beans, discarding any imperfect beans and debris. Soak in cold water for a few minutes and discard water. Repeat at least twice, retaining the last soaking water.

Place beans and 2 quarts soaking water in Dutch oven or 4-quart saucepan. Add bacon grease, salt and pepper. Bring to a boil and then reduce heat to simmer. Cover and simmer for 1 to 2 hours, stirring frequently and adding water as necessary to keep liquid above the expanding beans. Beans should be tender when cooked through. Serve with buttermilk cornbread.

Alternate method: After cleaning and rinsing, beans may be soaked in 2 quarts of cold water overnight prior to cooking.

Music and Charity in
"The Athens of The West"

The Kentucky Musical Society hosted its first concert in Lexington in 1805 and for decades gathered at Giron's second floor ballroom for concerts, cotillions, and quadrilles.

Public gatherings and cultural events ceased when a devastating series of Cholera epidemics struck Lexington in the mid nineteenth century. In 1833, hundreds of children were left destitute and orphaned by the devastating epidemic that took fifty citizens per day. Women from leading families…Gratz, Sayre, Hunt, Short…organized a public meeting at Lexington's court house to raise funds for The Lexington Orphan Asylum. The citizens raised $4,400 and engaged a matron and assistant to shelter the children, aged four to sixteen.

With the city's orphans protected, Lexington's cultural society had been revitalized, based on a humanitarian need. Citizens organized The Handel and Hyden Society to "present the new scientific music from Europe." The Harmonic Society presented concerts featuring 'Songs, Duets, Glees,' and a variety of instrumental pieces. Early Lexington organized Saxton's, the town band to perform at public events, concerts, and funerals. The "Athens of the West" supported two music stores, which offered instruments and songbooks.

Today, *The Lexington Singers,* 180 voices strong, is one of the oldest continuously performing independent community choral groups in America. Since its founding in 1959, the group has for fifty years entertained hundreds of audiences throughout the world.

The *Lexington Philharmonic Orchestra* began in 1961 as the Central Kentucky Philharmonic Orchestra, a group of 65 volunteer musicians, primarily music faculty from area universities and schools. Continuing the traditions of Lexington's first Philharmonic Society formed in 1870, the orchestra has become the region's preeminent symphony orchestra.

Limestone Bibb Lettuce Salad with Fruit and Poppyseed Dressing

SALAD

6	cups torn Bibb lettuce		1	cup strawberries, sliced or cut into chunks
1	cup spinach leaves		1	whole kiwi, peeled and thinly sliced
1	cup honeydew balls			Almond slices, optional
1	cup cantaloupe balls			

Clean lettuce, spinach and strawberries under running water and pat dry. Use a melon baller for making honeydew and cantaloupe balls. Assemble all ingredients into large salad bowl. Add poppyseed dressing to taste and mix. Sprinkle with almond slices if desired.

DRESSING

1½	cups sugar		3	tablespoons onion juice (from grated onion)
2	teaspoons dry mustard		2	cups olive oil
2	teaspoons salt		1	tablespoon poppyseeds
⅔	cup cider vinegar			

Mix all dressing ingredients in a quart jar. Shake well.

Serves 8

Bibb Lettuce

In 1856 retired Frankfort lawyer and amateur horticulturist, Judge John B. Bibb, developed a new variety of lettuce in his backyard greenhouse. Originally labeled limestone lettuce, Bibb is a beautiful soft head lettuce with crisp, deep green leaves that cluster like rose petals. After Judge Bibb began giving lettuce plants and seed to friends and neighbors, a Louisville greenhouse commercialized the 'Orchid of the Salad World' in 1919.

Spinach and Bibb Lettuce Salad with Hot Bacon Dressing

SALAD

3   heads Bibb lettuce, cleaned
    and separated

1   pound spinach, cleaned and torn

½   cup sliced celery

½   cup sliced fresh mushrooms

8   cherry tomatoes, halved

½   purple onion, thinly sliced

4   large hard-boiled eggs,
    cut into wedges

Layer each salad plate as follows: Bibb lettuce, spinach, celery and mushrooms. Garnish top of each salad with tomatoes, onion slices and egg wedges. Serve with Hot Bacon Dressing.

Serves 4-6

HOT BACON DRESSING

½   pound diced bacon

1   medium onion, chopped

1   cup water

1   cup vinegar

1   cup sugar

1   tablespoon salt

½   teaspoon pepper

2   tablespoons cornstarch

½   cup water

Fry bacon and onion together until onion is clear and bacon is crisp. Reserve bacon drippings. Combine 1 cup water and vinegar. Bring to a boil then add sugar, salt and pepper. Mix cornstarch, ½ cup water and bacon drippings into a smooth paste. Stir into water and vinegar mixture. Bring to a boil, stirring constantly. Mixture should thicken slightly. Simmer for about 10 minutes. Add onion and bacon. Pour over salad immediately before serving.

Asparagus Apple Salad

SALAD
2	cups (2-inch) diagonally cut asparagus		2	cups thinly sliced Gala apples
4	cups torn Romaine lettuce			

Cook asparagus in boiling water for 1 minute. Rinse under cold water; drain. Combine the asparagus, lettuce and apple in a large bowl. Drizzle with vinaigrette; toss gently to coat.

VINAIGRETTE DRESSING
¼	cup (1 ounce) crumbled blue cheese		2	teaspoons Dijon mustard
2	tablespoons chopped fresh parsley		1	teaspoon extra virgin olive oil
2	tablespoons white vinegar		¼	teaspoon salt
1	tablespoon water		¼	teaspoon ground black pepper
1	teaspoon sugar		⅛	teaspoon cinnamon

Combine all dressing ingredients and stir with a whisk.

Serves 8 (1 cup each)

McConnell Springs

Because of its significance in Lexington's history, McConnell Springs, located on Old Frankfort Pike, is listed on the National Register of Historic Places. It was on this site that William McConnell and his fellow pioneers named the city of Lexington in 1775, after hearing news of the first shots of the Revolutionary War at Lexington, Massachusetts. It is said that William McConnell claimed a preemption, built a small cabin, and cleared a piece of land on which he planted snap beans and apple seeds.

For the next 220 years, the property was the location of a distillery, gunpowder factory, and dairy farm. As the city of Lexington grew, the site was abandoned and covered with weeds, debris, and industrial development. In the late 1980s, citizens were successful in raising funds to preserve McConnell Springs, today a historical site but also a natural park interspersed with early rock fences, as well as a dam from the early mill, and the foundation of an early home.

Fresh Corn and Red Pepper Salad

¾ cup sour cream

1 teaspoon Worcestershire sauce

¾ teaspoon seasoned salt

3 cups fresh corn kernels (about 5 ears), uncooked

1 cup finely chopped red bell pepper

1 cup chopped green onions

¼ teaspoon ground black pepper

Combine sour cream, Worcestershire sauce and salt in a large bowl, stirring with a whisk. Add corn and remaining ingredients, stirring to combine. Cover and refrigerate at least 2 hours before serving.

Serves 8

Haricots Verts Salad

1½ tablespoons extra virgin olive oil

2 garlic cloves, minced

3 tablespoons pine nuts, toasted and divided

2 tablespoons red wine vinegar

½ teaspoon kosher salt, divided

½ teaspoon black pepper

16 large, fresh basil leaves (approximately ½ cup)

1½ pounds haricots verts

3 tablespoons chopped, ready to use sun-dried tomatoes

Heat oil and garlic in a small skillet over medium heat; cook 2 minutes, stirring occasionally. Remove from heat and cool slightly. Combine garlic mixture, 1 tablespoon nuts, vinegar, ¼ teaspoon salt, pepper and basil in a food processor; pulse until well combined. Cook beans in boiling water for 4 minutes or until crisp-tender; drain. Rinse under cold water; drain. Place in a large bowl. Add basil mixture and remaining ¼ teaspoon salt; toss to coat. Sprinkle with 2 tablespoons pine nuts and sun-dried tomatoes.

Serves 8

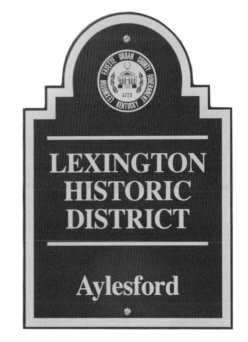

LEXINGTON HISTORIC DISTRICT

Aylesford

Grape Tomatoes with Capers

3 tablespoons drained small capers
3 tablespoons balsamic vinegar
2 tablespoons olive oil
½ teaspoon salt
½ teaspoon black pepper

2 pints grape tomatoes, halved
6 large basil leaves, shredded
3 tablespoons shredded fresh Parmesan cheese

Combine capers, vinegar, oil, salt and pepper. Drizzle over tomatoes, tossing to coat. Let stand at least 15 minutes or up to 1 hour. Sprinkle with basil and Parmesan cheese. Serve at room temperature.

Serves 6

Tomato Aspic

2 cups spicy tomato juice
⅓ cup chopped onion
¼ cup chopped celery leaves
2 tablespoons brown sugar
1 teaspoon salt
2 small bay leaves
4 whole cloves
2 cups regular tomato juice, divided

2 packages unflavored gelatin
1 teaspoon Worcestershire sauce
3 tablespoons lemon juice
¾ cup finely chopped celery
1 small cucumber, seeded and finely chopped
⅓ cup ripe olives, sliced
Lettuce leaves

In a saucepan mix 2 cups spicy tomato juice, onion, celery, brown sugar, salt, bay leaves and cloves. Simmer for 5 minutes. Strain.

Soften gelatin in 1 cup cold regular tomato juice and dissolve in hot mix. Add remaining 1 cup regular tomato juice, Worcestershire sauce and lemon juice. Chill until partially set. Add celery, cucumber and olives. Pour into a 5 cup mold or individual 1 cup molds and chill. Serve on lettuce leaf with chicken salad or shrimp salad.

Strawberry Pretzel Salad

2 cups crushed pretzels
¾ cup butter, melted
1¼ cups sugar, divided
1 (8 ounce) package cream cheese, softened

1 (16 ounce) container whipped topping, thawed and divided
2 cups pineapple juice
2 (3 ounce) packages strawberry gelatin
2 (10 ounce) packages frozen sliced strawberries

Preheat oven to 350 degrees. Mix pretzels, butter and ¼ cup sugar. Spread over a buttered 9x13-inch pan. Bake 10 minutes. Cool. Mix cream cheese, 2 cups whipped topping and 1 cup sugar; spread over cooled crust and refrigerate. Heat pineapple juice and add gelatin, stirring until dissolved; add strawberries. Set gelatin mixture in refrigerator until it starts to gel, then spread over cream cheese layer. When gelatin is set, cover with remaining whipped topping. Cover and refrigerate until ready to serve.

Serves 8-10

Red Mile Standardbreds

Excitement was building in September, 1875 at the new Red Mile. Aristides had won the first Kentucky Derby a few months earlier when the newly-reorganized Kentucky Trotting Horse Breeders Association sponsored the inaugural opening day of the Great Fall Trots at The Red Mile. Named for the mile-long red clay track, Red Mile is home to Standardbred racing, in which horses race in distinct gaits pulling two-wheeled sulkies. More harness racing two-minute miles have been established on this red clay track than at any other in the world.

The Standardbred horse performs or works in harness, as opposed to the Thoroughbred, which races under saddle. Slightly different bloodlines are found in trotters than pacers, though both can trace their heritage back to the greats, Hambletonian and Messenger. In order to be registered, every Standardbred must trot a mile within the "standard" of 2 minutes and 30 seconds, therefore the name Standardbred, coined in 1879. Early Fayette County Standardbred farms include Walnut Hall Farm (1892), Castleton Farm (1793), Almahurst, and Poplar Hill.

The Red Mile track hosts Spring and Fall race meets, including the Kentucky Futurity, a third jewel in harness racing's Triple Crown. In 2004, the Red Mile hosted its inaugural Quarter Horse meet, which marked the first time that breed had raced in the Bluegrass in more than a decade. Rounding out the Bluegrass parade of breeds, the Lexington Junior League Charity Horse Show, first leg of the Saddlebred Triple Crown, has been hosted at the Red Mile annually.

The White Thoroughbred

Over the years, good guys and heroes have ridden white horses...from George Washington to Hopalong Cassidy. As late as the 1960s there were no white Thoroughbreds registered with the Jockey Club, official breed registry, and until 1995 there had only been nine registered as white, since most were brown, bay, or gray. The Jockey Club now lists white as a "rare color not to be confused with the colors gray or roan. The entire coat, including the mane, tail and legs, is white and no other color should be present."

With the odds of foaling two white horses on the same farm measured in trillions, the white Thoroughbred is indeed a unique Bluegrass phenomenon. In 1963, a snow white filly, White Beauty, was foaled on acreage that is now Patchen Wilkes Farm. White Beauty became the matriarch of a family of white Thoroughbreds spanning several generations. Woodford County's Airdrie Stud bred a line of Thoroughbreds that produced the stallion Arctic White, and another family of white Thoroughbreds thrives.

Image: Barry Ezrine / Patchen Wilkes Farm

Precious Beauty and her 36-hour-old foal, Patchen Beauty

Grilled Hawaiian Chicken

1	teaspoon minced garlic	1	cup sherry wine vinegar
1	tablespoon unsweetened pineapple juice	½	cup white wine vinegar
¾	cup sugar	4	boneless, skinless chicken breasts

Mix garlic, pineapple juice, sugar and vinegars until sugar is dissolved. Marinate chicken for 48 hours. Grill on low heat approximately 30 to 40 minutes.

Serves 4

Sure Bet Parmesan Chicken

1	tablespoon butter	½	cup seasoned breadcrumbs
1	tablespoon vegetable oil	½	cup grated Parmesan cheese
4	(4 ounce) boneless, skinless chicken breasts	½	teaspoon dried basil
		2	large eggs

Preheat oven to 375 degrees. Place butter and oil in a 9x13-inch pan. Put in oven for about 5 minutes or until butter is melted. Flatten chicken to ¼-inch thickness. In a shallow bowl, combine breadcrumbs, Parmesan cheese and basil. In another bowl, beat the egg. Dip chicken into egg, then coat with breadcrumb mixture. Add chicken to buttered pan. Bake for 30 minutes.

Serves 4

Memorable Menus: The Navarre Café

A fancy new restaurant appeared for a short time on Lexington's Main Street in 1894, operated by Riley Grannon, and known to be 'elegant enough for the wealthiest horsemen.' The Navarre Café created quite a sensation with its elegant dining rooms, Brussels carpet, heavy silverware, and menus planned by an authentic French chef.

Winner's Circle Chicken Penne

2-3 heads of broccoli, cut into florets

¼ cup butter

2-4 boneless, skinless chicken breasts, cut into strips

3-4 garlic cloves, minced

Salt and freshly ground black pepper

12 ounces penne pasta

¾ cup dry white wine

1½ cups heavy cream

5-6 ounce package crumbled Gorgonzola cheese

Parmesan cheese

Plunge broccoli into a pan of boiling water with ¼ teaspoon salt. Bring back to a boil and boil for 2 minutes, drain in a colander and refresh under cold running water. Shake well to remove the surplus water and set aside to drain completely.

Melt the butter in a large skillet or pan. Add the chicken and garlic; season with salt and pepper to taste and stir well. Fry over medium heat until the chicken becomes white. Meanwhile, cook pasta for 8 to 10 minutes, or until al dente. Pour wine and cream over chicken mixture in the pan. Stir to mix, then simmer, stirring occasionally for about 5 minutes or until sauce has reduced and thickened and chicken is cooked through. Add broccoli to chicken mixture and toss until broccoli is heated through. Season with salt and pepper to taste. Drain pasta and add to chicken. Add Gorgonzola and toss well. Serve with grated Parmesan cheese.

Serves 4-6

Memorable Menus: Canary Cottage
1924-1951
"the South's Most Exclusive Soda Luncheonette."

During most of the twentieth century, The Canary Cottage, a popular Main Street 'tea room,' also operated locations in Cincinnati, Louisville and Indianapolis. Described by Duncan Hines, traveling food critic during a 1936 visit, as "the best dining facility in town," the Canary Cottage was considered 'cozy' with booths and a bar in the back.

The fried chicken was served in a basket accompanied by a card: 'Pick it up, Sir, Pick it up, Ma'am, You are at home in the Canary Cottage.'

Dinner — 65 cents
Alive Soft Shell Crabs (2)

served with Tartar Sauce

Shoestring Potato,

Cole Slaw,

Rolls-Muffins-Butter

Coffee, Tea or Milk

Menu: Betty Hoopes

Kentucky Hot Brown

At Louisville's Brown Hotel in the 1920s, an evening of dinner and dancing would often culminate in a late night supper of ham and eggs at the restaurant. The legend promoted is that the guests became tired of ham and eggs, or the chef was running low on supplies, so Chef Fred Schmidt created an open faced turkey and bacon sandwich covered with broiled cheese sauce...the Hot Brown was created and became a Brown Hotel favorite as well as a Bluegrass tradition. Many restaurants in Kentucky offer a version of the Hot Brown, and regional cookbooks often list this unique entrée.

The Legendary Hot Brown

THE BROWN HOTEL, LOUISVILLE

2 tablespoons whole butter

4 tablespoons all-purpose flour

1 quart heavy whipping cream

½ cup Pecorino Romano cheese, plus 1 tablespoon for garnish

Salt and pepper, to taste

2 slices of Texas toast (crust trimmed)

14 ounces sliced roasted turkey breast

2 Roma tomatoes, sliced in half

4 slices of crispy bacon

Paprika and parsley

In a 2-quart saucepan, melt butter and slowly whisk in flour until combined and forms a thick paste (roux). Continue to cook roux for 2 minutes over medium-low heat, stirring frequently. Whisk heavy whipping cream into the roux and cook over medium heat until the cream begins to simmer, about 2 to 3 minutes. Remove sauce from heat and slowly whisk in Pecorino Romano cheese until the Mornay sauce is smooth. Add salt and pepper to taste.

For each Hot Brown, place one slice of toast in an oven safe dish and cover with 7 ounces of turkey. Take the two halves of Roma tomato and set them alongside the base of turkey and toast. Next, pour one half of the Mornay sauce to completely cover the dish. Sprinkle with additional Pecorino Romano cheese. Place entire dish under a broiler until cheese begins to brown and bubble. Remove from broiler, cross two pieces of crispy bacon on top, sprinkle with paprika and parsley, and serve immediately.

Makes two hot browns

Grilled Bourbon Beef Tenderloin

1	cup bourbon	1	tablespoon Worcestershire sauce
1	cup firmly packed brown sugar	2	cups water
⅔	cup soy sauce	3-4	sprigs fresh thyme, chopped
6-7	sprigs fresh cilantro, trimmed and coarsely chopped	4½-5	pounds beef tenderloin with silver and fat removed
½	cup lemon juice		

Combine bourbon, brown sugar, soy sauce, cilantro, lemon juice, Worcestershire sauce, water and thyme. Pour over tenderloin, cover and refrigerate for 8 to 12 hours. Turn the filet over several times during the time the meat is marinating.

Preheat and oil grill. Remove tenderloin from marinade and place on preheated grill. Cook over high heat, with the grill lid closed, 5 minutes on each side. Reduce heat to medium and turn the filet about every 5 minutes until the degree of doneness is reached. Filet is cooked rare in approximately 30 minutes or when the meat thermometer registers 115 to 120 degrees; medium rare 130 to 135 degrees; medium 140 to 145 degrees; medium well 150 to 155 degrees; well done 160 to 170 degrees. Remove from grill; cover with foil to retain heat and let rest 10 minutes. Slice against the grain. Serve with Henry Bain Sauce.

Serves 8-10

Henry Bain Sauce

¼ cup ketchup

½ cup chili sauce

1½ tablespoons steak sauce

½ tablespoon hot pepper sauce

2 (9 ounce) bottles mango chutney

2 tablespoons Worcestershire sauce

1½ teaspoons dry mustard

Blend all ingredients in a food processor until thick and large pieces of chutney are blended. Place in an airtight container and store in refrigerator 2 to 3 days before serving to allow flavors to blend.

Henry Bain, headwaiter at the Pendennis Club in Louisville in the early 1920s, developed a version of this spicy steak sauce that remains a popular condiment to serve with beef, pork or chicken.

Grilled Jalapeño Basil Pork Chops

1	(10 ounce) jar jalapeño pepper jelly		4	(1 inch) thick pork loin chops
½	cup dry white wine		½	teaspoon kosher salt
¼	cup chopped fresh basil		¼	teaspoon freshly ground black pepper

Combine pepper jelly, white wine and basil in a small saucepan over low heat, stirring often until the pepper jelly melts. Remove from heat and let cool completely. Place pork chops in a large zip top bag and pour in ¾ cup of the pepper jelly mixture. Make sure that pork chops are coated well. Let stand at room temperature for 30 minutes, turning occasionally. Remove pork chops from the bag and discard the marinade. Sprinkle with salt and pepper. Grill over medium heat (with grill closed) 7 to 8 minutes on each side or until a meat thermometer registers 170 degrees when inserted into the thickest part of the meat. Remove from grill; spoon remaining pepper jelly mixture over pork chops; cover for 5 minutes with aluminum foil to allow meat to rest.

Serves 4

Keeneland

Braised Lamb Shoulder
with Rosemary and Black Olives

DUDLEY'S ON SHORT

4 tablespoons extra virgin olive oil, divided	2 cups dry white wine
2 pounds lamb shoulder, diced into 1-inch pieces	3 quarts chicken broth
2 medium yellow onions, finely diced	5 sprigs fresh rosemary bundled with kitchen twine
4 ribs celery, finely diced	2 tablespoons butter, softened
1 bulb fennel, finely diced	2 tablespoons flour
6 ounces Pernod liqueur	¾ cup coarsely chopped and pitted oil cured black olives

In a large Dutch oven heat 3 tablespoons olive oil. Begin to sear diced lamb in batches rather than all at once. This will insure even browning. Remove meat from pan and reserve.

Refresh pan with remaining olive oil being careful not to burn brown bits on bottom of pan. Add onion, celery and fennel. Sweat vegetables until translucent. Add Pernod and use a wooden spoon to scrape up brown bits in bottom of pan. Add white wine and simmer for 5 minutes; add broth. When broth returns to a simmer, add the lamb back into pan. Reduce heat to low and simmer for 35 to 45 minutes or until lamb is tender.

To finish, place rosemary bundle in stew. In a small mixing bowl mix butter and flour into a smooth paste. Ladle a scant cup of lamb stew into mixing bowl and whisk until smooth. Return contents to stew and bring to a strong simmer for 5 minutes. Add black olives, remove rosemary and season to taste with salt.

Serves 6

Dudley's On Short

Dudley's Restaurant, a mainstay of the Lexington dining scene for 28 years, relocated from historic Dudley Square to the heart of downtown Lexington in the Fall of 2009. After renovating the 1889 Northern Bank Building, owner Debbie Long and four investors opened Dudley's on Short in the Spring of 2010. The restaurant shares historically-hallowed ground at Cheapside, site of Lexington's early Public Square and Market House. Scene of early Lexington Court Days, Cheapside today is the permanent home of the Lexington Farmer's Market.

Dudley's on Short offers award-winning creative American cuisine, wine list, and service to local clientele while welcoming newcomers and visitors.

Tilapia with Lemon Vinaigrette

8   tablespoons extra virgin olive oil
3   shallots, thinly sliced
1   large head radicchio, coarsely chopped
1   (15 ounce) can cannelloni beans, drained

⅓   cup clam juice
   Salt and pepper, to taste
6   tilapia fillets
   All-purpose flour

Heat 5 tablespoons olive oil in a large saucepan. Add shallots and sauté until tender. Add radicchio and sauté until wilted. Add beans and clam juice and cook until beans are heated through, stirring often. Season to taste with salt and pepper.

Heat remaining olive oil in a skillet. Sprinkle fillets with salt and pepper; dredge in flour to coat. Fry fillets in skillet until golden brown. Spoon radicchio mixture over center of plate and top with fillets. Drizzle Lemon Vinaigrette over fish and serve immediately.

LEMON VINAIGRETTE

¼   cup lemon juice
¼   cup packed and chopped parsley leaves
2   cloves garlic, minced

2   teaspoons lemon zest
½   teaspoon salt
¼   teaspoon pepper
⅓   cup extra virgin olive oil

Whisk all ingredients together.

Serves 6-8

Shrimp and Artichoke Casserole

1   (14 ounce) can artichoke hearts, drained and quartered
1½   pounds raw shrimp, shelled and deveined
½   pound fresh mushrooms, sliced
8   tablespoons butter, divided
4½   tablespoons flour
1   cup heavy cream

½   cup milk
   Salt, to taste
½   teaspoon pepper
¼   cup dry sherry
1   tablespoon Worcestershire sauce
¼   cup grated Parmesan cheese
¼   teaspoon paprika

Preheat oven to 375 degrees. Place artichoke hearts on bottom of a 2½-quart casserole dish. Cover with raw shrimp. Cook mushrooms in 3½ tablespoons butter. Sprinkle over shrimp. In a medium saucepan, melt the remaining 4½ tablespoons butter. Add flour and cook for 3 to 5 minutes, stirring constantly. Gradually add cream and milk. Cook until thick. Add salt, pepper, sherry and Worcestershire sauce; pour over casserole. Top with Parmesan cheese and sprinkle with paprika. Bake, uncovered, 25 to 30 minutes until brown and bubbly.

Serves 6-8

Post Time Pasta

1	pound fresh broccoli, cut into florets	1	pound reduced-fat smoked sausage, sliced
1	(9 ounce) package refrigerated fettuccine	3	large eggs
2	tablespoons butter	¾	cup whipping cream
1	cup sliced fresh mushrooms	¾	teaspoon pepper
1	garlic clove, minced	1½	cups grated Parmesan cheese

In a Dutch oven, cook broccoli and fettuccine in boiling water 4 minutes or until broccoli is crisp-tender; drain. Rinse with cold water; drain. Place in a large bowl. Melt butter in a large heavy skillet. Add mushrooms and garlic; sauté 3 minutes or until tender. Add to fettuccine mixture. Cook sausage in skillet over medium-high heat 5 minutes or until done; drain and add to fettuccine mixture. Wipe skillet clean with a paper towel. Combine eggs, whipping cream and pepper and pour into skillet; stir until blended. Add fettuccine mixture; toss well. Cook over low heat, stirring constantly, 3 to 5 minutes or until thickened. Sprinkle with Parmesan cheese and toss. Serve immediately.

Serves 4

Keeneland

Starting Gate Spinach Lasagna

1 (16 ounce) container low-fat cottage cheese

1 (10 ounce) package frozen chopped spinach, thawed and well drained

3 cups shredded mozzarella cheese, divided

½ cup grated Parmesan cheese, divided

2 large eggs, beaten

1 (26 ounce) jar marinara sauce, divided

9 lasagna noodles

Preheat oven to 350 degrees. Mix cottage cheese, spinach, 2 cups mozzarella cheese, ¼ cup Parmesan cheese and eggs. Layer 1 cup marinara sauce, 3 lasagna noodles and ½ cup cottage cheese mixture in a 9x13-inch baking pan. Repeat layers. Top with remaining 3 noodles, sauce, 1 cup mozzarella cheese and ¼ cup Parmesan cheese. Bake uncovered 45 minutes. Let stand 10 minutes before serving.

Serves 8-10

Italian Crêpes

CRÊPES

4 large eggs

¼ teaspoon salt

2 cups flour

2¼ cups whole milk

¼ cup butter, melted

Combine eggs and salt. Gradually add flour, alternately with milk, beating with electric mixer or whisk until smooth. Beat in melted butter. Refrigerate batter at least 1 hour. Spray a 9-inch skillet with non-stick cooking spray. Cook batter 3 tablespoons at a time. Crêpe will be like a thin pancake when cooked.

FILLING AND SAUCE

1 cup small curd cottage cheese

3 tablespoons chopped parsley

1 tablespoon chopped onion

⅛ teaspoon salt

2 tablespoons butter, softened

1 large egg, beaten

1 tablespoon chopped chives

8 cooked crêpes

1 (15 ounce) jar Italian style marinara sauce

⅓ cup grated Parmesan cheese

Fresh basil, optional

Preheat oven to 350 degrees. Combine cottage cheese, parsley, onion, salt, butter, beaten egg and chives. Spoon 3 tablespoons of cheese mixture into center of each cooked crêpe. Roll up; place in a 9x13-inch baking pan. Pour marinara sauce over filled crêpes and sprinkle with Parmesan cheese. Bake 20 to 30 minutes. Garnish with fresh basil as desired.

Serves 8-10

Lexington Opera House

At the turn of the nineteenth century Lexington was one of the wealthiest and most cultured cities in the South. The modern Opera House, the city's second, planned by architect Herman L. Rowe and built at a cost of $45,000, opened its doors in 1887 on the corner of Broadway and Short Street. The lavishly-grand replacement quickly became known as "the best one night stand in the nation," with regular appearances by celebrities of the day including Will Rogers, Mae West, and Harry Houdini. The 1,250-seat house attracted audiences from all over the southeast for productions such as the 1890 musical "Henry Regatta" in which the entire stage was flooded for the show, as well as "A Country Circus" in 1893 that included a mile-long parade boasting more than 100 animals. One of the most impressive shows, however, was 1904s "Ben Hur" that featured an on-stage chariot race.

The curtain rang down on the last live performance in 1926, and for decades, the 'palace' operated as a movie theater. Lexingtonians banded together to save the dilapidated Opera House from the wrecking ball, and in 1975 restored it to its original grandeur, resplendent with plush décor, a grand stairway, velvet curtains, and queen boxes illuminated by massive crystal chandeliers.

Listed on the National Register of Historic Places, the Lexington Opera House remains a symbol of the past as well as a modern theatrical venue, offering ballet, opera, children's productions, family shows, comedy, music and professional national Broadway tours.

Interior Lexington Opera House 1898

Image: University of Kentucky Archives

Southern Cheese Grits

6	cups water	4½	cups shredded sharp Cheddar cheese, divided
2	teaspoons salt	3	cloves garlic, minced
1½	cups grits	⅛	teaspoon cayenne pepper
½	cup butter		
3	large eggs, well beaten		

Preheat oven to 350 degrees. Bring water to a rapid boil with salt; gradually stir in grits with a fork. Cook until all water is absorbed. Cut butter into small pieces and gradually add to grits. Combine eggs, 4 cups cheese, garlic and cayenne pepper and stir into grits mixture. Pour into a greased 2½-quart dish. Sprinkle top evenly with remaining ½ cup cheese. Bake 1 hour, 20 minutes.

Serves 8

Hash Brown Casserole

1	(32 ounce) bag frozen country-style hash browns	½	cup milk
1	(10¾ ounce) can cream of mushroom soup	3	large eggs, slightly beaten
1	(10¾ ounce) can cream of celery soup	2	teaspoons butter, melted
½	cup chopped onions	2	cups shredded Cheddar cheese, divided

Preheat oven to 350 degrees. In a large bowl mix all ingredients except ½ cup cheese. Pour into a 9x13-inch casserole dish. Bake 1 hour. Remove from oven and sprinkle remaining cheese. Return to oven and bake until cheese topping melts (approximately 10 minutes).

Serves 12

Purse to the Victor

Until the end of the nineteenth century, racing had been exclusively a man's sport. But then, many Fayette County women began to take an interest in the sport, some acquired their own stables and enjoyed watching horses race under personalized colors or silks. Turfwomen, as they were called even in that early day, made elaborate preparations. They vied in making silk and satin purses in which the race winnings were placed and hung on the finish wire, to be cut down and pocketed by the victor. First called the "take down purse," the term was later shortened to "purse," a term still used today.

Mac 'n Cheese with a "Kick"

1	(8 ounce) package elbow macaroni	½	teaspoon salt
2	tablespoons butter	½	teaspoon black pepper
2	tablespoons all-purpose flour	¼	teaspoon ground red pepper
2	cups milk	8	ounces shredded sharp Cheddar cheese, divided

Prepare pasta according to package directions. Keep warm.

Preheat oven to 400 degrees. Melt butter in a large saucepan over medium-low heat. Add flour and whisk until smooth. Gradually add milk, whisking constantly, 5 minutes or until thickened. Remove from heat. Stir in salt, black and red pepper, 1 cup cheese and cooked pasta. Spoon pasta mixture into a lightly greased 2-quart baking dish. Top with remaining cheese. Bake 20 minutes or until bubbly. Let stand 10 minutes before serving.

Serves 10-12

Tomato Onion Pie

1	(9 inch) deep dish pie crust
2	large tomatoes, sliced
1	cup chopped fresh basil
1	Vidalia onion, diced
1	cup grated Cheddar cheese
1	cup grated mozzarella cheese
½	cup mayonnaise
½	pound bacon, cooked and diced
	Salt and pepper, to taste

Preheat oven to 350 degrees. Brown crust in oven for 8 minutes. Layer sliced tomatoes in bottom of crust. Top with basil and diced onion. In a separate bowl, combine cheeses, mayonnaise and bacon. Press cheese mixture over tomatoes. Bake, uncovered, 15 to 20 minutes until golden brown. Allow pie to cool 5 to 10 minutes before serving.

Serves 6 to 8

Scalloped Cabbage

1 large head cabbage

TOPPING

1½ sleeves Ritz crackers

4 tablespoons butter

WHITE SAUCE

1 cup butter

4 tablespoons flour

2 teaspoons (scant) salt

Pepper, to taste

2 teaspoons sugar

2 cups milk

4 ounces Velveeta cheese

Place crackers in a zip top bag and crush with a rolling pin. Melt butter in microwave safe dish 20 to 30 seconds; mix with cracker crumbs and set topping aside.

Preheat oven to 400 degrees. Wash, cut, boil and drain cabbage. Pour into a 9x11-inch deep lasagna pan. In a medium microwave safe bowl, mix butter, flour, salt, pepper to taste, sugar and milk. Microwave 1 minute and whisk; repeat 4 to 5 times. Add cheese and microwave in 1 minute intervals until cheese melts. Pour cheese mixture over cooked cabbage. Top with cracker crumbs. Bake uncovered for 15 minutes.

Serves 12

Swiss Chard with Vinaigrette Reduction

2 strips bacon

2 cloves garlic, minced

¼ cup chopped green onions

½ pound Swiss chard, shredded in large pieces

¼ cup balsamic vinegar

1 small tomato, chopped

Salt and pepper, to taste

Fry bacon until crisp; remove from pan; drain and crumble into small pieces; set aside. Add garlic and green onion to bacon drippings in skillet. Sauté over medium heat 2 to 3 minutes. Add Swiss chard, stir and heat for 2 minutes or until slightly wilted. Add vinegar and reduce 2 to 3 minutes. Salt and pepper to taste. Garnish with chopped tomato and bacon.

Serves 2

Tuscan Artichokes

4	artichokes	Italian style breadcrumbs
	Kosher salt and black pepper, to taste	Olive oil
	Chopped garlic	Parmesan cheese
	Chopped parsley	½ cup beef broth

Select artichokes that are green, firm and the size of a small baseball. Rinse in cold water and trim off leaves that are bruised. Trim the stem leaving at least ½-inch or less. With a sharp knife cut the top of the artichoke about ¼ from the tip. With scissors cut the leaves that are pointed (this is more for presentation). To open the artichoke holding it from the bottom, tap it on the side of the sink using enough pressure to allow it to open, and then rinse again running cold water over the top. The artichoke may hold some water.

Place artichokes in a deep pan with cover. Add salt and pepper to taste. Sprinkle garlic and parsley over tops allowing the ingredients to go into artichoke. Generously sprinkle breadcrumbs over tops allowing the breadcrumbs to get into the leaves. The more breadcrumbs and seasonings, the tastier. Drizzle olive oil over each artichoke allowing the olive oil to get into the leaves and place some in the bottom of pan.

Place on stove on medium-high until steam is seen in pan; monitor closely-do not scorch artichokes. Add ½ cup beef broth once the artichokes have begun to cook (about 10 minutes). Continue cooking on low for about 1 hour until you can easily pull out a leaf and the meat at the base of the leaf is tender. Add more water if liquid evaporates. Drain and sprinkle with Parmesan cheese prior to serving.

Serves 4

Roasted Asparagus with Sesame Seeds

1	pound fresh asparagus		2	teaspoons kosher salt
2	tablespoons extra virgin olive oil		1	tablespoon sesame seeds

Preheat oven to 500 degrees. Snap off the bottoms (about 1-inch) of asparagus spears. Arrange asparagus spears in a single layer in a shallow baking dish and drizzle evenly with olive oil. Toss the spears to coat and sprinkle with kosher salt and sesame seeds. Bake until tender but still slightly firm, about 10 minutes. Serve immediately.

Serves 4

Elegant Broccoli

2   (10 ounce) packages frozen broccoli
    spears
1½ cups water
6   tablespoons butter, divided
1   (6 ounce) package cornbread stuffing
    mix
2   tablespoons all-purpose flour

1   teaspoon chicken flavored bouillon
    granules
¾   cup milk
1   (3 ounce) package cream cheese
¼   teaspoon salt
4   green onions, sliced
1   cup shredded Cheddar cheese
    Paprika

Preheat oven to 350 degrees. Cook broccoli according to package directions. Drain and set aside. Combine water and 4 tablespoons butter; bring to a boil. Remove from heat, stir in stuffing mix. Let stand 5 minutes. Spoon stuffing in a buttered 9x13x2-inch pan. Line broccoli spears with florets on stuffing, stems should be toward the center of pan.

Melt 2 tablespoons butter over low heat; add flour and stir until smooth. Cook 1 minute, stirring constantly. Add bouillon granules, stirring until dissolved. Gradually add milk, cook stirring until thick and bubbly. Add cream cheese and salt; stir until cheese has melted. Stir in onion. Spoon mixture over broccoli, covering the broccoli stems.

Garnish with Cheddar cheese and paprika. Bake until cheese has completely melted and is hot, approximately 30 minutes.

Serves 6-8

Hot Pineapple Delight

2   (20 ounce) cans pineapple tidbits,
    drained and juice reserved
10 tablespoons pineapple juice
    (reserved from tidbits)
1   cup firmly packed light brown sugar

3   tablespoons all-purpose flour
2   cups shredded Cheddar cheese
½   cup butter, melted
1   sleeve Ritz crackers, crushed

Preheat oven to 350 degrees. Combine pineapple juice, brown sugar and flour. Mix well, stirring until sugar and flour dissolve. Add pineapple and cheese. Combine butter and crackers; sprinkle over pineapple mixture. Bake in a greased 9x13-inch pan 20 to 30 minutes.

Serves 8-10

Whitney Farm

C.V. "Sonny" Whitney (1899-1992), lumber baron, mining magnate, co founder of Pan American Airways, horse breeder, movie maker, and later Director of Churchill Downs, became the third generation of Whitneys to achieve success in the Thoroughbred industry. He inherited a farm on Bryan Station Road from his father, Harry Payne Whitney, whose stables had bred Regret, the first filly to win the Kentucky Derby. To the farm later named Maple Hill, Sonny Whitney brought his bride, Marylou Shroeder Hosford Whitney, actress, cookbook author, food columnist, and hostess par excellence. In addition to publishing three cookbooks, Marylou Whitney penned a column in the Lexington Herald in the early 1960s: *One Cook's Tour, by Mrs. Cornelius Vanderbilt Whitney*.

The Whitney stables eventually produced 176 Stakes winners and four Kentucky Oaks winners. Maple Hill's orchards and gardens nurtured apple trees, acres of asparagus, and Bibb lettuce to supply the bountiful menus carefully planned by Mrs. Whitney. Known for the celebrated Derby eve dinner dance, the Whitneys often entertained dignitaries, celebrities, and members of the British Royal family.

Today the C.V. Whitney Farm and Marylou Whitney Stables are located on Bryan Station Road in Fayette County. With the leadership of Marylou Whitney and husband, John Hendrickson, the Stable has enjoyed success, owning Bird Town, Kentucky Oaks winner and Birdstone, Belmont and Travers Stakes winner.

Calumet

The first glimpse of Lexington from the air features a majestic, manicured Bluegrass farm embellished with green-roofed, red-trimmed barns, and infinite vistas of white plank fence. Lexington's Blue Grass Airport, anchored by life-sized bronze sculptures of Thoroughbreds, is located across Versailles Road from famed Calumet Farm. For decades, Calumet has been home to famous Thoroughbreds, no other farm matching its record of eight Kentucky Derby winners, seven Preakness Stakes winners (owner and breeder), and Five Triple Crown colt and filly winners.

Calumet Farm was named in honor of the business of its founder William Monroe Wright and

his Calumet Baking Powder Company of Chicago. Calumet began operations as a Standardbred farm and then evolved under the leadership of Wright's son, Warren, into a storied Thoroughbred tradition. The farm was owned by the Wright family heirs until 1991 when the late Count Henryk de Kwiatkowski purchased Calumet, preserved its storied legacy, and continued the tradition of family operation.

Cheese Biscuits

1	cup all-purpose flour	¼	cup shortening
1½	teaspoons baking powder	¾	cup shredded sharp Cheddar cheese
¼	teaspoon salt	¼	cup milk

Preheat oven to 450 degrees. Combine flour, baking powder and salt in a bowl; cut in shortening and cheese with a pastry blender. Add milk; stir with a fork until dry ingredients are moistened. Turn dough out onto a lightly floured surface; knead 3 to 4 times. Roll into ½-inch thickness; cut with a 2¼-inch round cutter. Place on a greased baking sheet. Bake 10 minutes or until golden brown.

Serves 8

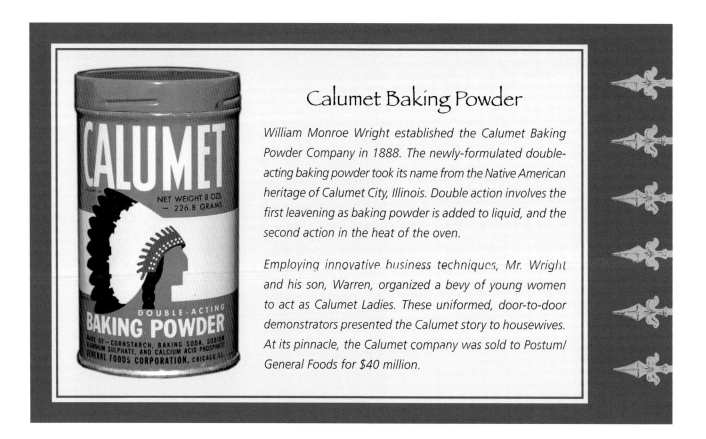

Calumet Baking Powder

William Monroe Wright established the Calumet Baking Powder Company in 1888. The newly-formulated double-acting baking powder took its name from the Native American heritage of Calumet City, Illinois. Double action involves the first leavening as baking powder is added to liquid, and the second action in the heat of the oven.

Employing innovative business techniques, Mr. Wright and his son, Warren, organized a bevy of young women to act as Calumet Ladies. These uniformed, door-to-door demonstrators presented the Calumet story to housewives. At its pinnacle, the Calumet company was sold to Postum/ General Foods for $40 million.

Special Occasion Rolls

1	cup boiling water	2	large eggs
⅓	cup sugar	3½	cups all-purpose flour
½	cup shortening		Butter
1	teaspoon salt		Sugar (for sprinkling)
1½	packages yeast		

Pour boiling water over sugar, shortening and salt. When lukewarm, pour mixture over yeast. When yeast dissolves, add eggs, mix well with flour. Cover and let rise in a warm place until double in size.

Punch dough down. Roll dough out onto a floured surface and cut with small round cookie cutter (about the size of juice glass rim). Place cut circles of dough in 8 or 9-inch round, greased pan. Spoon small dots of melted butter on dough. Top with another cut circle of dough. Dot tops with butter then sprinkle with sugar. Continue until pan is filled with double circles of dough, lightly touching. Let rise until double in size (about 1 hour, 30 minutes). Preheat oven to 400 degrees and bake 12 minutes or until brown.

These rolls are great for country ham sandwiches. This original recipe was a specialty at The Harberson, in Maysville, Kentucky and was shared throughout the Maysville community.

Makes 3-4 dozen

Pineapple Zucchini Bread

3	large eggs, beaten	3	cups all-purpose flour
1	cup oil	2	teaspoons baking soda
2	cups sugar	1	teaspoon salt
2	teaspoons vanilla extract	½	teaspoon baking powder
2	cups shredded zucchini	1½	teaspoons cinnamon
1	(8 ounce) can crushed pineapple, drained	½	cup pecans

Preheat oven to 350 degrees. Place beaten eggs in a large bowl. Gradually add oil, sugar and vanilla; beat until thick. Stir in zucchini and pineapple. In a separate bowl combine remaining ingredients. Gradually add to batter, mixing after each addition. Spoon into 2 greased and floured loaf pans. Bake 1 hour. Cool in pan 10 minutes. Remove to wire rack to cool completely.

Makes 2 loaves

Keeneland

The threads of tradition run throughout the tapestry of the Inner Bluegrass. Nowhere is that more evident than at Keeneland, Lexington's heritage-laden Thoroughbred racing and auction complex that was added to the National Register of Historic Places in 1986. Located in prime Bluegrass country on land first owned by Patrick Henry, steeped in history, graced by classic architecture, blessed by visionary leadership, and endowed with magnificent natural beauty framed by miles of iron, stone, and plank fencing, Keeneland has become a world-known landmark and treasured community institution.

After the 100-year-old Kentucky Association and its downtown track disbanded in the early 1930s, 200 racing enthusiasts and horse breeders met to form the Keeneland Association. Notable leaders were Hal Price Headley, Keeneland's first president, and land owner, John Oliver "Jack" Keene, who had begun construction of a track and farm-quarried stone stable, nucleus of Keeneland's modern Club House.

Establishing a philosophy that fosters innovation built on tradition, Keeneland installed the Kentucky Association's historic gatepost—KA— at the entrance to the Race Course. Keeneland sponsored its first race in 1936 and today, hosts three-week race meets in April and October, as well as prestigious Thoroughbred auctions.

The picturesque grounds are open to simulcasting from other tracks, or for special events in the Keene Barn and Entertainment Center or the Keene Mansion. Unique to Keeneland is its extensive sports library, founded in 1939, holding more than ten thousand volumes and an extensive clipping and photo collection. Unlike other racetracks, visitors are welcome in the paddock where prime Thoroughbreds are saddled before races, and in the barn and stable areas during morning workouts.

On Derby day, Lexington's Keeneland has become the place to be. The requisite Derby hats, fine food, and simulcasting are all on stage. Blooming dogwoods in April and blazing autumn color during the fall race meet provide a backdrop for a Bluegrass tailgating tradition. Fortunate are those who gather at picturesque Keeneland in the shade of historic trees and enjoy friends and good food on the very grounds that hosted the 1825 visit of the Marquis de Lafayette and more recently, Sheiks, Princes, Rulers, and Queen Elizabeth II of England.

In addition to operating a National Landmark, Keeneland embraces its heritage of giving back to the community. Since 1936, the Keeneland Foundation has donated millions of dollars to benefit educational, civic and industry-related service organizations.

Keeneland's Bread Pudding

Since the Keeneland Association's first race meet in the fall of 1936, Turf Catering has prepared traditional Bluegrass favorites. Ranking among the top three best sellers at the track's food venues, Bread Pudding is said to have originated in the 1200s in England, developed when early cooks found themselves with an excess of bread. Turf's recipe includes yeast rolls and Bourbon Sauce, definitely a Southern addition. 3,000 orders of the sweet pudding, comprising 80 percent of dessert sales, are enjoyed at the concession stands and dining rooms each week. "If it's not there, there's a revolt," comments Chef Ed Boutilier. "We're never out of Bread Pudding."

Bread Pudding

½ gallon milk

2 cups sugar

2 teaspoons vanilla

8 eggs beaten

2-3 quarts cubed white bread

1 cup golden raisins

1 tablespoon cinnamon

Whisk sugar into milk until dissolved. Add eggs and vanilla; stir. Soak bread into mix for several hours or overnight. Pour into Pyrex or stainless pan. Sprinkle with raisins and cinnamon and "push" into mix. Bake at 250° for approximately 1½ hours or until firm.

Maker's Mark Bourbon Sauce

1 pound butter

2 pounds powdered sugar

1 cup Maker's Mark Bourbon

Let butter become soft at room temperature and add powdered sugar. Whip bourbon into mix until it makes a frosting consistency. Ladle sauce over hot bread pudding and it will melt on its own.

Serves 10-12

Win, Place, Show Banana Pudding

1   (14 ounce) can sweetened condensed milk
1½ cups cold water
1   (3.4 ounce) box instant vanilla pudding
2   cups frozen whipped topping, thawed

1   (8 ounce) container sour cream
4   large bananas, sliced
1   (12 ounce) box vanilla wafers, divided

Whisk milk, water and pudding together; chill 10 to 15 minutes until thickened. Blend in whipped topping and sour cream. Add slices of 2 bananas and mix together. Line the bottom and sides of a 9x13-inch glass dish with vanilla wafers, reserving some to crush and sprinkle on top of pudding. Layer slices of 2 remaining bananas over vanilla wafers. Pour pudding mixture on top of sliced bananas and sprinkle with reserved crushed wafers. Refrigerate at least 2 hours before serving.

Serves 6-8

Rhubarb Custard Pie

4   cups rhubarb, sliced into 1-inch pieces
1½ cups sugar
3   tablespoons flour
¼   teaspoon salt

2   teaspoons vanilla extract
2   large eggs, beaten
1   (9 inch) pie shell, baked

Preheat oven to 400 degrees. Combine rhubarb, sugar, flour, salt, vanilla and eggs. Pour into lightly baked pie shell; bake 15 minutes. Remove from oven; reduce oven temperature to 350 degrees. Prepare topping.

TOPPING
1   cup flour
1   cup firmly packed brown sugar

½   cup butter, melted

Combine flour, brown sugar and butter; crumble over top of pie. Return to oven and bake an additional 30 minutes.

Strawberry-Rhubarb Custard Pie: use 2 cups quartered fresh strawberries and 2 cups chopped rhubarb and reduce sugar to 1 cup.

Serves 8

Ice Box Lemon Pie

½   cup butter, melted

2   cups sugar

4   large eggs

    Juice of 2 lemons

1   ready-made pie shell, unbaked

    Garnish: whipped topping, fresh mint leaves and fresh blackberries

Preheat oven to 350 degrees. Cream melted butter with sugar. Add eggs, one at a time, stirring constantly. Stir in lemon juice. Pour into unbaked pie shell and bake 10 minutes. Reduce heat to 325 degrees and bake 35 minutes more. Let cool and place in refrigerator. Cut pie into 8 slices. Garnish each slice with whipped topping, mint leaves or fresh blackberries, as desired.

Serves 8

Keeneland

Peanut Butter Pie

1	(8 ounce) package cream cheese, softened	1	cup whipping cream
½	cup sugar	1	(8 inch) prepared graham cracker crust
½	cup peanut butter	2	tablespoons chopped peanuts
1	teaspoon vanilla extract		

Combine cream cheese and sugar. Beat with a mixer at medium speed until smooth. Add peanut butter and vanilla; beat well. Set aside. Beat whipping cream until soft peaks form; fold into peanut butter mixture. Spoon into prepared graham cracker crust. Sprinkle top with peanuts. Cover and chill 3 hours before serving.

Serves 8

Overbrook Farm

Success with business ventures led W.T. Young (1919-2004), to develop Overbook Farm, 2,300 acres of manicured, plank-fenced Bluegrass. Since the 1980s, the farm has been home to numerous award-winning Thoroughbreds, including 1996 Derby winner Grindstone, and Preakness and Belmont winner, Tabasco Cat. Active in civic and educational ventures, W.T. Young was a leading Bluegrass philanthropist.

Americans have enjoyed a love affair with peanut butter since the new product was introduced at the 1904 St. Louis Universal Exposition. Fayette County's Overbrook Farm founder and owner, W.T. Young, participated in several food related businesses over the years: Royal Crown Cola, Kentucky Fried Chicken, but first peanut butter. The family founded W.T. Young Foods in 1946, and produced Big Top Peanut Butter until Proctor & Gamble and then the J.M. Smucker Company acquired the Winchester Road plant. Big Top became 'Jif' and today, Lexington's peanut butter production facility, the largest in the world, roasts and blends creamy, crunchy, Simply...the world's supply of Jif.

Chocolate Bourbon Pecan Pie

1	cup sugar		1	teaspoon vanilla extract
1	cup light corn syrup		¼	teaspoon salt
½	cup butter		6	ounces semisweet chocolate chips
4	large eggs, beaten		1	cup chopped pecans
¼	cup bourbon		1	(9 inch) pie shell, unbaked

Preheat oven to 325 degrees. In a small saucepan combine sugar, corn syrup and butter. Cook over medium heat, stirring constantly, until butter melts and sugar dissolves. Cool slightly.

In a large bowl combine eggs, bourbon, vanilla and salt. Mix well. Slowly pour sugar mixture into egg mixture, whisking constantly. Stir in chocolate chips and pecans. Pour mixture into unbaked pie shell. Bake 50 to 55 minutes or until set and golden. May be served warm or chilled.

Serves 8

Cooking with Bourbon

The world's only Bourbon Trail, in the heart of Kentucky, boasts four facilities located within forty-five minutes of Lexington and four more within a 100-mile radius. Cooking with bourbon is a Bluegrass tradition. An entire culinary business climate has developed around the Bourbon industry. The mellow liquid is folded into pies, candies, sauces, and marinades to create a distinct fragrance and flavor. The oaken, charred barrels in which bourbon is aged, have taken on a new life as flavoring agents for boutique soy sauce, flavored salts, and ale, as well as being recycled for flower planters and furniture. Byproducts of bourbon distilling are commonly utilized as animal feed.

Sideboard German Chocolate Cake

1   (4 ounce) package Baker's German's
    Sweet Chocolate
½   cup boiling water
1   cup butter
2   cups sugar
4   large egg yolks
1   teaspoon vanilla extract

1   teaspoon baking soda
½   teaspoon salt
2¼ cups all-purpose flour
1   cup buttermilk
4   large egg whites, stiffly beaten

Preheat oven to 350 degrees. Melt chocolate in boiling water; cool and set aside. Beat butter and sugar until creamy. Add egg yolks, one at a time, and beat until well blended. Add vanilla and cooled chocolate. Add baking soda and salt to flour. Add dry ingredients alternately with buttermilk to batter. Beat until smooth. Fold in beaten egg whites. Pour into 3 (9 inch) greased and floured cake pans. Bake 30 minutes or until toothpick placed in center comes out clean. Cool in pans for 10 minutes. Remove from pans and cool completely. Frost with Coconut Pecan Frosting.

COCONUT PECAN FROSTING

1   cup evaporated milk
1   cup sugar
3   large egg yolks
½   cup butter

1   teaspoon vanilla extract
1⅓ cups flaked coconut
1   cup chopped pecans

Combine milk, sugar, egg yolks, butter and vanilla in a saucepan. Cook over medium heat, stirring constantly until mixture thickens, about 12 minutes. Remove from heat; add coconut and pecans. Cool frosting until it is spreading consistency, beating occasionally. Frost between cake layers and on top of Sideboard German Chocolate Cake.

Serves 12

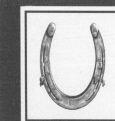

Bluegrass Superstition:

Lady Luck is a perennial companion to horse trainers, jockeys, owners, and those who wager at the track. The horseshoe that has been worn by a horse is considered a good luck charm.

14-Carrot Wedding Cake

2	cups sugar	4-5	carrots, peeled
2	cups flour	2	apples, cored
2	teaspoons baking powder	1½	cups vegetable oil
1½	teaspoons baking soda	4	large eggs
2	teaspoons cinnamon	½	cup chopped walnuts
1½	teaspoons salt		

Preheat oven to 350 degrees. Grease and flour 3 (8 inch) round pans. In a large bowl, sift sugar, flour, baking powder, baking soda, cinnamon and salt. In a large food processor, grind carrots and apples. Add oil and eggs; pulse to combine. Add wet mix to dry mix and stir to combine. Stir in walnuts.

Divide mixture between the baking pans and cook 35 to 40 minutes or until a toothpick inserted in the center of cake comes out clean. Let cakes cool in pan for 5 minutes; remove from pan and place on cake rack to cool before icing.

ICING

12	ounces cream cheese, softened	1½	teaspoons vanilla extract
¾	cup butter, room temperature	3	cups powdered sugar

Beat cream cheese, butter, vanilla and powdered sugar with a mixer until smooth. Apply a generous amount of icing between cake layers, sides and on top of cake.

Serves 12

Wedding in Gratz Park

Mary Todd Lincoln's White Cake

...Legend has it that Mary Todd Lincoln often made the cake for the president and he always commented, "Mary's White Cake is the best I have ever eaten." According to many Lincoln historians, the cake was never served with frosting.

1	cup butter	1	teaspoon vanilla extract
2	cups sugar	1	teaspoon almond extract
3	cups flour	1	cup finely ground blanched almonds
2	teaspoons baking powder	6	large egg whites
1	cup milk	¼	teaspoon salt

Preheat oven to 375 degrees. Cream butter and sugar until light and fluffy. Sift together flour and baking powder; remove 2 tablespoons and set aside. Add sifted ingredients, alternating with milk, to creamed mixture. Stir in vanilla and almond extract. Combine almonds with reserved flour and add to batter.

Beat egg whites until stiff; add salt. Fold into batter. Pour into greased and floured Bundt pan. Bake 55 minutes or until a toothpick inserted in the center of cake comes out clean. Cool 5 to 10 minutes; remove from pan and cool on rack.

Recipe Courtesy: Mary Todd Lincoln House Notecard Series

Mary Todd Lincoln House

The current Mary Todd Lincoln House at 578 West Main Street, since 1803 served as an inn, a brothel, and a grocery store, before being bought by Mary Todd's father in 1831. Robert Todd, a lawyer and businessman, was a member of the Kentucky General Assembly for 24 years. Mary Todd, born in Lexington in 1818, lived in this Lexington house from age 13-21 and visited several times after her marriage to Abraham Lincoln.

The Todd family entertained lavishly in Lexington. Nelson, the butler, was very popular for the mint juleps he created and served, perhaps from the dining room's antique sideboard, a rare and unusual Federal piece with revolving Lazy Susans at each end. Meals were prepared in a separate kitchen away from main house because of danger of fire and carried into a warming kitchen adjacent to the dining room.

The Mary Todd Lincoln House, opened in 1977 by the Kentucky Mansions Preservation Foundation, Inc, is the first house museum in America to honor a First Lady. The fourteen-room home currently contains period furniture, family portraits and items which belonged to both the Lincolns and the Todds.

Sweet Cream Pound Cake

1 cup butter, softened	½ pint whipping cream
3 cups sugar	1 teaspoon lemon juice
6 large eggs	1 teaspoon vanilla extract
3¼ cups all-purpose flour, divided	

Preheat oven to 325 degrees. Cream butter and sugar until smooth. Add eggs one at a time, beating 2 minutes after each egg. Add half the flour. Add whipping cream, lemon juice and vanilla. Add remainder of flour and mix well. Pour into a greased and floured tube pan. Bake 1 hour, 20 minutes.

Serves 12

Scotch Shortbread

2 cups butter	3 cups sifted flour (sift before measuring)
1 cup powdered sugar	1 cup rice flour

Preheat oven to 375 degrees. Cream butter; gradually add sugar, reserving 2 tablespoons. Work in flour. Turn dough onto floured board, using remaining powdered sugar. Roll to ¾-inch thickness. Cut with cookie cutters. Bake at 375 degrees 5 minutes. Lower temperature to 300 degrees and bake an additional 10 to 15 minutes until light brown. Remove immediately to prevent sticking and breakage.

Vanilla Pudding Cream Puffs

1	cup water		1	cup flour
½	cup butter		4	large eggs
¼	teaspoon (scant) salt			Garnish: whipped cream and cherries

Preheat oven to 450 degrees. In a medium saucepan bring water to a boil. Add butter and stir until melted. Add salt and flour, stirring vigorously, until mixture forms a ball that does not separate. Remove from heat. Add eggs one at a time, beating with a wooden spoon.

Fill greased muffin tins ¾ full with batter. Bake 10 minutes at 450 degrees then reduce heat to 325 degrees and bake an additional 20 minutes.

Remove puffs from tin and cool on wire rack. Cut tops of puffs off, removing some of inner puff to give more room for pudding. Fill with vanilla pudding. Replace tops of puffs and garnish with whipped cream and cherries.

Serves 12

VANILLA PUDDING

3 cups 2% milk
¾ cup sugar
⅓ cup cornstarch
2 large eggs, beaten
2 teaspoons vanilla extract
2 tablespoons butter

In a medium saucepan mix milk, sugar and cornstarch. Cook over medium-high heat, stirring constantly with a wire whisk, until mixture begins to boil, about 5 minutes. Add ⅓ cup of hot milk mixture to beaten eggs. Stir eggs into large pan of thickened milk. Reduce heat to medium-low. Stir in vanilla and butter. Cook mixture, stirring constantly, until mixture becomes a clear off white cream color. Cool pudding in refrigerator prior to filling cream puffs.

Double Chocolate Brownies with Ganache

1½	cups all-purpose flour	5	large eggs
2	teaspoons baking powder	2¼	cups sugar
1	teaspoon salt	2	teaspoons vanilla extract
1	cup butter	1	cup chocolate chips
6	ounces unsweetened chocolate		

Preheat oven to 350 degrees. Grease a 9x13-inch pan with butter. In a small bowl, combine flour, baking powder and salt; set aside. In a saucepan, combine butter and chocolate, melting over low heat until smooth; set aside. In a large bowl, beat eggs, sugar and vanilla until blended. Stir in warm chocolate mixture and flour mixture. Add chocolate chips and mix by hand until evenly distributed. Pour batter into prepared 9x13-inch pan. Bake 35 to 40 minutes or until toothpick inserted in center comes out with moist crumbs on it. When brownies are completely cooled, frost with Ganache.

GANACHE

¾	cup heavy cream	6	ounces semisweet chocolate chips

In a saucepan, melt cream and chocolate over low heat, stirring constantly. Pour over cooled brownies. Store brownies in refrigerator.

Serves 20-24

Pecan Chocolate Chip Cookies

1	cup butter	½	teaspoon salt
1	cup sugar	1	teaspoon baking powder
1	cup firmly packed brown sugar	1	teaspoon baking soda
2	eggs	½	(8 ounce) Hershey bar, frozen and finely grated
1	teaspoon vanilla extract		
2	cups all-purpose flour	1	(12 ounce) bag chocolate chips
2½	cups oatmeal	1½	cups chopped pecans

Preheat oven to 375 degrees. Cream together butter, sugar and brown sugar. Add eggs and vanilla; mix well. Combine flour, oatmeal, salt, baking powder and baking soda into a blender and blend until it resembles a powdery-like flour. Mix flour and butter mixtures together. Grate frozen chocolate bar using a cheese grater. Add chocolate chips, grated Hershey bar and nuts. Stir until evenly distributed. Form dough into golf ball size cookie balls and place on ungreased cookie sheet. Bake 6 to 8 minutes or until done.

Serves 24

Man O' War

Full grown horses generally eat nine quarts of oats per day, but one oversized superstar required twelve quarts to fill out his huge frame! Beloved Man O' War, twentieth-century Hall of Fame racer, stood 16.2 hands, with a huge girth and stride to match. "Big Red" carried more weight than his rivals, and still managed to win 20 of his 21 starts, breaking world, American, and track records across the country during his two years of racing. Known at the time as Lightning Legend and Yardstick of Greatness, Man O' War returned to Samuel D. Riddle's Fayette County Faraway Farm and was cared for by Will Harbut, his famous groom and constant companion. Will enjoyed recounting for visitors stories of Man O' War's fame, and requested that they sign the visitor ledger....63 of them containing 1,323,000 names! So beloved was Man O'War that he was the subject of four biographies and appeared on the cover of the September, 1941 Saturday Evening Post. As a sire, Man O' War produced more than 64 stakes winners and champions, including War Admiral, the 1937 Triple Crown winner.

At his death in 1947, the beloved racer was embalmed and lay in state in a specially made casket lined with his racing colors, a first for the racing industry. Thousands attended his funeral, as many more listened to the ceremony via radio. Big Red was buried at Faraway Farm and reinterred at the Kentucky Horse Park in 1977, where the Bluegrass star is memorialized by a life size statue.

Man O'War, # 1 of the top 100 U.S. Thoroughbred Champions of the 20th Century. Seen with Will Harbut, longtime groom, at his 21st birthday celebration. Broadcast by radio stations, the milestone was celebrated with two iced layer cakes and a fancy beribboned wreath... of apples and carrots.

Image: Keeneland

Equine Bill of Fare

"hay, oats, and…sweet potatoes!"

Although Bluegrass menus provide a wide variety of foods for humans, four-footed residents thrive on a standard routine diet. Horses are grazing animals with small stomachs designed to process food almost continuously, thus the amount of food a horse needs depends on its size, age, condition, and activity level. The most natural equine staple is good quality pasture grass. Hay, or dried baled grass, provides supplemental plant material, with Alfalfa being considered superior in protein content. Grain mixtures, usually including oats and molasses are fed, along with salt and vitamins. Completing the basic diet, horses drink from five to ten gallons of water each day.

Many horses have been known to prefer special treats: carrots, apples, peppermints. Others learn to drink cola or beer from a bottle or can…anything sweet is appealing. Woodford County neighbor, Airdrie Stud's 2008 Oaks Winner and three-Year-Old Filly of the Year, Proud Spell, favors raw sweet potatoes as does her sire, Proud Citizen!

SUMMER

MENU

Cheapside Kiss

Parmesan Stuffed Cherry Tomatoes

Spicy Coleslaw

Home Run Barbeque Pork

Block Party Baked Beans

Cheesy Summer Zucchini

Best Peach Pie

Summer Lemonade

SUMMER

"In the words of the pioneers, Kentucky is a land flowing with milk and honey."

Far from arid deserts and humid beaches, the protected emerald plateau of the Inner Bluegrass Region ensures an extended Summer season. Fruits, vegetables, and grain crops are afforded long warm days in which to mature and ripen, but farmers must be prepared for a hot dry summer or a rainy period, as Kentucky's weather can prove unpredictable.

The fresh greens of watercolor spring give way to summer's multicolored oil painting of jewel fruits and vegetables. Local farmers and gardeners reap the rewards of planting and sowing as new strawberries, peaches, blackberries, green beans, and finally the first ripe red tomatoes and juicy sweet corn are ready for the table. Many communities support Farmers Markets, beginning on crisp Spring weekends and flourishing in the four to five months of Summer. Continuing a tradition established decades ago, Lexingtonians gather on Saturday mornings at Cheapside Park's Farmers Market to enjoy the bounty of fruits, vegetables, and locally-produced goods.

Lexington's calendar bursts with picnics, parties, festivals, weddings, and parades celebrating Summer holidays. Polo matches in the Park and summer outings provide the perfect venue for warm weather tailgating, community gatherings, and seasonal fare. Brides prefer to schedule weddings during the warm months of summer, taking advantage of a lush garden setting or the unique aura of a historic museum house.

Central Kentucky hostesses plan summer menus featuring the garden or market's bounty, and enjoy greeting guests in lush gardens and on comfortable porches bordered by fancy iron filigree. Taking advantage of nature's bounty, many build on the heritage of Southern cuisine by preserving, pickling, canning, making conserves and jelly, realizing the long, hot days will shorten and fade and another growing season will soon end.

As they have done for generations, livestock farmers take advantage of the warm days of summer to preserve and stockpile food sources for winter feeding. During the progression of the Summer season, pastures are transformed into nature's art galleries, showcasing sculptural bales of hay… large 1000-pound rolls or smaller square bales of preserved grass and forage. Bluegrass farmers, ever mindful of nature's design, acknowledge the admonition to "make hay while the sun shines."

The sun does, indeed, shine bright on my Summer Kentucky home.

Image: Summer Divider Page, Hope House, Dr. and Mrs. Elvis Donaldson

Ornamental Iron

Elaborate iron fences and gates guarding the historic homes, gardens, and public parks may have been forged at Joseph Bruen's Foundry in Lexington. Established in 1816 and operating for half a century, the foundry was supplied by Red River Iron Works and Owingsville's Slate Creek Ironworks, both transporting supplies to Lexington via Iron Works Pike. Blacksmiths traditionally hammered

horseshoes, hoes and shovels, but the demand for highly decorative work grew as Lexington's historic houses and gardens multiplied. A few former blacksmiths began to specialize in fences, railings, arched doorways and grill patterns, and became known as whitesmiths. A number of fences and gates in historic neighborhoods exhibit the symbol of Springfield Iron Works, others of Stewart Ironworks. Winner of the 1904 St. Louis World's Fair Grand Prize and Gold Medal of Merit, Stewart's of Northern Kentucky produced wrought iron fencing, gates, benches, and fountains for some of Lexington's finest homes, parks, and cemeteries.

Market Houses

"..here the Lexington housewife comes marketing..."

*"The government of the Commonwealth of Kentucky
was organized in Lexington on June 4, 1792"*

Lexington's early market houses provided a center of political and economic activity for the pioneer city, serving as public marketplace, gathering ground, and courthouse. In addition to being a shopping center for local housewives, it was here that the first Kentucky legislature met: "The government of the Commonwealth of Kentucky was organized in a ceremonial meeting in Lexington on June 4, 1792. Isaac Shelby of Lincoln County was appointed governor. Assembled in a log building, perhaps the public market house, near the corner of Main Street and Broadway, the governor-elect took the oath of office. Three days following, Isaac Shelby met with legislators on the upper floor of the same log house."

Cheapside, between Main and Short streets, was set aside in the 1780 town plat as the public square. Named for its counterpart in London, England, Cheapside accommodated the area's first school buildings and was a popular horse trading center, particularly during 'court' or 'market' days. G.W. Ranck in the 1872 History of Lexington: "Cheapside, located on the west side of the old Fayette County Courthouse on Main Street, was the site of both slave auctions and impassioned abolitionist speeches before the Civil War."

Image: University of Kentucky Archives

November Court Day, 1897

Cheapside Kiss

CHEAPSIDE BAR AND GRILL

1½ ounces Stoll Ohranj (orange-flavored Vodka)	½ ounce cranberry juice
¾ ounce Pama (pomegranate liqueur)	½ orange, sliced
	Club soda

Chill martini glass by filling with ice and club soda prior to preparing recipe. Fill martini shaker half full with ice. Add vodka, liqueur and cranberry juice. Shake vigorously for at least 60 seconds or until metal cup frosts. Strain into chilled martini glass and garnish with orange slice.

Serves 1

Banana Punch

6 cups water	Juice of 2 lemons
4 cups sugar	6 ripe bananas, mashed
4 (6 ounce) cans frozen orange juice	3 quarts lemon-lime soda
1 (64 ounce) can pineapple juice	

To make syrup, mix sugar and water; cook until sugar is dissolved; cool. Add orange juice, pineapple juice, lemon juice and bananas; stir well. Freeze in two separate containers. Two hours before serving remove from freezer, add lemon-lime soda, and slush down with potato masher.

Makes 1 gallon

Early Schools

"It is said that the first school in Lexington was founded to keep younger boys occupied so that they would not be roaming through the forests where they might be picked up by prowling Indians." John McKinney taught early classes in a log cabin near Main Street. Lexington later saw a series of private or semi public schools: Van Doren's, Mrs. Beck's, Dr. Ward's, Madame Mentelle's, Layfayette Academy, and Sayre College were among the more prominent early schools. Sayre, organized in 1854 by David A. Sayre, a prominent Lexington businessman, was first located on Mill Street, and two years later moved to Limestone. The school operated as Transylvania Female Institute until 1876 when it was renamed Sayre School. Today Sayre educates students from preschool through twelfth grade.

Sangria

3 liters white wine
Juice of 3 lemons
6 tablespoons sugar

¾ cup triple sec
3 (8 ounce) bottles club soda
Garnish: lemon slices

Mix together white wine, lemon juice, sugar and triple sec. Chill. Add club soda immediately before serving. Garnish with lemon slices.

Serves 20

Strawberry Slush Punch

1 (6 ounce) box strawberry gelatin
½ cup sugar
2 cups boiling water
1 (6 ounce) can frozen orange juice concentrate

1 (6 ounce) can frozen lemonade
6 cups cold water
1 (64 ounce) can pineapple juice
1 liter ginger ale

Dissolve strawberry gelatin and sugar in boiling water. Add orange juice and lemonade. Stir in cold water and pineapple juice; mix well. Place mixture in 2 large zip top freezer bags and place in freezer until ready to serve. When serving, remove bags from freezer and allow to partially thaw until slushy. Place in serving container and pour ginger ale over fruit punch mixture.

Summer Lemonade

3 lemons
1 cup sugar

5 cups water, divided
1 cup fresh lemon juice

Peel lemons, leaving pith on fruit. Cut lemon rind into ¼-inch strips. Combine lemon strips, sugar and 2 cups water in a medium saucepan. Bring to a boil; boil 7 minutes. Let cool. Transfer mixture to a pitcher, discarding lemon strips, if desired. Add remaining 3 cups water and lemon juice; stir well. Cover and chill thoroughly.

Makes 1½ quarts

Kentucky's Other Beverage: Wine

In addition to being known for its long tradition of bourbon culture, the Bluegrass was home to America's first commercial vineyard. As early as 1798, Jean J. DuFour, Swiss winemaker for the Marquis de Lafayette, recognized Kentucky's friendly climate, rich soil, and limestone-filtered water as similar characteristics of the wine making regions of France and Italy...ideal qualities for grape culture.

Joining prominent Kentucky statesmen, including Henry Clay, DuFour established the Kentucky Vineyard Society and planted First Vineyard, located in a deep bend of the Kentucky River southwest of Lexington. Although short lived, First Vineyard provided the basis for a Kentucky wine industry that became the nation's third largest by the late 1800s, until Prohibition brought a halt to all spirit production in the 1920s.

Within the past decade, as Bluegrass farmers search for alternative crops to replace the long standing tobacco tradition, the Kentucky wine trail has grown to 52 wineries, with Fayette County and its neighbors boasting a dozen of these agritourism facilities. Hosting public events and weddings, many vineyards provide an entertainment venue in the Commonwealth's magnificent countryside.

Classic Sweet Tea

2½ quarts cold, filtered water

2 family-size tea bags or 6 regular-size bags

½ cup granulated sugar

In a clean kettle bring 2 cups water to a rolling boil. Place tea bags in a heat-resistant container and pour boiling water over. Cover and steep for 7 minutes. Discard tea bags…do not squeeze. Add sugar to tea concentrate, stir and add 2 quarts filtered cold water. Serve over ice with or without lemon or a sprig of mint.

May use 4 tablespoons loose tea instead of tea bags; strain out leaves before adding sugar. If making green tea, use warm water, not hot in the brewing process. Do not use the same utensils or containers for tea and coffee, as coffee oils will infuse into the tea.

Southern Sweet Tea

'Sweet tea'…'house wine,' or 'champagne of the South'

During the mid-nineteenth century, green tea was the tea of choice. An 1839 cookbook, The Kentucky Housewife, by Mrs. Lettice Bryan, printed a typical American tea punch recipe, including very strong tea, loaf sugar, rich sweet cream, and claret or champagne. The punch could be served hot or cold in glass cups. Fifty years later, black tea appeared in printed recipes.

Ice tea was popularized and quickly commercialized at the 1904 World's Fair in St. Louis, as visitors searched for cool drinks in the extremely hot weather. By World War I, Americans were buying tall 'ice tea' glasses, long spoons, and lemon forks.

*1928 – **Southern Cooking,** by Henrietta Stanley Dull, Home Economics Editor for the Atlanta Journal, lists the recipe that remained standard in the South for decades thereafter.*

Freshly brewed tea, after three to five minutes' infusion, is essential if a good quality is desired. The water, as for coffee, should be freshly boiled and poured over the tea for this short time…The tea leaves may be removed when the desired strength is obtained…Tea, when it is to be iced, should be made much stronger, to allow for the ice used in chilling. A medium strength tea is usually liked. A good blend and grade of black tea is most popular for iced tea, while green and black are used for hot…To sweeten tea for an iced drink, less sugar is required if put in while tea is hot. Iced tea should be served with or without lemon, with a sprig of mint, a strawberry, a cherry, a slice of orange, or pineapple. This may be fresh or canned fruit. Milk is not used in iced tea.

Peddlers and Provisions

Itinerant peddlers were the first entrepreneurs in early Lexington. With the opening of stores and taverns, Lexington soon became a supply center for travelers between East and West. Merchants replenished stocks from Philadelphia and Baltimore, as goods were brought on pack horses to Pittsburgh, then floated down the Ohio to Maysville and carted overland to Lexington. The Bluegrass region bartered hides, skins, furs, ginseng, homemade linens, hams, lard, lumber, butter, and toward the close of the eighteenth century, whiskey, tobacco and hemp were sent to New Orleans. As early as 1787, flatboats and wagons brought teapots, chinaware, linens, coffee, tea and chocolate, sugar, spices, and seasonings to the frontier town.

During the late nineteenth century Lexington Roller Mills produced its popular "Lexington Cream" flour for decades.

The first modern post offices in Lexington were located on the Northwest corner of Broadway and Short Streets circa 1870. Afterwards a series of grocery stores appeared on the site: Voght & Foley grocery, Piggly-Wiggly, and finally Kroger. Piggly Wiggly became America's first self-service grocery store, founded in Memphis, Tennessee in 1916. The store was unlike any to that date, featuring shopping baskets, open shelves, no clerks to shop for the customer....revolutionary!

Piggly Wiggly, 133 North Broadway and Short Street – June 20, 1931

Image: University of Kentucky Archives

Overnight Pancakes with Brown Sugar Syrup

1½	cups dry old-fashioned oatmeal	2	teaspoons baking powder
½	cup yellow cornmeal	1	teaspoon salt
2½	cups buttermilk	2	eggs, beaten
½	cup whole wheat flour	5	tablespoons melted butter
2	tablespoons brown sugar		Milk, if necessary
1	teaspoon baking soda		

In a large bowl, combine oats, cornmeal and buttermilk. Cover and refrigerate overnight. The next morning, sift together flour, sugar, baking soda, baking powder and salt twice, then add to the oat mixture. Stir in eggs and butter. If thinner pancakes are desired, add milk. Spoon batter onto hot griddle or skillet, greased with butter. Turn when bubbles appear on top and remove to a warm platter until ready to serve.

Serves 6

BROWN SUGAR SYRUP

½	cup light corn syrup	½	cup water
½	cup light brown sugar		Dash salt, to taste
½	cup sugar		Vanilla extract, to taste

In a saucepan, bring corn syrup, brown sugar, sugar and water to a boil. Turn down heat and allow mixture to simmer for 2 minutes. Add salt and vanilla to taste. If thicker syrup is desired, boil for several more minutes. May store in refrigerator for several weeks.

Makes 2 cups

Creamy Scrambled Eggs

3	eggs	¼	teaspoon salt
¼	cup milk	⅛	teaspoon pepper
½	(3 ounce) package cream cheese, cubed	3	tablespoons chopped green onions
		1½	tablespoons butter

Combine eggs, milk, cream cheese, salt and pepper in a blender; cover and process at medium speed until frothy (7 to 10 seconds). Stir in onion. Melt butter in a large nonstick skillet over medium heat, tilting pan to coat bottom; pour in egg mixture. Cook without stirring until mixture begins to set on bottom. Draw a spatula across bottom of pan to form large curds. Continue cooking until eggs are thickened but still moist.

Serves 2-3

Notable Neighbor: CastlePost

Forty years ago, massive 12-foot stone walls and corner turrets of a mysterious structure began to rise on the western border of Fayette County. Surrounded by historic farms in neighboring Woodford County, the unfinished castle remained a landmark protected by massive, lion-headed gates, the subject of curiosity, intrigue, and rumor for more than thirty years.

In 2003, Miami attorney and University of Kentucky graduate, Thomas Post purchased the castle property including 50 acres of land and a tobacco barn. Today, CastlePost, a luxury tourist inn, features 16 guest suites, an elegant ballroom, billiard room, tennis court, basketball court, swimming pool, and full complement of staff equipped to provide royal accommodations in the Bluegrass.

Crab Cakes

THE MOUSETRAP

1	(16 ounce) can blue crab lump meat	1	teaspoon Old Bay Seasoning
1	(16 ounce) can blue crab claw meat	2	large eggs
1	red pepper, finely diced	⅓	cup mayonnaise
½	cup finely chopped parsley	¼	cup canola oil
1	cup fine breadcrumbs		

Open cans of crabmeat and remove any shell fragments from within. Mix together with red pepper, parsley, breadcrumbs and Old Bay Seasoning, reserving a small amount of parsley. Add eggs and mayonnaise and mix until ingredients bind together. Form mixture into 3½ to 4 ounce cakes, making a shape similar to a hockey puck. Warm oil in a sauté pan to medium heat and gently place cakes in the oil. Sauté until golden brown on one side, about 3 minutes. Flip and brown the other side. Remove cakes from oil and place on paper towels to absorb any extra oil. Garnish with reserved parsley.

Makes 12 crab cakes

Party Burger Bites on Rye

1	pound ground beef	1	teaspoon garlic powder
1	pound hot sausage	1	teaspoon cayenne pepper
1	pound American cheese slices	2	loaves party rye bread
1	teaspoon oregano		

Preheat oven to 350 degrees. Brown ground beef and sausage in skillet; drain. Add cheese and simmer until melted. Add oregano, garlic powder and cayenne pepper. Mix well. Spread on party rye bread and bake 10 to 15 minutes. Serve hot.

Serves 18

Farmers Market Fresh Salsa

3	ripe tomatoes, seeded and diced	1	tablespoon finely chopped fresh cilantro
½	cup chopped onion	2	teaspoons salt
4-6	fresh serrano chili peppers (or jalapeño peppers), seeded and finely chopped	2	teaspoons fresh lime juice

Stir all ingredients together in a bowl and let stand at least 1 hour before serving. Serve with tortilla chips.

Serves 12

Parmesan Stuffed Cherry Tomatoes

2-3 pints cherry tomatoes
4 cups finely grated fresh Parmesan cheese
4 teaspoons chopped green onion
4 tablespoons mayonnaise
(enough to moisten)

6 strips bacon, cooked crisp and crumbled in small pieces
¼ teaspoon black pepper

Using a very small melon baller or ¼ teaspoon, scoop out cherry tomatoes. In food processor, pulse together Parmesan cheese, green onion, mayonnaise, bacon and black pepper. Fill centers of cherry tomatoes with mixture. Serve as appetizer or side dish.

Serves 12-18

Tomato Basil Parmesan Dip

1 (8 ounce) package cream cheese
½ cup sour cream
½ cup shredded Parmesan cheese
5 Roma tomatoes, diced

5 green onions, diced
1 tablespoon fresh chopped basil
Salt and pepper, to taste

Beat together cream cheese, sour cream and Parmesan cheese. Stir in tomatoes, green onion and basil. Add salt and pepper, to taste. Refrigerate at least 2 hours before eating. Serve with crackers, pretzels or vegetable sticks.

Serves 12-15

Avocado, Tomato and Feta Cheese Dip

2 avocados, peeled and chopped
4 Roma tomatoes, chopped
1 small red onion, chopped
1 small bunch cilantro, trimmed and chopped
4 ounces feta cheese, crumbled

¼ cup olive oil
1 tablespoon red wine vinegar
1 tablespoon ground cumin
1 teaspoon kosher salt
1 tablespoon lime juice

Combine avocados, tomatoes and onion in a bowl; mix gently. Stir in cilantro. Add feta cheese, olive oil, vinegar, cumin, salt and lime juice; mix until combined. Cover and chill in refrigerator. Serve with tortilla chips or crostini.

Serves 20

Gratz Park

*....".....A community where neighbors know each other's names
and share responsibility for preserving the beauty of the neighborhood and its
historic character. Most of the large homes accommodate groups, and neighbors
gather often, with food as the centerpiece."*

Cooking in the Park 2003

On the north boundary of Lexington's business district, majestic shade trees shelter a historic green commons bordered by handsome iron gates and adorned with a bronze-statued fountain honoring children. Gratz Park is anchored by the Carnegie Center for Literacy and Learning, (formerly Lexington Public Library) and Transylvania University. The Historic District includes three early churches, two public museum houses, and dozens of private homes, architectural gems dating from the 1790s to the 1970s. Christened Centennial Park in 1876, the site of community concerts, horse shows, and public meetings, the neighborhood was later renamed for the Gratz family, who remained pivotally active in the Park's preservation for generations.

The heritage of the Gratz Park Historical District is entwined with that of a young city that was known in the early nineteenth century as the "Athens of the West." After serving as the first campus of Transylvania University, the park became a parade ground and bivouac area for Union and Confederate troops during the Civil War. It was then rescued by Howard Gratz, who repaired much of the damage suffered during the War and planted many of the park's tulip poplar trees. Among other improvements, a wrought iron fence was constructed around the entire commons perimeter with highly-arched double gates at the four corners. The arch installed in the park today is an exact replica, and the attached gates are original.

In 1958 Gratz Park was named the first local historic district in the Commonwealth, and twenty years later, was listed on the National Register of Historic Places. Today, Gratz Park is maintained by the Lexington Fayette Urban County Government Division of Parks and Recreation and overseen by an active Gratz Park Neighborhood Association.

Roasted Red Pepper Soup

GREENTREE TEAROOM

1   sweet onion, chopped
     Vegetable oil

4   cloves garlic, minced

5-6 fully ripe red sweet bell peppers,
       roasted, peeled and chopped

3   cups vegetable broth

1   (10 ounce) can tomato paste

Pinch of sugar (just to accentuate flavors, not to sweeten)

White pepper and/or cayenne pepper, to taste

Sea salt

½   cup heavy cream

Sauté sweet onion in a small amount of oil until translucent. Add garlic and cook briefly, but do not brown. Add roasted peppers. Using a food processor or food mill, process onions, garlic and roasted peppers until relatively smooth; preserving a bit of texture. Combine roasted pepper mixture with vegetable broth, tomato paste, sugar, pepper and salt in a pot and simmer for about 5 minutes. Remove from heat and finish with heavy cream.

Serves 6

Corn and Crab Chowder

6	slices bacon	3	cups fresh corn, cut from ears (about 6 ears)
2	celery ribs, diced	1	pound fresh lump crabmeat
1	medium green pepper, diced	1	cup whipping cream
1	medium onion, diced	¼	cup chopped fresh cilantro
1	jalapeño pepper, seeded and diced	1	teaspoon kosher salt
4	cups unsalted chicken broth	½	teaspoon coarse black pepper
3	tablespoons all-purpose flour		Garnish: crumbled bacon, fresh cilantro

Cook bacon until crisp; drain; crumble into small pieces. Reserve 2 tablespoons bacon drippings. Sauté celery, green pepper, onion and jalapeño pepper in bacon drippings until tender. Whisk together broth and flour until smooth. Add to celery mixture. Stir in corn. Bring to a boil; reduce heat and simmer, stirring occasionally for approximately 30 minutes. Gently stir in crabmeat, whipping cream, cilantro, salt and pepper. Cook for 5 minutes or until thoroughly heated. Garnish with crumbled bacon and fresh chopped cilantro.

Serves 6

Mexican Bean Soup

2	(14 ounce) cans chicken broth	1	smoked sausage ring, cut in bite-sized pieces
1	can roasted garlic chicken broth	½	(1 pound) box rotini pasta, cooked by box directions
2	cups water		
1	small can diced tomatoes with green chilies	1	can Mexi-corn, drained
2	tablespoons minced fresh cilantro	1	can black beans, rinsed and drained
1	teaspoon chili powder	1	tablespoon lime juice

Combine broths, water, tomatoes, cilantro and chili powder in a large pot; bring to a boil. Cover, reduce heat and simmer 10 minutes. Add sausage, pasta, corn and black beans to broth mixture. Simmer 10 to 12 minutes. Stir in lime juice. Do not overcook or pasta will lose its shape. Serve while hot.

Serves 6-8

Saddlebreds and Lexington Junior League

In addition to the Thoroughbred and Standardbred, the American Saddlebred is the third breed of horse found on Bluegrass farms. Descended from a cross between an 1830 American Thoroughbred Denmark, and easy-gaited Bluegrass mares, the Kentucky Saddle Horse became important in the day when horses provided the major means of transportation, and was a major Kentucky export in the mid nineteenth century. As motorized vehicles were introduced, the Saddlebred evolved into a show horse, performing in gaited, harness and pleasure divisions. Bluegrass breeders were instrumental in developing and improving bloodlines, as exemplified by Wing Commander, considered one of the first Saddlebred celebrities. Owned by Fayette County's Dodge Stables, now Castleton-Lyons Farm, the World Champion title holder during the decades of the 1940s and 50s, became a leading sire of famous Saddlebreds.

Lexington was the scene of one of America's first horse shows in 1816, and the tradition continues

today with the annual Lexington Junior League Charity Horse Show. Celebrating more than seventy years of operation, the Show has generated millions of dollars for the local community, becoming one of the most prestigious events in the industry, as well as the first leg of the Saddlebred Triple Crown. In addition to its charitable activities, Lexington's Junior League maintains the historic Bodley-Bullock House in Gratz Park as a museum and public event facility.

As the need for saddle and carriage horses increased, England's London and Newmarket sales facilities, founded by Richard Tattersall, expanded to the United States in 1892 as Tattersall's Light Horse Sales Facility. Located near downtown Lexington and the Red Mile, Tattersalls has offered Standardbreds and Saddlebreds through the auction ring for decades.

Almond Salad with Red Wine Dressing

SALAD

½	cup almonds	1	cup chopped celery
2	tablespoons sugar	2	whole green onions, chopped
½	head iceberg lettuce	1	can Mandarin oranges
½	head romaine lettuce		

Place almonds in a nonstick pan with sugar and cook until sugar is dissolved and almonds are coated and brown. Cool; break apart. Mix both types of lettuce, celery, onion and oranges. Chill. When ready to serve, toss with Red Wine Dressing and top with almonds.

RED WINE DRESSING

2	tablespoons sugar	1½	tablespoons grated yellow onion
1½	teaspoons Dijon mustard	1	cup canola oil
⅓	cup red wine vinegar	1½	tablespoons poppy seeds
¼	teaspoon salt		

Blend sugar, mustard, vinegar, salt and onion in a food processor or blender for 1 minute. Slowly add oil with processor running. Stir in poppy seeds.

Serves 5

Headley-Whitney Museum

George Headley III (1908-1985), accomplished West Coast jewelry designer, returned to his family's Fayette County farm, La Belle, to design jewelry and bibelots. Along with his wife, Barbara Whitney Henry Peck, sister of Cornelius Vanderbilt Whitney, Headley opened a jewel room and library on the picturesque farm grounds. The Headley-Whitney Museum, completed in 1970, features a Shell Grotto, exhibit facilities, and a venue for elegant Bluegrass weddings.

Headley-Whitney Museum showcases the famous Whitney doll houses, miniature replicas of C.V. and Marylou Whitney's Maple Hill in Fayette County. Having traveled the country raising funds for charity, the four dollhouses feature Aubusson carpets, table settings, chandeliers, functional piano and harp, as well as miniature diamond rings and readable books, all faithful details of the Whitney home.

Old Fair Grounds and Floral Hall

The Kentucky Agricultural & Mechanical Association hosted early fairs at Maxwell Springs, modern site of the UK Campus. After the original amphitheater burned in 1861, the group purchased a tract of land on South Broadway and constructed a race course anchored by a succession of elaborate grandstands. The Association's first annual fair was held in August, 1872, boasting trotting horse races each day at the Red Mile trotting track. The fairgrounds hosted carnivals, circuses, and the first Blue Grass Fair.

Remaining on the grounds of the Red Mile as a heritage of the Kentucky Association is Floral Hall, a unique octagonal building designed in 1879 by Lexington architect, John McMurtry. Originally, the three-story structure housed poultry exhibits, homegrown products, flowers, and canned goods during the fairs. In later years it was known as the Berry Barn in honor of trainer, Tom Berry, and in 1971 was designated the Standardbred Stable of Memories, housing collections of antique racing carts, carriages, sleighs, and other equine memorabilia.

Image: University of Kentucky Archives

Golden Beet Salad

6   medium-size golden beets
     (about 6 ounces each)
1   cup pecan halves
¼   cup rice wine vinegar
1   large shallot, minced
2   tablespoons light brown sugar
½   teaspoon salt

½   teaspoon freshly ground pepper
¾   teaspoon vanilla extract
¼   cup canola oil
1   (5 ounce) package gourmet mixed salad
     greens, thoroughly washed
1   cup (4 ounces) crumbled Gorgonzola
     cheese

Preheat oven to 400 degrees. Trim beet stems to 1-inch; gently wash beets thoroughly. Wrap individually in aluminum foil and place on jelly-roll pan or cookie sheet. Bake 1 hour or until tender. Transfer to a wire rack, and let cool, wrapped in foil 30 minutes.

Meanwhile, decrease oven temperature to 350 degrees. Bake pecans in a single layer in a jelly-roll pan or cookie sheet 5 to 7 minutes or until lightly toasted and fragrant. Cool completely on wire rack (about 15 minutes).

In a small bowl, whisk together vinegar, shallot, brown sugar, salt, ground pepper and vanilla. Add oil in a slow, steady stream, whisking constantly until smooth.

Peel beets and remove stem ends. Cut beets into ½-inch wedges; gently toss with ⅓ cup vinegar mixture.

Arrange greens on a serving platter. Top with beet mixture, Gorgonzola cheese and pecans. Serve with remaining vinaigrette.

Serves 4-6

Expression: Get Your Goat

Most thoroughbreds hate to be alone, therefore, some enjoy a mascot or buddy. Goats are particularly favored to keep high-strung thoroughbreds calm. An old racetrack trick to throw your opponent's horse off his form, or excite him, was to steal his mascot, therefore, the expression "get your goat," still means to upset someone rendering him vulnerable.

Spicy Coleslaw

COLESLAW

4   pounds cabbage (green, red, savoy), thinly sliced

3   cherry tomatoes, halved

1   large sweet onion, thinly sliced

3   cucumbers, peeled, sliced and diced

1   small red bell pepper, cut into thin strips

1   small yellow bell pepper, cut into thin strips

Combine all vegetables in a large salad bowl and toss with dressing to coat.

SALAD DRESSING

1½   cups mayonnaise

½   cup cider vinegar

¼   cup sugar, or to taste

1   tablespoon Tabasco sauce

2   teaspoons kosher salt

½   teaspoon freshly ground pepper

Whisk together mayonnaise, vinegar, sugar, Tabasco sauce, salt and pepper until sugar is dissolved.

Serves 12

Hot Sweet Pickles

1   (32 ounce) jar dill pickle chips

1   tablespoon minced garlic

2   cups sugar, divided

2   ounces Tabasco sauce

Drain pickles well and put back in jar. Combine garlic, 1 cup sugar and Tabasco sauce and add to the pickles. Close jar and shake until well dissolved. Add remaining sugar and shake again until dissolved. Store in refrigerator for up to 1 week, shaking occasionally.

Home Grown Tomato Salad with Cucumber Dressing

MERRICK INN RESTAURANT

Lettuce leaves

Fresh home grown tomatoes, sliced

Place 2 to 3 tomato slices on each salad plate that has been lined with a lettuce leaf. Add a dollop of Cucumber Dressing.

CUCUMBER DRESSING

6	cucumbers	3	tablespoons sugar
4	bunches green onions	1	tablespoon white pepper
½	gallon mayonnaise	1	teaspoon garlic
3	cups sour cream	½	teaspoon salt

Peel and remove seeds from cucumbers; slice. Wash and chop green onions. Using a food processor, finely chop cucumbers and green onions together. Place in strainer to drain excess liquid. Combine mayonnaise, sour cream, sugar, white pepper, garlic and salt together in a large bowl. Add drained cucumbers and green onions to mixture. Mix well.

Makes approximately 3 quarts

Merrick Inn

Fayette County horseman Cal Milam trained many thoroughbreds, but his favorite was Merrick. The thoroughbred won 62 races and lived a record 38 years. Interred in 1941 near the manor house, Merrick's headstone reads: "Noble in Character, Worthy in Deeds."

The Manor House on one of Lexington's famous horse farms was built before the Civil War. On this site, the Murray family has owned and operated the Merrick Inn for more than 35 years, providing casual dining and traditional cuisine in the stately manor house. Known for innovative southern cuisine, served in a historic Bluegrass setting, Merrick Inn is a Bluegrass institution.

Corn Cornucopia

1   (12 ounce) can shoepeg corn
1   (15 ounce) can Le Sueur peas
1   (15 ounce) can black beans, rinsed and drained
1   cup chopped celery
1   cup chopped green onion
1   whole green pepper, chopped
1   (4 ounce) jar pimentos, drained

1   (14½ ounce) can French green beans, drained
1   cup sugar
½   cup vegetable oil
¼   cup cider vinegar
1   teaspoon salt
1   teaspoon pepper

In a large bowl mix corn, peas, beans, celery, green onion, green pepper, pimentos and green beans. In a saucepan, mix together sugar, oil, vinegar, salt and pepper. Boil 3 minutes and cool. Pour over vegetables and refrigerate.

Serves 12-15

Summer Garden Salad

3½ cups fresh or frozen corn
¾   cup peeled and diced cucumber
¼   cup diced onion
2   small tomatoes, seeded and diced
¼   cup sour cream

2   tablespoons mayonnaise
1   tablespoon vinegar
½   teaspoon salt
¼   teaspoon dry mustard
¼   teaspoon celery seed

In a large bowl mix corn, cucumber, onion and tomatoes. In a separate bowl mix together sour cream, mayonnaise, vinegar, salt, dry mustard and celery seed. Pour over corn mixture and mix well. Place in refrigerator for 2 to 3 hours prior to serving.

Serves 8

Kentucky Wonder Green Bean Salad

1	cup chopped walnuts		¼	teaspoon salt
¾	cup olive oil		¼	teaspoon pepper
¼	cup white wine vinegar		1½	pounds fresh green beans
1	tablespoon chopped fresh dill		1	small purple onion, thinly sliced
½	teaspoon minced garlic		1	(4 ounce) package crumbled feta cheese

Preheat oven to 350 degrees. Bake walnuts, stirring occasionally, 5 to 10 minutes until toasted.

Combine oil, vinegar, dill, garlic, salt and pepper; cover and chill. Break green beans into thirds. Steam over boiling water 15 minutes, or until tender crisp. Plunge into cold water; drain and pat dry. Combine walnuts, beans, onion and feta cheese in a large bowl. Toss, cover and chill. Pour oil mixture over bean mixture 1 hour before serving. Toss and serve.

Serves 6

Ambrosia

4	ounces cream cheese, softened	1	cup mini marshmallows
¼	cup sour cream	½	cup sweetened shredded coconut, plus
1¼	cups Mandarin oranges, drained		1-2 tablespoons for garnish
1	cup crushed pineapple, drained		

In a mixing bowl, whip cream cheese and sour cream together until lightened. Gently stir in oranges, pineapple, marshmallows and coconut. Sprinkle with remaining coconut. Cover and chill for at least 4 hours.

Serves 10-12

Lemon-Pineapple Salad

2	(3 ounce) packages lemon-flavored gelatin	1	(8 ounce) container frozen whipped topping, thawed
2	cups boiling water	1	(15 ounce) can crushed pineapple, undrained
1	(21 ounce) can lemon pie filling	2	teaspoons grated lemon rind

Stir together gelatin and boiling water in a large bowl until dissolved. Chill 1 hour or until consistency of unbeaten egg whites. Whisk in lemon pie filling and whipped topping until smooth. Fold in pineapple and lemon rind. Spoon mixture into a lightly greased 2-quart mold or serving dish. Chill 8 hours or until firm.

Serves 10-12

Bluegrass Superstition:

Perhaps the most popular superstition is that the horseshoe should be displayed with the open end up, so your luck won't run out!

Cattle

Almost every settler who traveled to Kentucky through the Cumberland Gap brought a cow, as bovines were hardy travelers who adapted readily to primitive conditions. Supplying milk and beef, cattle became important to the Bluegrass almost immediately upon settlement.

In the early nineteenth century Henry Clay began building his livestock herds by importing purebred Hereford cattle from England, and since that time the region has been known for cattle production and sales.

Lexington has been home to the largest cattle marketing system east of the Mississippi for decades. Bluegrass Stockyards remains among the largest in the country and draws cattle from

most Kentucky counties and many surrounding states. "The Bluegrass Region has the largest assembly of cattle brokers in the United States. Eastern Livestock, the largest order buyer in the nation, has offices in Lexington. S&B Cattle Company and Eugene Barber & Sons are national players that are also based in Lexington."

Business Lexington, 2007.

Today, as the largest cattle-producing state east of the Mississippi River, Kentucky is home to over 1.17 million beef cows and ranks 5th nationally in the total number of cattle farms. Stocker and feeder commercial herds join registered Angus, Limousin, and Charolais seen here.

Fruity Peanut Chicken Salad

2	pounds boneless, skinless chicken breasts		1	cup chopped celery
2	tablespoons extra virgin olive oil		2	tablespoons lemon juice
1	tablespoon dried rosemary		2	tablespoons pineapple juice
2	cups halved seedless red grapes		1	cup mayonnaise
1	(20 ounce) can pineapple tidbits, drained (reserve 2 tablespoons juice)		1	cup coarsely chopped honey-roasted peanuts

Boil chicken in water with olive oil and rosemary until fully cooked; drain in colander, reserving rosemary. Chop chicken into bite-size pieces. Place chicken and rosemary in large bowl. Add grapes, pineapple, celery, lemon juice and pineapple juice. Cover and refrigerate for at least 2 hours. Just before serving, gently fold in mayonnaise and honey-roasted peanuts. Serve on a bed of lettuce or on bun for sandwiches.

Serves 8-10

Expression: Cooking From Scratch

To cook a dish with basic ingredients, no boxed mixes or convenience foods, is termed "from scratch."

The expression "Starting from Scratch" originated in sports, particularly cricket and boxing, meaning a line or mark that indicated a boundary or starting point. Applied figuratively the expression means 'from nothing or with no favorable odds.'

The Bluegrass version involves two horsemen who were preparing their horses for a heated race. One scratched a line in the dirt street to indicate where the front hooves should be placed, therefore, the race began from 'scratch.'

Finger Lickin' Chicken

2-3 pound fryer, cut up or 8-10 small chicken pieces	1 teaspoon salt
2 quarts water	1-2 teaspoons black pepper
2 tablespoons salt	3-4 cups shortening or lard
2 cups all-purpose flour	Salt and pepper, to taste

Immerse small fryer pieces in salted water for at least 3 hours (or overnight) to pull out impurities and to tenderize meat. Heat shortening or lard in a well-seasoned 10 to 12-inch cast iron skillet on medium heat. Season flour with salt and pepper; dredge chicken pieces in flour mixture. Chicken should be immersed about halfway in the hot shortening. Avoid overcrowding pieces in the skillet.

Brown chicken for 8 to 10 minutes on each side; turning once with tongs. (When frying, do not puncture pieces or juices will be lost.) Place lid on skillet for approximately 3 minutes. Remove lid and finish frying for approximately 5 to 7 more minutes or until chicken is thoroughly browned. Chicken cooks fast; do not over cook. Remove and drain on paper towels or rack.

Serves 8-10

Kentucky Fried Chicken

Chicken has been a staple of Bluegrass menus since pioneer days. During the great depression, Harland Sanders' fried chicken was the most popular item at the Corbin, Kentucky Sanders Café and Gas Station. Due to the popularity of the chicken and marketing savvy of Colonel Sanders, by the early 1960s more than 200 United States outlets were preparing chicken with the secret recipe and frying method. Today a subsidiary of Yum! Brands based in Louisville, Kentucky, KFC or Kentucky Fried Chicken is served at 15,000 outlets in 105 countries and territories around the world.

The Colonel's secret recipe of '11 herbs and spices' remains such a highly secured trade secret that portions of the classified mix are created in different locations in the United States and shipped to headquarters to be blended. One copy of the secret spice mix, written in pencil on a single sheet of notebook paper and signed by Sanders, is guarded at corporate headquarters in a vault, only accessible to two unnamed executives at any one time.

Peachy Chicken

4	boneless, skinless chicken breasts	⅓	cup firmly packed brown sugar
	Flour, to dredge	1	(15 ounce) can peaches in juice (reserving juice)
2	tablespoons oil		
2	cups orange juice	1	tablespoon cornstarch

Lightly coat chicken with flour. Heat oil in a large skillet; add chicken and cook until brown. Combine orange juice, brown sugar and juice from peaches. Pour over chicken. Cook covered over medium heat for 25 minutes, or until done. Add peaches and heat 5 minutes. Remove chicken from skillet and thicken sauce with cornstarch. Serve over rice with sauce.

Serves 4

Fayette County's Courthouses

Lexington has seen a series of courthouses, the first being a simple log structure constructed in 1782. It was replaced by a two-story stone structure in 1788, which housed Kentucky's first provisional government until the state's capital city of Frankfort was selected. The third was constructed in 1806, and the fourth, built in 1884, burned three years later. Lexington's fifth courthouse (1900) serves as the modern Lexington History Museum. A few blocks away, Circuit and District Courts are housed in the newest complex, The Robert F. Stephens Courthouse Complex (2001). A series of distinctive fountains graces the plaza adjacent to the Courthouses, joining downtown's family of unique and welcoming water features.

Grilled Chicken with Warm Tomato Dressing

THE KENTUCKY GOVERNOR'S MANSION

4	(6 ounce) boneless, skinless chicken breasts	2	tablespoons chopped fresh rosemary leaves
¼	cup fresh squeezed lemon juice	2	teaspoons salt
⅓	cup olive oil	1	teaspoon freshly ground white pepper

Place chicken, lemon juice, olive oil and rosemary in a resealable 1-gallon plastic bag. Let marinate for 1 hour at room temperature.

Preheat a grill pan to high heat. Remove chicken from plastic bag; place on platter and sprinkle with salt and pepper. Place chicken smooth-side down on the grill and cook for 4 minutes. Rotate 45 degrees and cook an additional 4 minutes or until thoroughly cooked. Place on serving platter and drizzle with Warm Tomato Dressing.

WARM TOMATO DRESSING

2	teaspoons olive oil	¼	cup balsamic vinegar
10	ounces (1 pint) cherry tomatoes	1	tablespoon sugar
3	garlic cloves, crushed	¼	teaspoon salt
⅔	cup red wine	1	teaspoon red wine vinegar

Heat oil in skillet; add tomatoes and cook, stirring often until skins are blistered. Stir in garlic, red wine and balsamic vinegar. Continue to cook until liquid has reduced by half (about 5 minutes). Stir in sugar, salt and red wine vinegar and cook for 1 minute more. Spoon over chicken and serve.

Serves 4

The Governor's Mansion—Frankfort

Notable Neighbors: Kentucky Executive Mansions

Kentucky's capital city, Frankfort, is located thirty minutes northwest of Lexington. The Commonwealth is unique among the states in maintaining two Executive or Governor's Mansions. The Old Mansion (1798) is two years older than the White House, and served as home to 33 governors and 10 lieutenant governors for more than 200 years. Seat of government, office of the chief executive, private residence, museum…the 20-room Federal mansion, listed on the National Register of Historic Places, currently serves as the Commonwealth's Guest House.

Joining the Old Mansion on the National Register of Historic Places is the 'new' Governor's Mansion (1914), home and official residence of Kentucky's chief executive. The French-inspired, four-story, Beaux-Arts residence patterned from Marie Antoinette's Versailles Palace,is widely regarded as one of the most elegant in the United States.

Executive entertaining, beginning in 1798 and continuing to modern times, has been bountiful and stately. In addition to being available for public tours, the executive residences, with guest houses and staffs, have served thousands for luncheons, receptions, dinners, meetings, and gala parties. Holiday and Derby entertaining usually encompass weeks, bringing a round of parties, celebrity house guests, and thousands of visitors. Serving the finest Kentucky foods and offering classic hospitality, the Mansions and the resident chief executives represent the best of the Commonwealth.

Kentucky Beef Roast

1	(3 pound) rump roast	⅛	teaspoon pepper
¼	teaspoon garlic powder	½	package beef onion soup mix
¼	teaspoon seasoned salt	1	(10½ ounce) can cream of mushroom soup, undiluted
2	tablespoons Worcestershire sauce		

Preheat oven to 350 degrees. Place roast in 13x9x2-inch pan. In a small bowl combine garlic powder, salt, Worcestershire sauce, pepper, onion soup mix and cream of mushroom soup. Pour soup mixture over roast. Cover with aluminum foil and bake 2 hours, 30 minutes, or until tender.

Serves 6-8

Lexington Public Library

Established in 1795, Lexington's Public Library is the oldest institution of its kind in Kentucky. In the years after Kentucky was granted statehood, the subscription-based library occupied a room in M. Giron's Confectionary building on North Mill Street for which the 'Sharers of the Lexington Library' paid $115 annual rent.

The next evolution in the library's history began in 1906 when The Andrew Carnegie Foundation built a new $75,000 Bedford stone, Neo-Classical building at the southern end of Gratz Park. The Carnegie Library operated here until the late 1980s, when Lexington Public Library's central branch relocated to East Main Street in order to accommodate its growing collection. The atrium of the modern downtown Library is renowned for showcasing the world's largest ceiling clock, fueled by a Foucault pendulum which moves with the earth's rotation.

The 1906 Carnegie building is now home to the Carnegie Center for Literacy and Learning, which provides free, public programs promoting literacy and childhood reading.

Home Run Barbeque Pork

6	pounds pork roast		2	cups firmly packed brown sugar
3	(18 ounce) bottles BBQ sauce		⅔	cup dark Karo syrup
½	teaspoon ground red pepper		¼	cup yellow mustard
2	shakes Louisiana hot sauce		2	tablespoons A-1 sauce

Cook pork roast in crockpot until tender (approximately 8 hours) and meat shreds easily from the bone. Tear apart with fork. Mix BBQ sauce, red pepper, hot sauce, brown sugar, syrup, mustard and A-1 sauce in a saucepan and simmer over low heat for 45 minutes. Drain liquid from meat; return meat to crockpot and pour sauce over shredded pork. Continue to cook in crockpot 10 to 15 minutes. Thin mixture with water and/or red wine to desired thickness.

Serves 20

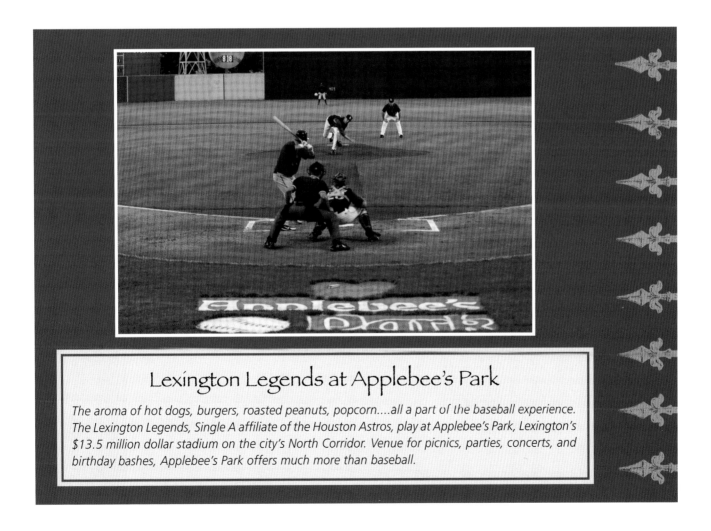

Lexington Legends at Applebee's Park

The aroma of hot dogs, burgers, roasted peanuts, popcorn....all a part of the baseball experience. The Lexington Legends, Single A affiliate of the Houston Astros, play at Applebee's Park, Lexington's $13.5 million dollar stadium on the city's North Corridor. Venue for picnics, parties, concerts, and birthday bashes, Applebee's Park offers much more than baseball.

Stuffed Pork Chops

SAL'S CHOPHOUSE

2	pork chops		¼	ounce red bell pepper
¼	ounce prosciutto		1	basil leaf
¼	ounce fresh mozzarella cheese			

Preheat oven to 500 degrees. Make a thin slit into pork chops and stuff with prosciutto, mozzarella, bell pepper and basil. Seal slit with a skewer or butcher's twine. Cook in oven until pork chops reach on internal temperature of 165 degrees.

SAUCE
2   ounces marinara sauce
½   ounce demi-glace
1   tablespoon butter

In a saucepan, heat marinara, demi-glace and butter. After reduced, puree and ladle over pork chops.

Serves 2

Sal's Chophouse

Sal's Chophouse on Tates Creek Road with its open-design kitchen, began as an Italian eatery and evolved into a restaurant specializing in bone-in steaks, veal, lamb, and pork. Sal's bakery provides fresh bread and homemade desserts, as well as crème brûlée, New York cheesecake, and homemade chocolate chip cookies for the 5-restaurant Bluegrass Hospitality Group.

Asian Grilled Salmon

3	pounds fresh salmon	6	tablespoons olive oil
2	tablespoons Dijon mustard	½	teaspoon minced garlic
3	tablespoons soy sauce		

Brush grill rack with oil and preheat. Lay salmon skin-side down and cut into 4 equal pieces. Whisk together mustard, soy sauce, oil and garlic. Drizzle half of the marinade over fish and allow to sit for 10 minutes. Place salmon skin-side up on hot grill. Grill 4 to 5 minutes, depending on thickness of fish. Turn carefully with a wide spatula and grill another 4 to 5 minutes. Salmon will be slightly raw in center, but will keep cooking as it sits.

Remove salmon from grill by gently inserting wide spatula between salmon and skin, leaving skin on the grill. Transfer to plate and drizzle with remaining marinade.

Serves 4-6

Memorable Menu: Wing's Teahouse

Lexington's first Asian restaurant was located upstairs at Main and Lime and later moved out to North Lime, offering Chinese and American food.

NOVEMBER, 1961

Wing's Family Style Dinners...three courses for $2.25.

To Our Patrons:

It is our aim to acquaint the people of
Lexington and Central Kentucky with the authentic Chinese
dishes, prepared by our master chefs. It is also our desire
that our patrons will cultivate a fondness for the real
Chinese dishes and convey their impression to their friends

Menu: Jerome and Virginia Redfearn

Breaded Catfish with Lemon Sauce

6   (6 ounce) catfish fillets
½   teaspoon salt, divided
½   teaspoon black pepper, divided
1   cup plain dry breadcrumbs
½   teaspoon garlic powder

½   teaspoon ground red pepper
4   egg whites
    Vegetable cooking spray
    Lemon Sauce (see below)
    Garnish: Orange slices, parsley sprigs

Preheat oven to 375 degrees. Sprinkle catfish evenly with ¼ teaspoon salt and black pepper. Set aside. Combine breadcrumbs, remaining salt and black pepper, garlic powder and ground red pepper in a shallow bowl. Whisk egg whites in a shallow bowl until frothy. Dip fillets in egg whites and dredge in breadcrumb mixture. Arrange fillets on a wire rack coated with nonstick cooking spray in an aluminum foil-lined 15x10-inch jelly-roll pan. Do not overlap fillets. Lightly coat fillets evenly on both sides with nonstick cooking spray. Bake 25 to 30 minutes or until fish is golden brown. Serve with Lemon Sauce. Garnish with orange slices or parsley sprigs, if desired.

LEMON SAUCE

1   (8 ounce) container sour cream
1   tablespoon chopped fresh parsley
½   teaspoon grated lemon rind

2   tablespoons fresh lemon juice
¼   teaspoon salt

Stir together sour cream, parsley, lemon rind, lemon juice and salt until blended. Cover mixture and chill until ready to serve.

Serves 6

Jerrico

"We traveled the country from coast to coast, borrowing the best ideas..."

Warren Rosenthal

Lexington is known for its dining establishments. But many don't know the city has been an incubator for a number of restaurants with a world-wide presence today. Warren Rosenthal, graduate of the University of Kentucky and owner of Fayette County's Patchen Wilkes Farm, collaborated with Jerome Lederer, Founder of White Tavern Hamburgers, and spent 24 years at the helm of Jerrico. In addition to pioneering restaurant franchising in 1957, Jerrico premiered a number of restaurants in Lexington: the first Jerry's Drive-In, the first Long John Silver's on Southland Drive (1969), and among others, Gratzi's, which later became Fazoli's (1989).

Warren Rosenthal lists the development of the frozen French fry as a monumental occurrence in the restaurant business, replacing a labor intensive practice with convenience. Before the advent of frozen fries, staff peeled pounds and pounds of fresh potatoes, blanched them, and finish-fried at service.

Pesto Shrimp Pasta

2 tablespoons butter

2 tablespoons olive oil

1-2 tablespoons minced garlic

1 pound medium to large raw shrimp, peeled and deveined

¼ teaspoon pepper

½ teaspoon salt

1 (10 ounce) can Rotel tomatoes, undrained

1 (4½ ounce) box penne pasta cooked as directed on package

2-3 tablespoons prepared basil and garlic based pesto sauce

1 cup finely grated Parmesan cheese, divided

Fresh chopped basil

In a large skillet melt butter and olive oil over medium-high heat. Add minced garlic and cook 1 to 2 minutes until slightly brown. Add shrimp to skillet and sprinkle with salt and pepper to taste. Cook shrimp on medium-high heat thoroughly until slightly brown, approximately 8 to 10 minutes. Add Rotel tomatoes and simmer on low heat 3 to 5 minutes. While the shrimp is simmering, mix hot pasta with pesto and ¾ cup Parmesan cheese together in a large serving bowl. Pour shrimp mixture on top and mix well. Top with remaining Parmesan cheese and fresh basil.

Serves 3

Linguine Seta Sapore
DUDLEY'S ON SHORT

1½ pounds dry linguine

4 tablespoons olive oil, divided

6 medium vine-ripened red tomatoes

3 ribs celery, thinly sliced

3 cloves garlic, smashed

10-12 torn fresh basil leaves

2 teaspoons kosher salt

8 ounces grated Parmesan cheese

Cook linguine in salted boiling water; drain (do not rinse). Toss with 2 tablespoons olive oil; set aside. Cut tomatoes into wedges. Combine with celery, garlic, basil and salt. Working in batches, pulse mixture 7 or 8 times in a food processor until you have achieved a chunky sauce. Do not over process or sauce will be too thin. In a large skillet heat remaining 2 tablespoons olive oil. Carefully add sauce. Once sauce is hot, add pasta and stir together with tongs. Finish with additional oil, if needed, and freshly grated Parmesan cheese.

Serves 6

Lexington Farmers Markets

Cheapside Park, named for its counterpart in London, England, was the setting for market days during Lexington's early years, and Jackson Hall, covering a city block between Limestone and Upper, Water and Vine streets became the Market House from the mid 1870s until 1940. A 1930s publication detailed the activity: "All sorts of edibles may be found—old-fashioned country butter, Kentucky home-cured hams, bee-tree honey, and other products peculiar to the bartering age, together with a variety of fruits, vegetables, meats, and fish. Here the Lexington housewife comes marketing as her forebears have done for generations."

Today, Kentucky's largest outdoor Saturday Farmers Market has returned to Cheapside Park, after operating on Vine Street for several decades. The Lexington Farmers Market began in 1975 as an agricultural cooperative, supplied by more than sixty farmers during the peak season. Participating with the Kentucky Department of Agriculture's Kentucky Proud program, the Market showcases the best of Kentucky produce, meats, flowers, herbs, baked goods, ice creams and specialty items. April of 2010 brought a sparkling new feature to Cheapside Park. The Fifth Third Bank pavilion, a glass exhibition structure covering 5,700 square feet, will shelter shoppers on Saturdays, as well as visitors to art shows, festivals, and concerts throughout the year.

Country Fried Potatoes

3   large Idaho baking potatoes, peeled
      and sliced evenly into ⅛-inch slices
      (each potato should yield 12-16 slices)

¾   cup canola vegetable oil

1   white onion, thinly sliced

1   tablespoon black pepper

2   tablespoons plain or seasoned flour

     Salt, to taste

Soak sliced potatoes in heavily salted water for 15 to 20 minutes. Drain in colander; do not rinse. Heat oil in 12 to 14-inch skillet (iron or stainless steel) on medium to high heat. Place potatoes in single layer; cover with sliced onion and pepper, to taste. Sprinkle flour over potatoes. Cover with lid approximately 15 minutes. Remove lid and turn potatoes. Fry on other side 15 to 30 minutes, checking and turning to prevent sticking. Add salt to taste. Remove and drain on paper towels.

The Potato Chip

Mrs. Cornelius Vanderbilt, 'Marylou' Whitney, mistress of Fayette County's C.V. Whitney Farm, published The Potato Chip Cookbook in 1977 to honor the 124th birthday of the snack favorite. Inspirational credit for the potato chip is given to her husband, C.V. 'Sonny' Whitney's great, great grandfather, Commodore Cornelius Vanderbilt.

The Commodore frequented Moon's Lake House at Saratoga Lake, New York, in the 1850s. He returned a plate of fried potatoes to the chef, reporting that they were too thick for his taste. The chef, known to be an 'ornery' character, sliced another batch paper thin, fried them to a crisp, and salted them heavily, by one account to render them inedible. Whatever the rationale, the Commodore loved them, and crisp potato wafers, also known as Saratoga Chips, were soon added to menus around the country. Bulk Potato Chips became available in grocery stores in 1895, and appeared in packaged form in 1926.

Block Party Baked Beans

8	slices bacon	¾	cup firmly packed brown sugar
4	large onions, chopped	½	cup vinegar
1	teaspoon garlic powder	2	large cans baked beans, undrained
¼	teaspoon salt	3	(15 ounce) cans butter beans, drained
1	teaspoon mustard		

Preheat oven to 350 degrees. Fry bacon in nonstick pan until crisp; drain; crumble into small pieces. Reserve bacon drippings. Sauté onion in bacon grease, covering with lid until onion is tender. Add garlic, salt, mustard, brown sugar and vinegar. Simmer 15 minutes, covered, to make a "dressing." Combine baked beans, butter beans, cooked bacon and the dressing. Put in 13x9x2-inch pan sprayed with nonstick cooking spray. Bake 1 hour, 30 minutes, uncovered.

Serves 12-14

Shucky Beans

FAMILY OF JOHNNY DEPP, *Native Kentuckian, Movie Actor*

½	pound shuck beans	½	teaspoon salt, optional
6	ounces salt pork		

Wash shuck beans, discard any dark or discolored beans. Break beans in half, place in a slow cooker with water to cover (about 6 cups). Cover and chill. Soak beans for 24 hours; do not drain. Transfer beans to a stockpot and bring to a boil, uncovered. Reduce heat to medium, and cook 30 minutes. Drain and rinse beans.

Return beans to slow cooker, add salt pork and salt, if desired. Add cold water to cover beans by at least 1-inch (about 4 cups). Cover slow cooker with lid and cook all day.

Serve with chopped raw onion, buttermilk cornbread and fried pork chops.

Serves 4-6

Shucky Beans

As opposed to green beans that are traditionally broken into pieces before cooking, Shucky, Shuck Beans, 'leather britches,' or hull beans are left whole and strung on slender canes or string and allowed to air dry. Favored in the South, white half runners or beans with a large mature seeds are chosen for the process. The dried hulls are carefully stored or frozen and slowly rehydrated before being cooked with ham or bacon.

Fried Green Tomatoes

4-6	green tomatoes	1	teaspoon onion powder
4	tablespoons kosher salt	2	teaspoons salt
2	cups flour	1	teaspoon freshly ground black pepper
5	eggs	½	teaspoon dried sage
1½	cups milk	1	teaspoon dried thyme
4	cups yellow cornmeal	¼	teaspoon cayenne pepper
1	teaspoon garlic powder	1	cup vegetable oil

Slice green tomatoes into ¼-inch slices. Lay sliced tomatoes onto a baking sheet. Sprinkle kosher salt evenly over tomatoes. Let tomatoes sit at room temperature for 1 hour. Salt will draw out excess moisture from tomatoes. Set tomatoes aside. Place flour in a medium-size bowl. Set aside. Thoroughly mix eggs and milk together. Set aside. In a large mixing bowl, mix cornmeal, garlic powder, onion powder, salt, black pepper, sage, thyme and cayenne pepper. Set aside. In a large skillet preheat oil to 350 degrees. Dust green tomatoes in the flour. Dip tomatoes, one at a time, in egg and milk mixture. Then transfer into cornmeal mixture. Repeat process until all tomatoes are breaded in cornmeal. Place a few green tomatoes in the skillet at a time and sauté for about 2 to 3 minutes on each side. Remove from pan and place on a tray lined with paper towels. Repeat until all tomatoes are cooked.

Serves 6

Jonathan at Gratz Park

Historic Gratz Park Inn, Lexington's only boutique hotel, is home to Jonathan at Gratz Park, a specialty restaurant featuring upscale Southern cuisine with a twist. Since 1998, husband and wife team, Jonathan and Cara Lundy, have treated guests to 'redefined regional cuisine' in Jonathan's elegant Dining Room, English Pub Room, and Courtyard Patio.

Cheesy Summer Zucchini

3	cups cooked rice	3	large tomatoes, sliced
2	(4 ounce) cans chopped green chilies, drained	2	cups sour cream
		2	green onions, chopped
1	pound Monterey Jack cheese, shredded	1	teaspoon dried oregano
4	medium zucchini, thinly sliced and steamed until tender	1½	teaspoons garlic salt

Preheat oven to 350 degrees. Put rice into a greased 13x9x2-inch casserole dish. Place green chilies on rice. Cover with half of cheese. Top with zucchini and tomato slices. Combine sour cream, onion, oregano and garlic salt; spread over tomatoes. Top with remaining cheese. Bake, uncovered, 20 minutes.

Serves 10-12

Fresh Squash Casserole

3	pounds fresh yellow squash	2	eggs
½	cup chopped onion	1	tablespoon sugar
½	teaspoon pepper	8	ounces butter, melted and divided
1	teaspoon salt	½	cup cracker meal

Cook squash until tender; drain and mash. Preheat oven to 375 degrees. Add onion, pepper, salt, eggs, sugar and 4 ounces butter to squash. Pour mixture into 8x8-inch baking dish. Sprinkle cracker crumbs on top and pour remaining 4 ounces melted butter over breadcrumbs. Bake 1 hour or until brown on top and bubbly.

Serves 6-8

Expression: Bring Home The Bacon, Chew The Fat

When early settlers were able to obtain prized pork, or bring home the bacon, they might hang up the full sides to show off. As a sign of wealth, hosts would often cut off a little to share with guests and all would sit around and 'chew the fat.'

Vidalia Onion Pie

2	pounds Vidalia onions, sliced		½	teaspoon pepper
3	tablespoons butter		½	teaspoon Tabasco sauce
3	eggs		1¼	cups shredded Parmesan cheese
1	cup sour cream		5-6	slices bacon, cooked and crumbled
¼	teaspoon salt		1	(9 inch) pie shell, unbaked

Preheat oven to 425 degrees. Sauté onion in butter; set aside. Beat together eggs, sour cream, salt, pepper and Tabasco sauce in a large bowl. Combine egg mixture and sautéed onions. Pour into unbaked pie shell. Top with Parmesan cheese and bacon bits. Bake 15 minutes. Reduce oven temperature to 325 degrees until nicely brown and a knife inserted into middle comes out clean, approximately 25 minutes.

Serves 8-12

Creamy Sweet Onions

1	pound Vidalia onions, sliced and separated		¾	teaspoon salt
1	egg, beaten		½	teaspoon pepper
1	cup heavy whipping cream		½	cup shredded Cheddar cheese
				Paprika

Preheat oven to 350 degrees. In a medium saucepan, bring water to a boil. Drop onion in boiling water and boil for 1 minute. Drain and place in a 8-inch dish. Combine egg, cream, salt and pepper. Pour over onion. Sprinkle with cheese and paprika. Bake 25 minutes.

Serves 6-8

Tomato and Havarti Cheese Bake

¼	cup butter		½	teaspoon dried basil or ½ tablespoon fresh
2	large onions, sliced			
1	(6 ounce) package plain croutons		½	teaspoon salt
6	large tomatoes, sliced		3	cups grated Danish Havarti cheese

Preheat oven to 350 degrees. In a skillet, heat butter and sauté onion for 5 minutes. Add croutons and sauté 3 minutes. In a greased 9x13-inch casserole dish, layer half crouton-onion mixture and half tomato slices. Sprinkle with ¼ teaspoon basil, ¼ teaspoon salt and half of cheese. Repeat layers, ending with cheese. Bake 40 minutes.

Serves 6-8

Artistry in Marble

Joel T. Hart (1810-1877) migrated to Lexington from his birthplace in Clark County to engrave tombstones at Lexington's marble yards. He later traveled to Italy to study sculpture, returning to the Bluegrass as a skilled artisan. Perhaps his most treasured gift to Lexingtonians was "Woman Triumphant," which was exhibited in the 1885 Fayette County Courthouse, only to be crushed during a fire that destroyed the building. The "pride and joy of the city" was reduced to fragments gathered by souvenir hunters.

Image: Kentucky Historical Society

Zucchini and Red Onion Flatbread

1	(10 ounce) tube refrigerator pizza dough	1	small red onion, cut into ⅛-inch slices
¾	cup garlic and herb cheese spread		Olive oil
1	cup grated Parmesan cheese		Kosher salt
3	tablespoons chopped fresh Italian parsley		Freshly ground black pepper
1	(8 inch) zucchini, cut crosswise into ⅛-inch slices		Nonstick cooking spray

Preheat oven to 400 degrees. Line baking sheet with parchment paper and spray with cooking spray. Unroll pizza dough onto the parchment paper. Spread half the herb cheese over half the dough, leaving ½-inch border. Sprinkle with ½ cup Parmesan cheese and 2 tablespoons parsley. Fold plain dough over the filled half. Do not seal the edges. Spread remaining herb cheese over top and sprinkle with remaining ½ cup Parmesan cheese.

Arrange one row of zucchini slices down both of the outer sides of long side of dough. Arrange onion slices in the middle between the two rows of zucchini. Brush with olive oil. Sprinkle with salt and pepper. Bake approximately 20 to 25 minutes, until bread is puffed and deep brown around edges. Sprinkle with 1 tablespoon parsley.

Serves 6-8

The Arboretum

Encircled by the clamor and hubbub of a major University, two hospitals, and miles of traffic-burdened streets, Lexington's 100-acre Arboretum affords area residents a tranquil green space within the city. A collaboration of the University of Kentucky and Lexington-Fayette Urban County Government, Kentucky's State Botanical Garden offers a two-mile paved walkway leading the trekker through seven physiographic landscapes of Kentucky, Children's outdoor learning environment, sixteen acres of inner Bluegrass woodland, as well as acres of roses, trees, and colorful annuals. Gardeners benefit from the All American Trial Gardens, gaining a glimpse of vegetables and annuals that thrive in the local climate.

Buttermilk Cornbread

FAMILY OF JOHNNY DEPP, *Native Kentuckian, Movie Actor*

1	tablespoon bacon grease	1	cup self-rising flour
2½	cups self-rising cornmeal (plus a small amount for skillet preparation)	2	cups buttermilk
		2	large eggs, beaten

Preheat oven to 350 degrees. In a 10-inch cast iron skillet, heat bacon grease and sprinkle a small amount of cornmeal to cover bottom of skillet. Mix remaining ingredients and pour into hot skillet.

Place hot skillet into oven and bake 35 to 45 minutes until golden brown and pulling away from sides of skillet.

Serves 8-10

Strawberry Pecan Bread

3	cups all-purpose flour	1	cup vegetable oil
2	cups sugar	4	large eggs, beaten
3	teaspoons ground cinnamon	2	(10 ounce) packages frozen strawberries, thawed
1	teaspoon baking soda		
1	teaspoon salt	¼	cup chopped pecans

Preheat oven to 325 degrees. Combine flour, sugar, cinnamon, baking soda and salt in a large bowl. Add oil and eggs; mix well. Stir in strawberries and pecans. Divide batter evenly into two greased and floured 9x5x3-inch loaf pans. Bake 1 hour, 15 minutes or until toothpick inserted in center comes out clean.

Serves 20 (Makes 2 loaves)

Giron's Confectionary

Monsieur Mathurin Giron, jovial, fastidiously-dressed French immigrant, established an early confectionary and ballroom on Lexington's North Mill Street, and was credited for being one of the individuals who brought European culture to Kentucky. Monsieur Giron claimed to have been a grenadier in Napoleon's army before leaving France for America, arriving in Lexington in 1811. He was remembered for parties he hosted in his second-floor Lexington ballroom, and delicacies he concocted, particularly the monumental cakes created for weddings, dances, and banquets honoring visiting dignitaries.

John D. Wright, Jr. in *Lexington, Heart of the Bluegrass:* "On the second floor was the ballroom with its great, paneled doors of polished cherry, opening to the high frescoed ceiling. Giron served delectable banquets here, ably assisted by his famous Swiss chef, Dominique Ritter. And when the tables were cleared and the dancing began (Mary Todd is said to have loved the dances at Giron's), the dancers could rest and cool themselves on the small, graceful balcony, lean on the delicately wrought iron railing, and look down on the street below." On a more literary note, an 1819 Public Library occupied the Lincoln Room on the ground floor of M. Giron's ballroom.

"1825 General Lafayette (aide to General Washington and man for whom Fayette County is named) visited Lexington and Giron honored him with an elaborate tiered white cake. The first 'castellated' cake seen in the region was so glorious, that no one could bear to cut it, and it remained on display until the next day. Young Mary Todd, a favorite customer, acquired Giron's white cake recipe, which later became a favorite of her husband, Abraham Lincoln." (Recipe on page 66)

Ale-8-One Strawberry Pie

10 ounces Ale-8-One soft drink

3 tablespoons cornstarch

1 cup sugar

1 (6 ounce) box strawberry gelatin

2 pints fresh strawberries, cleaned and sliced

2 prepared graham cracker or shortbread crusts

1 (12 ounce) container frozen whipped topping, thawed

In a saucepan, combine Ale-8-One, cornstarch and sugar. Bring to a boil. Add gelatin and mix until dissolved. Remove from heat. Place strawberries into prepared crusts. Pour gelatin mixture over strawberries. Chill in refrigerator 4 to 6 hours. Before serving, top slices with whipped topping.

Ale-8-One is a beloved central Kentucky soft drink. Any lemon-lime soda may be substituted.

Serves 12-14 (2 pies)

Notable Neighbor: Ale-8-One

Ale-8-One, the soft drink unique to Kentucky, has been bottled in the Bluegrass since 1926. Only retailed locally and in surrounding states, the Winchester beverage maintains an avid fan base all over the world. The family-guarded secret recipe yields a caffeinated, mildly-carbonated, ginger-flavored soft drink. Ale-8 purists prefer the older returnable glass bottles, known as long necks. Employees of one of two returnable bottle companies in Kentucky have seen some strange circumstances surrounding the product. "A man once brought back probably 1,400 bottles in a Volkswagen Beetle. They were stacked floor to ceiling, and he had just enough room to drive and shift!"

Since 2003, the historic company has launched new products and expanded its distribution area to surrounding states. Diet Ale 8 was premiered a few years ago as the first new product since 1926. Lollipops, Salsa, Apple Butter, and Barbeque Sauce, all featuring Ale 8 in the recipes have made their debut in recent years.

Peach Pudding

2	cups sliced peaches	1	teaspoon baking powder
1¼	cups sugar, divided	½	cup milk
4	tablespoons butter	1	tablespoon cornstarch
1	cup flour	1	cup boiling water
¾	teaspoon salt, divided		

Preheat oven to 325 degrees. Layer peaches in a 8x8-inch pan. Cream ½ cup sugar and butter together. Add flour, ½ teaspoon salt, baking powder and milk to butter mixture to form a batter. Pour over peaches.

Combine remaining ¾ cup sugar, cornstarch and ¼ teaspoon salt. Sift over batter. Pour boiling water over topping. Bake 50 minutes or until crusty.

Serves 6

Peach Cobbler

3⅓	cups all-purpose flour, divided	2	cups sugar
1½	teaspoons salt	¾	cup water
¾	teaspoon baking powder	½	cup butter, melted
¾	cup shortening	1½	teaspoons ground cinnamon
½-⅔	cup cold water	¾	teaspoon almond extract
8	cups peeled and sliced fresh peaches		

Preheat oven to 350 degrees. Combine 3 cups flour, salt and baking powder; cut in shortening until mixture is crumbly. Sprinkle enough cold water (adding 1 tablespoon at a time) over surface to moisten dry ingredients, stirring with a fork after each addition. Shape into a ball. Set pastry aside.

Combine peaches and ⅓ cup flour. Toss gently to coat peaches. Stir in sugar and remaining ingredients. On a floured surface, roll ⅔ of pastry to a 11x15-inch rectangle. Place in a lightly greased 9x13x2-inch baking dish. Spoon peach mixture over pastry in baking dish. Roll remaining pastry to ¼-inch thickness; lattice design over peach mixture. Bake 1 hour, 15 minutes or until pastry is golden brown.

Serves 8-10

Best Peach Pie

CRUST

1¼	cups flour	½	cup unsalted butter
½	teaspoon salt	2	tablespoons sour cream

Preheat oven to 425 degrees. Combine all ingredients in a food processor and blend until a ball forms. Press into a buttered pie pan and bake 10 minutes.

FILLING

3   large egg yolks
1   cup sugar
2   tablespoons flour
⅓   cup sour cream
3   fresh peaches, peeled and sliced

Reduce heat to 350 degrees. Beat egg yolks slightly and combine with sugar, flour and sour cream. Arrange peaches in pie shell and pour mixture over peaches. Cover with foil. Bake 35 minutes at 350 degrees, then increase temperature to 375 degrees and bake 15 minutes more.

Serves 6-8

Banana Cream Pie

CRUST

1 cup flour	3 tablespoons milk
½ teaspoon salt	⅓ cup oil

Preheat oven to 400 degrees. Combine flour and salt. Add milk and oil; mix with fork. Roll out between 2 pieces floured waxed paper. Remove waxed paper from top of crust and flip crust into a 9-inch pie plate. Bake 10 to 12 minutes. Let cool.

FILLING

2 bananas, sliced	2 cups milk
1 (3.4 ounce) box vanilla instant pudding	1 cup sour cream
1 (3.4 ounce) box banana instant pudding	

Lay sliced bananas on bottom of crust. Combine both boxes of pudding with milk and sour cream. Mix until thick. Pour into cooled crust.

TOPPING

12 ounces whipping cream	2 tablespoons sugar

Beat whipping cream until stiff. Add sugar and beat until sugar is dissolved. Spread on pie and refrigerate.

Serves 8

Bodley-Bullock House

The Bodley-Bullock House (1814-1815) was built for Lexington's Mayor Thomas Pindell, and then sold to 1812 War veteran, General Thomas Bodley. During the Civil War the house served as headquarters for military forces during the occupation of the city. After the war, the house was owned by a series of prominent Lexingtonians, including Dr. Waller Bullock, a sculptor and founder of the Lexington Clinic. Minnie Bullock, avid gardener, was the founder of the Lexington Garden Club. Today, the Gratz Park jewel at 200 Market Street is operated by the Lexington Junior League as a house museum and event facility.

Buttermilk Blackberry Shortcakes

3	cups all-purpose flour		¾	cup buttermilk
⅓	cup sugar		½	teaspoon vanilla extract
1	teaspoon baking powder		1	large egg yolk
½	teaspoon baking soda		2	tablespoons heavy cream
½	teaspoon salt		1	tablespoon raw sugar
½	teaspoon cinnamon		4	pints fresh blackberries
½	cup butter flavored vegetable shortening, cut into cubes		¾	cup blackberry syrup
				Garnish: fresh whipped cream

Preheat oven to 425 degrees. Line a baking sheet with parchment paper; set aside. In a large bowl, combine flour, sugar, baking powder, baking soda, salt and cinnamon. Using a pastry blender, cut the shortening into the flour mixture until it resembles coarse meal. In a small bowl, combine the buttermilk and vanilla extract. Make a well in the center of flour mixture and pour the milk mixture into the well. Stir with a fork until mixture just comes together. Turn dough onto a floured work surface and knead 4 to 5 times. Roll dough out to 1-inch thickness. Using a 3-inch fluted round cutter, cut shortcakes. In a small bowl whisk together egg yolk and cream. Using a pastry brush, lightly coat the tops of shortcakes with egg wash and then sprinkle each evenly with raw sugar. Place shortcakes on prepared baking sheet. Bake 12 to 14 minutes or until golden brown. Set aside until cool enough to handle. When cooled, cut shortcakes in half horizontally. In a medium bowl, combine the blackberries and blackberry syrup. Stir gently to coat. Spoon the prepared berries evenly over shortcake bottom and garnish each with fresh whipped cream. Replace shortcake tops and serve.

Serves 12

Spindletop

Among the palatial residences in Central Kentucky, Spindletop Hall occupies a high ranking. The $1 million, 40-room mansion with solid bronze doors and chandeliers, was completed in 1937 after two years of construction. Pansy Yount, widow of Texas oil millionaire, Miles Frank Yount, relocated her nationally-known Saddlebred farm to Kentucky, selecting acreage on Iron Works Pike as the site of her estate. Plans included a greenhouse, swimming pool, bath house, tennis court, two aviaries, three kennels, and mansion with 14 bathrooms; plumbing, roofs, and window screens of solid copper. A remote-controlled organ, buoyant dance floor, and massive kitchen complex promoted elegant entertaining.

In early 1959, Spindletop Farm was sold/donated to The University of Kentucky for $850,000, and since 1962, Spindletop Hall has served as the University of Kentucky Faculty, Staff, and Alumni Club.

Frosted Peanut Butter Cake

½	cup buttermilk		2	large egg yolks, beaten
1	teaspoon baking soda		3	tablespoons peanut butter
½	cup water		1	teaspoon baking powder
½	cup butter		1½	cups all-purpose flour
1½	cups sugar		2	large egg whites, stiffly beaten

Preheat oven to 350 degrees. In a small bowl, mix buttermilk, baking soda and water; set aside. In a large mixing bowl, cream butter and sugar. Add beaten egg yolks and peanut butter to butter mixture. Add baking powder to flour and mix alternately with buttermilk mixture to batter. Fold beaten egg whites into batter. Pour into 2 greased and floured 9-inch cake pans. Bake 25 minutes. Cool 5 minutes before removing from pans. Remove cake from pans and allow to cool completely on wire racks.

FROSTING

1	(1 pound) box powdered sugar		1	teaspoon vanilla
4	tablespoons shortening		½-¾	cup evaporated milk
4	heaping tablespoons peanut butter			Garnish: peanut butter cup candies

Mix powdered sugar, shortening, peanut butter and vanilla with ½ cup evaporated milk. Beat until smooth. Add rest of milk, as needed. Frost cooled cake and decorate top with peanut butter cup candies, as desired.

Serves 12

Waveland

Fayette County's Waveland State Historic Shrine, jewel in the crown of Kentucky's Park System, features an excellent example of Kentucky Greek Revival architecture and pre-Civil War hemp plantation. Visitors may tour the fully-furnished Mansion and outbuildings—"slave quarters, smokehouse, and icehouse, that are important reminders of the social and economic climate of the time."

Built in 1847 by Daniel Boone's grandnephew Joseph Bryan, the edifice is reputed to have been designed by John McMurtry, noted Lexington architect, and typical of construction projects of the era, built with locally-acquired materials... bricks were burned on the farm, stone quarried at Tyrone, iron wrought at the Waveland smithy, and lumber harvested from local forests. During its operational period, Waveland Plantation was a thriving community estate of 2,000 acres including a gunsmith shop employing as many as 25 men, grist mill, blacksmith shop, distillery, paper mill, Baptist church, and female seminary.

Early Bluegrass Authors

James Lane Allen (1849-1925) born in Lexington, has been called Kentucky's first important novelist. A graduate of Transylvania University, Allen delivered the Salutatorian address to his fellow graduates in Latin. Perhaps it was from his family's Scarlet Gate Farm on Harrodsburg Road that James Lane Allen penned nineteen books, fourteen set in Kentucky or related to Kentucky subjects...*King Solomon of Kentucky, The Reign of Law, A Tale of the Kentucky Hemp Fields*. At his death in 1925, James Lane Allen was buried in the Lexington Cemetery, having willed funds for a Gratz Park fountain dedicated to the children of Lexington.

Judge James H. Mulligan (1844-1915), prominent attorney and poet, founder of the "Cakes and Ale Club," and resident of Lexington's Maxwell Place, penned the famous poem, *In Kentucky*, and delivered it to an audience of Kentucky legislators at the Phoenix Hotel in 1902. It was reported that the Judge was "constantly interrupted by applause that burst into a grand napkin salute at its close." Reprinted in newspapers and set to music, the poem is the most often quoted rhyme featuring Kentucky, and concludes with the following stanza:

Thunder peals the loudest,
The landscape is the grandest
And Politics-the damndest
In Kentucky

Italian Cream Cake

½ cup butter, room temperature
½ cup vegetable oil
2 cups sugar
5 large egg yolks
1 teaspoon baking soda
1 cup buttermilk

2 cups soft wheat, low-protein flour
5 large egg whites, stiffly beaten
1 cup coconut
1 teaspoon vanilla extract
1 cup chopped pecans

Preheat oven to 350 degrees. Set aside a small amount of coconut and pecans for the icing. In a large bowl, cream butter, oil and sugar together. Add egg yolks, one at a time, beating well after each addition. In a small bowl, combine baking soda and buttermilk; stir until dissolved. Add flour to batter alternating with buttermilk and baking soda mixture. Always begin and end with flour. Fold in stiffly beaten egg whites, coconut, vanilla and pecans. Bake in 3 (9-inch) greased and floured baking pans lined with wax paper. Bake 25 minutes. Start testing after 20 minutes. Do not overbake.

CREAM CHEESE ICING

1 (8 ounce) package cream cheese, room temperature
¾ cup butter, room temperature

5 cups powdered sugar
2-3 tablespoons whipping cream
1 teaspoon vanilla extract

Cream cheese and butter together. Slowly add powdered sugar and cream, alternating. Add vanilla and beat well. If icing is too thick add more cream, if too thin add more powdered sugar. Spread on cooled cake and sprinkle with reserved coconut and pecans.

Serves 12-14

Just Picked Strawberry Cake

1	plain white cake mix		½	cup sugar
1	(3 ounce) package strawberry gelatin		4	large eggs
4	tablespoons all-purpose flour		½	cup chopped fresh strawberries, with juice
1	cup vegetable oil			
½	cup whole milk			

Preheat oven to 350 degrees. Lightly grease 2 (9-inch) round cake pans or 3 (8-inch) round cake pans. Dust with flour.

Place cake mix, gelatin, flour, oil, milk, sugar, eggs and strawberries in a large mixing bowl. Blend with mixer on low speed for 1 minute. Scrape down sides of bowl and beat 2 minutes more on medium speed. Divide batter among prepared pans and bake 30 to 35 minutes. Remove from oven and cool 10 minutes. Invert each layer and allow to cool completely.

ICING

½	cup butter, softened		½	cup chopped fresh strawberries with juice
4	cups powdered sugar, sifted			

Garnish: fresh strawberries

In a large bowl, blend butter with mixer until fluffy. Add sifted powdered sugar and ½ cup strawberries with juice. Blend until frosting is creamy. Refrigerate 1 hour. Spread frosting between layers and on top and sides of cake. Decorate with fresh strawberries.

Serves 12

Polo in The Park

Directions to a Lexington Polo Club match might include the terms Secretariat field, Man O'War or John Henry field. The Lexington chapter of the Kentucky Polo Association plays matches on Kentucky Horse Park fields named for famous champions.

Picnics and tailgating are traditional companions to Polo, as combining social activities and equine sport is a favorite practice in the Bluegrass. The Lexington Polo Club, hosts of the USPA National Amateur Cup, joins forces with land preservation agencies, Bluegrass Conservancy and The Fayette Alliance for Polo in the Park. Good food and music add to the excitement of a summer match.

A 'hand' is approximately 4 inches, the unit of equine measurement. The horse is measured from the ground to the withers (where the back and neck meet.) A horse that measures 62 inches tall would be 15.2 hh or 'fifteen two hands high.' In the early twentieth century polo ponies could only be 14.2 hands tall, which was the dividing measurement between a pony and a horse, but today there is no size limit...they're still called polo ponies.

Duncan Hines

"If the soup had been as warm as the wine,
if the wine had been as old as the turkey,
and if the turkey had had a breast like the maid,
it would have been a swell dinner."

Duncan Hines

Unlike Betty Crocker or Mrs. Butterworth, Duncan Hines was a real character who became one of the first modern food critics, traveling the United States with his wife, Florence, sampling much of America's culinary offering. A native Kentuckian, Hines had a discriminating palate and definite opinions regarding food establishments: "I would like to be food dictator of the U.S.A. just long enough to padlock two thirds of the places that call themselves cafes or restaurants."

Adventures in Good Eating for the Discriminating Motorist was published annually from 1936 until 1962. A favorable listing in Mr. Hines' book became a coveted measure of quality, along with a stamp of approval that was displayed in the deserving restaurant, "Recommended by Duncan Hines."

The following excerpt was recorded in Louis Hatchett's, *The Man Behind the Cake Mix*:

"The next day 10 October, 1936, they made a quick day trip to Bowling Green, Kentucky, to visit Hines' family..... Hines and Florence stopped for the day in Lexington where they consumed supper at the best dining facility in town, the Canary Cottage. There they ate country ham and fried chicken served with homemade rolls and cornsticks."

Ale-8-One Pound Cake

SHARON THOMPSON, *Lexington Herald Leader Food Writer*

1	cup butter	1	teaspoon lemon extract
½	cup vegetable shortening	3	cups all-purpose flour
3	cups sugar	7	ounces Ale-8-One soda
5	large eggs		

Preheat oven to 300 degrees. In a large bowl, cream butter, shortening and sugar. Add eggs, one at a time, beating after each addition. Add lemon extract. Add flour and Ale-8-One soda, beating after each addition. Pour batter into a greased and floured tube pan. Bake 1 hour, 30 minutes or until toothpick inserted comes out clean. Let cool in pan 10 minutes before turning out onto a cake pan.

Three Chimneys

The handsome barns on Old Frankfort Pike's Three Chimneys Farm have been home to winning Thoroughbreds, including Triple Crown winner Seattle Slew and Derby winners Silver Charm and Genuine Risk. Today beloved 2004 and 2008 Derby winners Smarty Jones and Big Brown reside, and hold court, at Three Chimneys. On 1,800 acres of prime Bluegrass land, champion Thoroughbreds enjoy personal attention in exquisite natural settings protected by miles and miles of black plank fence. Three Chimneys stallions are ridden every day, a rarity in the thoroughbred industry and an example of the personal attention given to each resident.

Founded and owned by the Clay family since 1972, the working farm maintains a philosophy of providing access to visitors. Three Chimneys participation with the Make-A-Wish Foundation and other charities has given worthy individuals an opportunity to get up-close-and-personal with all-star Thoroughbreds. The farm retains a staff tour director to oversee tens of thousands of guests who visit the farm by appointment each year. Passionate about land preservation, the Clay family has protected major portions of Three Chimneys through land conservancy programs.

Company's Coming Cheesecake

CRUST
1   cup graham cracker crumbs
3   tablespoons sugar

3   tablespoons margarine, melted

Preheat oven to 325 degrees. Combine crumbs, sugar and margarine. Press into bottom of a 9-inch springform pan. Bake 10 minutes.

CAKE
3   (8 ounce) packages cream cheese, softened
¾   cup sugar
2   tablespoons flour

3   large eggs
2   tablespoons whole milk
1   teaspoon vanilla extract

Preheat oven to 450 degrees. In a large bowl, combine softened cream cheese, sugar and flour. Beat with a mixer on medium speed until well blended. Add eggs, one at a time, mixing well after each addition. Blend in milk and vanilla. Pour mixture over crust; bake 10 minutes. Reduce oven temperature to 250 degrees and continue baking 25 to 30 minutes.

TOPPING
1   pint sour cream
¼   cup sugar

½   teaspoon vanilla extract
Garnish: fresh strawberries or chocolate sauce

Preheat oven to 475 degrees. Combine sour cream, sugar and vanilla. Spread over baked cheesecake. Bake 5 minutes. Loosen cake from sides. Cool on wire rack. Chill. Garnish as desired.

Serves 12

Lemon Cream Strawberries

½   cup whipping cream
3   tablespoons powdered sugar
½   cup sour cream
⅛   teaspoon ground cinnamon

2   tablespoons lemon juice
Garnish: fresh mint leaves
2   pints fresh strawberries

Beat whipping cream until foamy; gradually add powdered sugar. Beat until soft peaks form. Combine sour cream, cinnamon and lemon juice. Fold into whipped cream. Garnish with mint leaves. Serve with strawberries.

Makes 1¼ cups cream

Homemade Peach Ice Cream

1½ cups sugar, divided
¼   cup all-purpose flour
¼   teaspoon salt
3   large eggs, beaten
1   cup whole milk

1½ tablespoons vanilla extract
4   cups peeled and chopped peaches
2   cups heavy whipping cream
2   cups half-and-half

Combine 1 cup sugar, flour and salt in a heavy saucepan; mix well. Stir in eggs and milk. Cook mixture over medium heat until thick and bubbly, stirring constantly. Remove from heat and stir in vanilla. Cool mixture completely. Cook peaches over low heat 5 to 10 minutes. Cool. Add remaining ½ cup sugar and let sit 5 minutes. Combine cooled mixture, whipping cream and half-and-half, mixing until mixture is smooth. Fold in peach mixture. Pour into freezer can of a 1 gallon ice cream maker. Freeze according to manufacturer's instructions, using 1 part rock salt and 6 parts ice. Let ice cream ripen at least 1 hour.

Makes 2½ quarts

Oatmeal Marble Brownies

1   cup butter, softened
2   cups firmly packed light brown sugar
2   teaspoons vanilla extract
2   large eggs
3   cups old-fashioned oats
1½ cups all-purpose flour
1   teaspoon baking soda

1   teaspoon salt
1   (12 ounce) package chocolate chips
1   cup sweetened condensed milk
2   tablespoons butter
1   cup chopped walnuts, optional
2   teaspoons vanilla extract

Preheat oven to 350 degrees. In a large bowl, cream butter and brown sugar until smooth. Add vanilla and eggs; beat well. Stir in oats. In a separate bowl, combine flour, baking soda and salt; stir until mixed well. Gradually add dry mixture to butter mixture, stirring until mixed well. Spread ⅔ of mixture in a 9x13-inch glass pan.

In a glass bowl, microwave chocolate chips, condensed milk and butter for 1 minute on high. Stir. If not smooth, microwave on high for 30 seconds more (repeat if needed) and stir. Stir in nuts and vanilla. Pour chocolate filling on top of oatmeal butter mixture in pan. Using a spoon, dot the top with remaining ⅓ of oatmeal butter mixture.

Bake 25 to 30 minutes until oatmeal mixture is beginning to brown on top. Cool completely and cut into 2x2-inch squares.

Lucretia Clay's Ice Cream

"...daily piles of strawberries and towers of ice cream were welcome luxuries."

1835 Visitor to Ashland

Ashland, the 600-acre Henry Clay Estate, was home to five generations of the Clay family. Following an extensive renovation between 1990 and 1993, twenty acres of the original farm remain, with the house, gardens, and dependencies, or outbuildings, on display.

Among the dependencies are two 1834 brick ice houses and the dairy cellar. Clay's ingenious design involved subterranean brick houses with conical roofs from which straw-packed ice melt flowed into the dairy house to cool cream, milk, and butter for at least three seasons of the year.

Lucretia Clay oversaw the Ashland estate as her husband, prominent Senator and perennial candidate traveled for many years. Henry Clay noted her practical abilities and thrift during these long periods away from home, saying, "Again and again has she saved our home from bankruptcy."

Cows on Ashland's 600-acre estate provided rich milk, from which Lucretia Clay churned good quality butter which she sold to local hotels and restaurants. Clay family lore noted that Lucretia was known for her ice cream, particularly served with strawberries. An Ashland visitor commented in 1835: "...daily piles of strawberries and towers of ice cream were welcome luxuries." Modern visitors may see the beautiful china dessert service believed to have been brought from Paris, France, for Lucretia Clay by her sister, Nancy Hart Brown.

General Marquis de Lafayette

In all of Kentucky's history, it is likely that no event occasioned more lavish entertainment than the 16-month triumphal tour of "the nation's hero," the Marquis de Lafayette. General Lafayette, a member of the French Royal Army, served as a commander under General George Washington during the American Revolution and became the inspiration for "Fayette County."

Image: Kentucky Historical Society

A May, 1825 Journal: "...In Lexington a ball and dinner were given at the Grand Masonic Hall which, although still unfinished, was lavishly decorated in patriotic motif. The piece de resistance was a magnificent castellated cake, made by Mathurin Giron, the confectioner; a cake so magnificent, in fact, that no one could bring himself to cut it and it was preserved for display at breakfast in the morning and then at the next meeting of the lodge. Lafayette, alas, feasted on it only with his eyes."

During his whirlwind trip to Lexington, General Lafayette sat for an hour with Lexington's great portrait painter, Matthew Harris Jouett (1788-1827) as the artist completed a life-size portrait of the hero. Lafayette's portrait hangs in Frankfort's Old State Capitol.

Early Portrait Artists

Among the first artists seen in the Bluegrass were itinerate painters who worked and lived on many Bluegrass estates. **Samuel H. Dearborn** advertised in the *Lexington Gazette* on May 1, 1809, that he planned to be in the city for several weeks. **William Edward West** (1788-1857) watchmaker and inventor, came to Lexington in 1788 to paint portraits as did **John Grimes** (1799-1837) and **Joseph H. Bush**, a protégé of Henry Clay. **Oliver Frazer** (1801-1864) painted Cassius Marcellus Clay, the noted abolitionist, as well as charming portraits of children. Others included **Thomas Noble** (1835-1907) and **William P. Welsh,** a painter who grew up in Lexington and began his artistic career as a graphic artist at Kaufman Men's Clothing Company.

Matthew Harris Jouett, (1788-1872) Transylvania educated, is known as Kentucky's great portrait painter. It was he who painted the life-size portrait of General Lafayette in 1824-25, beginning the work in Washington and completing it as Lafayette completed his triumphal tour of Kentucky in 1825.

Henry Faulkner 1924-1981, painted in the modern era in a style labeled "sophisticated primitive," but was more well known for his Bohemian, flamboyant lifestyle.

FALL

MENU

Mulled Wine

Kentucky Blue Cheese Ball

Pumpkin Soup with Cranberry Relish

Romaine Apple Nut Salad

Quail with Blackberry Wine Sauce

Nutty Wild Rice

Harvest Acorn Squash

Spalding's Doughnut Bread Pudding with
Wild Turkey Honey Liqueur Sauce

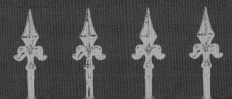

FALL

" Kentuckians' historical definition of a good dinner is a turkey at one end of the table, a ham at the other, six vegetables down one side, and seven down the other, pickles and jelly sprinkled in between, with a side dish of oysters."

The Kentucky, Thomas D. Clark

Nature's summer bounty provides the culinary excesses of fall. Sparkling days shorten to golden haze as majestic shade trees transform the landscape with palettes of gold, russet, brown, and vibrant yellow. Autumn days in the Bluegrass may be steamy or crisp, leading to the first frost that chills warm weather crops into submission. Indian Summer, a brief return to warmer days oftentimes appears in late fall, reminiscent of an earlier season and a reminder to prepare for winter's cold winds to come.

Farmers and gardeners prepare for harvest, bringing in the bounty of fruits, vegetables, grains, and produce. Bluegrass kitchens, fragrant with the aroma of roasting squash, apples, pumpkin, and spices, produce a wealth of traditional and modern dishes. From fresh, cold foods to warmer comfort foods, soups and stews take center stage and palates require heartier fare.

Autumn's glory brings three weeks of racing back to Keeneland, and an opportunity to picnic with friends in nature's picturesque settings. The Bluegrass Region holds a wealth of historic parks and house museums, many planning events to coincide with the last warm days of the season. Horseback trail riding, Iroquois Hunt Club events, and sports activities round out the calendar. Football fans anticipate the opening kickoff and an opportunity to tailgate with fellow fans before the game. The Horse Capital of the World is in the spotlight as Thoroughbred sale rings once again reverberate with the auctioneer's chant, offering world-class Thoroughbreds who command world-class prices.

Founded on a Rock

"Outside of scripture, no people were ever so founded on a rock."

~ James Lane Allen, 1892

Historic stone fences provide the perfect embellishment for Bluegrass autumnal glory. 'Dry Stack,' 'mortared,' 'capped'…all terms associated with one of the largest collections of stone fencing in the world. Although 'rock fence' has traditionally been associated with a looser form of construction, the terms 'rock fence' and 'stone fence' are used interchangeably today.

Many fieldstone fences were constructed between 1820 and the Civil War. In preparing fields for tilling and planting, farmers removed rock and piled them along the edges of cropland, thus creating a loose form of fence.

Concerned with keeping his blooded livestock pure, Robert A. Alexander removed split rail fencing and hired Irish immigrants to build five-foot stone fences around the perimeter of Woodburn, his Woodford County estate. They in turn, taught the art of fence building to local craftsmen, and by the turn of the twentieth century the rock fence had become a visual icon of the Bluegrass and the pride of generations of master artisans.

The oldest type of stone fence found in the Bluegrass Region is the dry stack fence, a marvel of engineering, laid in a double course with largest interlocking stones at the base. The more modern mortared fence is constructed with a mortar core and faced with stone, occasionally

in elaborate patterns. Assisted by preservation organizations such as the Dry Stone Conservancy in endeavoring to protect the region's heritage, local governments have drafted ordinances and regulations that address protection of one the most treasured symbols of the Bluegrass, the stone fence.

Agriculture

The heritage of the Bluegrass revolves not only around the equine industry but a strong general agricultural economy. Farms and fortunes have been built on crops such as corn and other grains, cattle, mules, sheep, hogs, hemp, and then tobacco. Today fruit and vegetable crops, as well as grapes grown for wine are making a reappearance.

The Works Progress Administration noted in 1930, "The rich limestone soil of the region, the abundant rainfall and plenitude of spring water, and above all the quick-growing perennial grass that took possession of the soil as soon as the heavy timber and canebrake were cleaned away, formed a natural foundation for a profitable livestock industry. Fields of native grass, known in parts of the eastern United States as June grass, supplied central Kentucky with prime

pasturage. From the prevalent blue of its delicate flowers, the name of the region was derived."

Soon after the first wave of settlers arrived to clear timber and vast canebrakes of 'Kentucke,' a second wave of settlers arrived, bringing or importing, the best blood lines in horses, cattle, and sheep. As the frontier moved westward, excellent Bluegrass livestock became foundation sires and dams for improving breeds. The sale of cattle on Henry Clay's estate amounted to $30,000 in 1839. (Gray, 1958).

In 2007, Fayette county led the state in agricultural production… $504,125,000 in total sales. But farming in Fayette County is more than cash receipts; agritourism is also a major industry, contributing more than a billion dollars each year to the regional economy.

Mulled Wine

2	cups water	3	(2½-inch) cinnamon sticks
2	cups sugar	11	whole cloves
1	orange, sliced	13	whole allspice
1	lemon, sliced	2	(750 ml) bottles dry red wine

In a saucepan, combine water, sugar, orange, lemon, cinnamon sticks, cloves and allspice and bring to a boil over medium heat. Reduce heat and simmer 5 minutes. Add wine and simmer 10 minutes. Pour mixture through a wire mesh strainer into a container; discard solids. Serve warm or at room temperature.

Serves 10

Gainesway and Stonestreet

WINE AND THOROUGHBREDS

John Gaines (1929-2005), industry leader and founding father of the Breeders Cup Championships, the National Thoroughbred Racing Association, and the Kentucky Horse Park, developed a Thoroughbred division at Gainesway Farm in 1962. The 1,500-acre farm, whose original acreage was moved to Paris Pike, was home to champions and sires of champions under the ownership of three generations of Gaines horsemen. The farm's heritage involves an award-winning Standardbred farm, a feed business that developed Gaines Dog Food, and a Thoroughbred farm that managed many of the industry's top stallions.

Graham Beck, founder of South Africa's Graham Beck Wines, purchased Fayette County's Gainesway Farm in 1989. Antony Beck operates the farm today, where famed stallions Afleet Alex and Birdstone stand. The farm is known for its rich horticultural mission, featuring acres of specialty trees and exquisite flower and vegetable gardens.

Joining the family of vintner/Thoroughbred farm owners are Californians Jess Jackson and Barbara Banke, founders of Kendall-Jackson Wine Estates. Stonestreet Farm was developed in 2005 by the purchase of Fayette County's Buckram Oak Farm and Adena Springs in neighboring Woodford County. Majority owners of Curlin, 2007 and 2008 Horse of the Year, and 2009 Kentucky Oaks and Preakness champion, Rachel Alexandra, the Jacksons name Stonestreet barns for grapes, thus the Chardonnay Barn. There's also Rachel Alexandra Pinot Noir!

Spiced Tea

4	quarts water	2	family-size tea bags (or 6 small)
2	cinnamon sticks	6	lemons
2	tablespoons whole cloves	6	navel oranges
1	teaspoon whole allspice	1	(46 ounce) can pineapple juice
2½	cups sugar		

Heat 2 quarts water to almost boiling point. Place spices in a cheesecloth and tie. Drop in water. Add sugar, cover and steep 30 minutes. In another kettle, pour in 2 quarts water. Bring to a boil then add tea bags. Steep 7 minutes. Juice lemons and oranges; strain. Add a little of the pulp to the mixture. Stir in pineapple juice. Mix all together and serve hot.

Serves 16

Mock Mint Julep

4 mint sprigs
2 cups cold water
1½ quarts Ale-8-One (6 pack of Ale-8-One)
1½ cups sugar
¾ cup fresh lemon juice
Thin lemon slices

Rinse mint and discard stems. Place sugar, water and lemon juice in a medium-sized bowl. Mix and stir in mint leaves. Allow to stand 30 minutes. Fill a large pitcher with ice and stir liquid over ice. Add Ale-8-One soda and lemon slices. Pour into tall glasses.

Serves 10

Notable Neighbor: Highbridge Spring Water

*"In 1830, the water from Fayette County's Maxwell Springs
was in such demand that for a time, it was bottled for public sale."*

High Bridge, America's highest railroad bridge spanning a navigable body of water, casts a shadow on the Highbridge Spring Water Company, operating from a Jessamine County limestone quarry cave deep below the earth. What began in 1976 as a mushroom farm venture in Jessamine County has developed into a thriving, Kentucky Proud business.

 Bill Griffin was told that the cave he owned would never be any good for storage or any other venture until he dealt with the water flowing from the spring in the back...an underground aquifer. Developing an ingenious system of catch basins, reservoirs, piping, and bottling machines, the Griffin family began marketing the water from their cave in 1982. At that time, the only bottled product on the grocery store shelves was distilled water used in steam irons.

Today, family owned and operated, Highbridge Spring Water is described as a pure, no sodium, 'not-spring-water-with-minerals,' reverse osmosis-filtered water. Marketed in nine states, Highbridge has been bottled with custom labels and caps to become the official beverage for many Bluegrass events.

Fayette County's Early Churches

The earliest churches in Fayette County were established by settlers who brought their religious culture with them, and some survive today. South Elkhorn Baptist, Town Fork Baptist, Bryan Station Baptist Church, Mt. Zion Church, Walnut Hill, Mt. Horeb on Iron Works Pike, and Bethel on the western side of the county served pioneers of the Bluegrass.

Constructed in 1801, Walnut Hill Presbyterian Church in southeastern Fayette County holds the distinction of being the oldest Presbyterian Church building in Kentucky. Christ Church Episcopal, circa 1796, one of three churches within the Gratz Park area and the first Episcopal congregation west of the Allegheny Mountains, was designed by Thomas Lewinski, famous Lexington architect. Neighboring First Presbyterian Church on Mill Street, founded in 1784, is one of the oldest congregations in Lexington.

Image: Bullock Photograph Collection, Transylvania University Library

At the beginning of the 20th century, Historic Pleasant Green Baptist Church
carried out its baptisms in a pond that was once situated between Bolivar and Scott Streets.
With roots planted as early as 1790, the historic African-American Church remains one of the oldest in the region.

Sweet Saturday Oatmeal Bake

3	cups instant oats	2	large eggs, beaten
1	teaspoon baking soda	1	cup whole milk
2	teaspoons baking powder	½	cup canola oil
¼	teaspoon salt	½	cup real maple syrup
1	teaspoon cinnamon	1	teaspoon vanilla extract
½	cup dried cranberries	1½	cups fresh blueberries
½	cup chopped walnuts		

Preheat oven to 350 degrees. In a large bowl, mix oats, baking soda, baking powder, salt, cinnamon, dried cranberries and walnuts. In a separate bowl, beat eggs; add milk, oil, maple syrup and vanilla extract. Add to oat mixture and mix well. Bake in a greased 8x8-inch pan 40 to 50 minutes or until firm. Serve warm and top with fresh blueberries.

Serves 8-9

Hash Brown Brunch Strata

1	teaspoon vegetable oil	½	teaspoon coarse ground black pepper
1	(22½ ounce) package frozen hash browns, thawed	8	ounces thickly sliced ham, coarsely chopped or 2 cups cooked and crumbled pork sausage or 1 pound bacon, cooked and crumbled
2	cups shredded Colby and Monterey Jack cheese blend, divided		
1	(8 ounce) package cream cheese	4-5	green onions with tops, divided (1 cup sliced)
12	large eggs	3	plum tomatoes

Preheat oven to 450 degrees. Lightly brush a 15½x10-inch jelly-roll pan with oil. Place hash browns in pan and press gently into an even layer. Sprinkle half of cheese evenly over hash browns. Bake 13 to 15 minutes or until crust starts to brown and cheese is melted.

Meanwhile, in a large mixing bowl, whisk cream cheese until smooth. Gradually add eggs and black pepper. Whisk until smooth. Coarsely chop ham. Slice green onions, reserving ¼ cup of tops for garnish. Place meat and remaining green onions in a 8-inch sauté pan. Cook and stir over medium heat 2 to 3 minutes or until hot. Stir meat mixture into egg mixture.

Remove pan from oven. Pour egg mixture over crust. Return pan to oven. Bake 8 to 10 minutes or until center is set. Slice tomatoes in half lengthwise, scrape out seeds and dice. Remove pan from oven. Top with remaining cheese, tomatoes and reserved green onion. Cut into squares and serve.

Serves 12

Fasig-Tipton

Established in 1898 by William B. Fasig and Edward A. Tipton and headquartered at New York's Madison Square Garden, Fasig-Tipton's Auction Company initially sold high-quality road and carriage horses in addition to Thoroughbred and Standardbred racing stock.

In 1972, Fasig-Tipton established its permanent headquarters in Lexington, from which it initiates a year-round sales schedule for Thoroughbred auctions across the country. Prominent Kentucky graduates include 1994 Kentucky Derby winner Go For Gin, 1999 champion sprinter Artax, two-time champion filly Silverbulletday, Dubai World Cup winner Captain Steve, 2008 Kentucky Derby and Preakness winner Big Brown, and 2009 Kentucky Derby winner Mine That Bird.

Financed in equal parts by buyers, consignors, and Fasig-Tipton, the company established Blue Horse Charities in 2001 to assist those caring for Thoroughbreds no longer suitable for breeding or racing. Synergy Investments Ltd., a Dubai-based company headed by Abdulla Al Habbai, purchased Fasig-Tipton Co. in 2008 from the Hettinger family.

Commonwealth Crab Dip

1 (8 ounce) package cream cheese, softened
3 tablespoons finely chopped green onion
1 tablespoon prepared horseradish
2 tablespoons mayonnaise

1 tablespoon ketchup
¼ teaspoon Worcestershire sauce
8 ounces fresh lump crabmeat, drained
¼ cup sliced almonds, toasted
⅛ teaspoon smoked paprika

Soften cream cheese and beat with mixer until smooth. Stir in green onion, horseradish, mayonnaise, ketchup and Worcestershire sauce. Gently fold in crabmeat. Cover and chill at least 2 hours. Top with smoked paprika and toasted almonds before serving.

Serves 12-14

Ham Stuffed Jalapeño Peppers

12 jalapeño peppers
1 (8 ounce) package cream cheese, room temperature
½ cup shredded Cheddar cheese
4 slices deli ham, thinly sliced and chopped

1 tablespoon lime juice
1 teaspoon chili powder
2 green onions, finely chopped
½ teaspoon salt

Preheat oven to 350 degrees. Put oven rack in middle. Cut jalapeños lengthwise through stem. Combine cream cheese, Cheddar cheese, ham, lime juice, chili powder, green onions and salt in a bowl. Fill each jalapeño with cream cheese mixture. Place jalapeños on baking sheet. Bake 20 minutes or until hot. Cool slightly and serve warm.

Serves 10-12

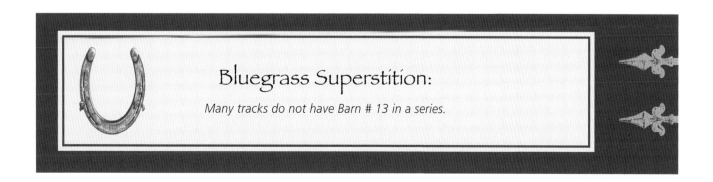

Bluegrass Superstition:

Many tracks do not have Barn # 13 in a series.

Olive-Nut Filling

GINGKO TREE CAFÉ AT ASHLAND: THE HENRY CLAY ESTATE

1 (8 ounce) package cream cheese, softened
1 tablespoon teriyaki sauce (thick)
¼ teaspoon ground white pepper

¼ teaspoon minced garlic
1 tablespoon mayonnaise
¾ cup chopped salad olives with pimentos
½ cup coarsely chopped pecans

Combine softened cream cheese, teriyaki sauce, white pepper, garlic and mayonnaise. Fold in olives and nuts. Store chilled. Let soften to spread for sandwiches or to fill celery boats. This may be thinned with milk or cream to make a dip or crudités.

Recipe was based on fond memory of the olive-nut sandwich served for many years at McAdams and Morford's lunch counter in downtown Lexington.

Always Popular Pimento Cheese

1 pound sharp Cheddar cheese
2 pounds mild Cheddar cheese
1 pound Swiss cheese
4-6 ounces pimentos
  Juice of 1 lemon

2 cloves garlic, minced
1 teaspoon dry mustard
1 teaspoon Worcestershire sauce
½ teaspoon sugar
¾ cup mayonnaise

Grate cheeses in food processor (may have to work in batches). Add pimentos, lemon juice, garlic, mustard, Worcestershire sauce and sugar to the cheeses in food processor and pulse to combine. Moisten with mayonnaise to desired consistency. Serve with crackers or as a sandwich on grainy wheat bread.

Makes 4 pounds

Memorable Menus: Hutchison Drug

Hutchison Drug, one of Lexington's early drugstores, operated from 1926 until 2007. Opening on the corner of East Main and DeWeese, the drugstore moved several times and located finally at Broadway and Short. Visitors were greeted with a penny scale beside the front door and treated at the old-fashioned soda fountain to pimento cheese sandwiches, fresh squeezed lemonade and ice cream sundaes.

Kentucky Blue Cheese Ball

1 (8 ounce) package cream cheese

1½ cups (12 ounces) shredded sharp Cheddar cheese

3-4 ounces blue cheese, crumbled

1 tablespoon Worcestershire sauce

1 teaspoon onion salt, or to taste

Garnish: parsley flakes and chopped pecans

Combine all ingredients with a mixer. Roll in a ball or log. Cover with parsley flakes and nuts. Serve with raw vegetables, crackers or pretzels.

Serves 15-20

Hot Artichokes and Feta Dip

1 (14 ounce) can artichoke hearts, drained and chopped

8 ounces crumbled feta cheese

1 cup mayonnaise

½ cup shredded Parmesan cheese

1 (10 ounce) package frozen chopped spinach, thawed and squeezed dry

1 clove garlic, minced

⅓ cup chopped fresh basil

Garnish: chopped tomatoes and sliced green onions

Preheat oven to 350 degrees. Mix all ingredients together except garnish. Pour into an ungreased 9-inch pie pan. Garnish with chopped tomatoes and sliced green onion. Bake 20 to 25 minutes or until lightly brown. Serve warm with crackers, tortilla chips or pita bread.

Serves 4-8

Joyland Park and Dance Casino

Hot dogs and cotton candy are legendary amusement park foods. One of Fayette County's first facilities was Bluegrass Park, opened in 1910 on US 60 at South Elkhorn. Reportedly operated by the Sauer family, the park featured a roller coaster, the Scenic Railway. Record indicates that the family removed rides and equipment from US 60 to Paris Pike when Joyland Park and Dance Casino opened to great fanfare in 1923. For almost forty years the park featured carnival rides, roller coasters, the area's first public swimming pool and Big Band concerts.

Programme of
J O Y L A N D
Dance Casino

JOYLAND PARK
2 1-2 Miles Paris Pike
LEXINGTON, KENTUCKY

Featuring the
Kentucky Kernels'
Orchestra

Season 1924

A.M. James, *Manager*

Courtesy: Betty Hoopes Collection

Paris Pike

Decades ago, the road from Lexington to Paris, U.S. 27/68, was a picturesque but dangerous two-lane road with an increasing volume of traffic. Native Americans first followed this trail behind herds of grazing buffalo, and later Paris Pike became one of the first commercial roads built west of the Allegheny Mountains, providing a primary route connecting the Ohio River port of Maysville with Lexington. Officially designated a historic scenic route, the 13.5-mile thoroughfare passes through some of the most valuable farms in the Region. It was along this historic byway that early Fayette County farm owners established Bluegrass estates.

Modern Paris Pike is the result of 30 years of public/private planning, negotiating, legal battles, and trips back to the drawing board. The completed project expands the road to four lanes and incorporates numerous unique features, particularly preservation of handsome estate entrances, rock walls, and architectural elements of Paris Pike's historic farms. The Dry Stone Conservancy brought expert masons from Scotland to train area residents in the craft of rebuilding the historic stone fences, resulting in displays of early drystone fences showcased alongside miles of modern reproductions, standing as median monuments commemorating the past and present of the unique Bluegrass Region. Worthy of a historical marker, some early collections are memorialized as to builder, date, and style.

Retaining a park-like aesthetic in the roadway corridor and maintaining an ultimate mission of adapting to the land, the 2003, multi-million-dollar Paris Pike Project has won national acclaim, environmental and landscape awards, and serves as a model for highway projects involving sensitive historic landscapes.

Pumpkin Soup with Cranberry Relish

1	tablespoon extra virgin olive oil	2	teaspoons poultry seasoning
2	tablespoons butter	2	teaspoons hot sauce
1	bay leaf, preferably fresh	6	cups low-sodium chicken broth
2	celery stalks with tops, finely chopped	1	(28 ounce) can pumpkin puree
1	medium yellow onion, finely chopped	2	cups heavy cream
	Salt and pepper, to taste	½	teaspoon nutmeg
3	tablespoons all-purpose flour		

In a medium soup pot, heat oil and melt butter on medium heat. Add bay leaf, celery and onion. Sprinkle with salt and pepper, to taste. Cook until tender, about 9 minutes. Add flour, poultry seasoning and hot sauce. Cook 2 minutes. Whisk in chicken broth and bring to a boil. Whisk in pumpkin puree one large spoonful at a time. Bring to a simmer and cook 15 minutes, whisking occasionally. When mixture begins to thicken, add cream and nutmeg. Keep warm until ready to serve. Garnish with Cranberry Relish.

CRANBERRY RELISH

1	Granny Smith apple, finely chopped	2	teaspoons honey
¼	red onion, finely chopped	½	teaspoon ground cinnamon
2	tablespoons lemon juice	1	teaspoon chili powder
½	cup finely chopped dried sweetened cranberries		

In a small bowl, combine all ingredients and mix well.

Serves 6

Baked Potato Soup

4	very large baking potatoes		4	green onions, chopped
⅔	cup butter		12	slices bacon, cooked crisp and crumbled
⅔	cup all-purpose flour		1¼	cups shredded sharp Cheddar cheese
6	cups milk		1	(8 ounce) container sour cream
¾	teaspoon salt			Garnish: chopped green onions, optional
½	teaspoon pepper			

Preheat oven to 400 degrees. Bake potatoes until soft and cooked thoroughly; allow to cool. Cut cooled potatoes in half lengthwise and scoop out potato pulp. Set potato pulp aside. In a large saucepan, melt butter over low heat. Add flour and stir until smooth. Cook 1 minute, stirring constantly. Gradually add potato pulp and milk to flour mixture over medium heat, stirring constantly until thick. Add salt, pepper, onion, bacon and cheese. Remove from heat when cheese melts and stir in sour cream. Serve immediately. Garnish with chopped green onion, if desired.

Serves 8

Baby Portabello Mushroom Bisque

4½	cups unsalted chicken broth		3	bay leaves
⅓	cup butter		1¼	pounds baby portabello mushrooms, sliced
⅓	cup finely chopped onion		1	cup whipping cream
¼	cup finely chopped celery		1	teaspoon salt
6	tablespoons all-purpose flour		1	tablespoon lemon juice
½	teaspoon dried thyme, crumbled		¼	teaspoon ground white pepper
½	teaspoon dried basil, crumbled		1	teaspoon Worcestershire sauce
½	cup dry sherry		⅛	teaspoon hot pepper sauce

In a heavy medium saucepan, bring chicken broth to a boil. In a large saucepan, melt butter over medium heat; add onion and celery; sauté approximately 5 minutes. Add flour, thyme and basil; stir 4 minutes. Whisk in sherry. Add hot chicken broth and bay leaves; bring to a boil. Reduce heat and simmer 3 minutes, stirring constantly. Add mushrooms and cook 20 minutes, stirring occasionally. Add remaining ingredients and simmer until slightly thickened, about 10 minutes.

Ultimate Tomato Soup

½ medium onion, chopped

1 tablespoon butter

2 (26 ounce) cans tomato soup

2 (11 ounce) cans stewed tomatoes

1 quart half-and-half

2 (8 ounce) packages cream cheese, softened

2 (12 ounce) cans V8 juice

1 tablespoon dried basil

¼ teaspoon salt

⅛ teaspoon ground black pepper

Garnish: mozzarella cheese and packaged croutons

Sauté onion in butter until tender. In a large pot, combine onion and remaining ingredients, except garnish, and simmer over low heat for 30 minutes. Garnish with cheese and croutons.

Makes 14 cups

The Kentucky Association

During Lexington's settlement days every man depended on the horse for transportation and industry. Early challenges involved impromptu sprints organized along roads and through town streets, which were dirt paths from which stumps and other debris had not been thoroughly cleared. Lexington's Main Street was such a course until the Kentucky General Assembly, responding to safety concerns, restricted racing to 'special paths.'

As early as 1787, the Commons and Lee's Woods became popular settings for races. Two years later, Henry Clay and other Lexington racing enthusiasts established the Kentucky Association Track in that area, and organized the Commonwealth's first Jockey Club. Soon, race winners' names were as famous as governors, celebrities, and U.S. Senators.

In the early nineteenth century, The Kentucky Association purchased sixty-five acres of land and built a mile-long track, grandstand, stables, and other buildings. For the next 100 years, the Kentucky Association track, in addition to sponsoring race meets, became the site of county fairs and livestock shows, operating continuously through the Civil War. During the depression years of 1932-33, the Kentucky Association disbanded and the Race Street track was razed a few years later.

The Kentucky Association's heritage lives today, exemplified by the historic wrought iron monogrammed gatepost that Keeneland's first president, Hal Price Headley, rescued during the dismantling of the old track facility. Standing guard at the entrance to Keeneland, 'KA' has been the Keeneland Association's emblem since that time.

Ole Kentucky Chili

4	pounds ground beef		1½	tablespoons sugar
2	large onions, chopped		1	tablespoon paprika
1	clove garlic, minced		1½	teaspoons salt
2	tablespoons wine vinegar		½	teaspoon white pepper
1	(2 ounce) can tomato paste		½	teaspoon allspice
2	(4 ounce) cans tomato sauce		2	bay leaves
2	tablespoons chili powder		2	quarts water
½	teaspoon cinnamon			Garnish: shredded Cheddar cheese and diced onion, optional
1	teaspoon crushed red pepper			
2	tablespoons Worcestershire sauce			

In a large pot, brown beef, onion and garlic. Drain excess grease. Stir in remaining ingredients, except garnish, and bring to a boil. Lower heat and simmer for about 3 hours, stirring occasionally. Serve in bowl over rice or pasta. Garnish with Cheddar cheese and onion, as desired.

Serves 20

Ale

During a 1906 interview, the owner of The Lexington Brewing Company (1794), attributed the success of the brewery to "the splendid quality of the limestone water, which has proved the best for making the famous Kentucky whiskeys the finest on earth, is also the best to be used in brewing beers." At that time the Brewery was producing one million cases of ale annually. Lexington Brewery's Dixie Beer was manufactured for years near the corner of Main and Rose Street. Today, Lexington Brewing Company is independently owned and operated by Alltech, a major supplier of yeast and other fermentation products.

Iroquois Hunt Club

Founded in 1880 by General Roger D. Williams and named in honor of the first American Thoroughbred to win the English Derby, the Iroquois Hunt Club is dedicated to "keeping coyotes dispersed so they do not become a threat to livestock and house pets." The annual season begins in early November with the "Blessing of the Hounds" by an Episcopal bishop, a custom dating back to St. Hubert, patron saint of huntsman. The riders, outfitted in full traditional regalia including red coats and black hats, are accompanied over the ten square miles of hunt country by 30 hounds searching for foxes, rabbits and raccoons.

Although originally founded as a foxhunt club, the primary focus of the club today is to prevent coyotes in the area from forming packs and harming livestock. In 1928 the club moved its headquarters to Grimes Mill on Boone Creek, on the Fayette-Clark County border. At the 1813 stone clubhouse headquarters, excellent food and hospitality is provided during the season, and the annual Hunt Ball is hosted on the first Saturday in November. The Iroquois Hunt club remains one of four in Kentucky, and the third oldest hunt club in the United States continually utilizing traditional rituals, practices, and British customs in protecting animals and land.

Image: University of Kentucky Archives

Blessing of the Hounds – November 7, 1936

157

Lexingtonian House Salad

MALONE'S

SALAD
4   slices bacon, cooked crisp and crumbled

2-3 cups romaine and iceberg lettuce mix

1½ ounces diced tomatoes

Ranch Dressing

Preheat oven to 400 degrees. Cover baking sheet with a layer of wax paper. Arrange bacon slices on baking sheet and bake until bacon reaches preferred crispiness, approximately 30 minutes. Place bacon on paper towels to drain excess grease. Once grease is drained, wrap bacon with a fresh paper towel and crush to make bacon bits.

Toss lettuces, tomatoes, bacon bits and 4 ounces Ranch Dressing in a frozen bowl.

Serves 2

RANCH DRESSING
1   (16 ounce) container sour cream

1   package Hidden Valley ranch dip mix

⅛   teaspoon dry mustard

2   cups mayonnaise

½   cup buttermilk

½   cup whole milk

Mix all ingredients and store in an airtight container for no more than one week.

Makes approximately 5 cups

Malone's

Since 1998, Malone's has brought to Lexington the finest cuts of Chicago style Prime Beef and fresh seafood, as well as a Wine Spectator award-winning wine list. Brian McCarty and Bruce Drake's Bluegrass Hospitality Group operates Malone's in three Lexington locations, Lansdowne, Hamburg, and Palomar Center.

Romaine Apple Nut Salad

SALAD
1   large head Romaine lettuce (10 cups)
1   cup shredded Swiss cheese
1   red or green apple, cubed
1   red or green pear, cubed
½   cup dried cranberries
1   cup salted cashews

Wash and clean lettuce. Tear up to make about 10 cups in a large salad bowl. Sprinkle cheese, apple, pear and dried cranberries over lettuce. Just before serving, pour dressing over salad mixture and toss. Sprinkle cashews on top.

DRESSING
½   cup sugar
⅓   cup lemon juice
2   teaspoons chopped onion
1   teaspoon Dijon mustard
¼   teaspoon salt
⅔   cup oil
1   tablespoon poppy seeds

In a blender, add sugar, lemon juice, onion, mustard and salt. Process until blended. With blender running, slowly add oil. Add poppy seeds and mix a few seconds.

Serves 12

Celebration Fruit Salad

¾   cup powdered sugar
1   (8 ounce) package cream cheese
1   (20 ounce) can crushed pineapple, drained
1   (10 ounce) package frozen strawberries, thawed, with juice
2   bananas, diced
8   ounces frozen whipped topping, thawed
1   cup chopped pecans

In a medium bowl, blend powdered sugar and cream cheese with a mixer on medium speed until smooth. Fold remaining ingredients in by hand. Pour into serving bowl and chill in refrigerator 4 to 6 hours.

Serves 6-8

Cranberry Waldorf Salad

3 cups coarsely chopped fresh cranberries	½ teaspoon cinnamon
1½ cups sugar	¾ cup chopped walnuts, toasted
1½ cups unpeeled, diced Red Delicious apples	½ cup whipping cream, whipped
1½ cups halved, seedless green grapes	½ cup mayonnaise
1½ cups fresh orange sections (about 3 large)	1½ tablespoons powdered sugar

Combine cranberries and sugar; stir well. Place mixture in a colander and place colander inside a large bowl; cover and chill at least 8 hours.

Transfer cranberry mixture to a large bowl; discard liquid. Add apple, grapes, orange sections, cinnamon and walnuts to cranberry mixture; toss lightly. Spoon mixture evenly onto individual salad plates. Combine whipping cream, mayonnaise and powdered sugar; stir gently. Top salads evenly with whipped cream mixture and serve.

Serves 6

The Phoenix Handicap

The first horse races were run up and down the main streets of towns. Lexington's early Main Street resembled an obstacle course, with stumps protruding from the dirt path.

Five years after Kentucky became a state, the owner of Postlewaite's Tavern in pioneer Lexington presented a silver pitcher to the winner of a Main Street horse race, and America's earliest stakes race was founded. Postlewaite's Tavern became the Phoenix Hotel, and today, The Phoenix Handicap is run annually at Keeneland Race Course.

Edamame and Bean Salad

2   cups shelled edamame, fresh or frozen

1   (16 ounce) can wax beans

2   green onions, thinly sliced including green tops

1   cup grape tomatoes or 2 Roma tomatoes, seeded and diced

1   tablespoon fresh basil

1   tablespoon rice vinegar

1   tablespoon fresh lime juice

1   teaspoon honey

1   teaspoon Dijon mustard

2   teaspoons olive oil

½   teaspoon salt

¼   teaspoon pepper

Steam edamame until tender crisp, about 5 minutes. Drain. In a large mixing bowl, combine edamame, wax beans, green onions, tomatoes and basil. Toss to mix.

In a small bowl, combine vinegar, lime juice, honey and mustard. Whisk in olive oil. Add dressing to vegetables. Toss to coat. Season with salt and pepper.

Serves 8 (½ cup servings)

Loaded Baked Potato Salad

7   pounds baking potatoes

Extra virgin olive oil, for brushing

2   pounds bacon, cut crosswise into 1-inch pieces

1   cup butter, softened

2   pints sour cream

Salt and pepper, to taste

1   bunch green onions, thinly sliced

1   pound Cheddar cheese, shredded

Preheat oven to 400 degrees. Pierce potatoes with a fork and brush with oil. Bake until tender, about 1 hour. Let cool and cut into bite-size pieces.

In a skillet, cook bacon until crisp, about 10 minutes. Drain on paper towels.

In a large bowl, combine butter and sour cream; season with salt and pepper. Stir in potatoes, bacon, green onions and cheese. Serve at room temperature.

Serves 20

Barns of The Bluegrass

Bluegrass barns embellish the rural landscape and serve as reminders of the importance of the horse in local culture and industry, since one horse may be worth more than the entire barn. The Thoroughbred farm typically incorporates a number of specialized buildings—stallion barn, breeding "shed," foaling barn, training barn, and more. Many of these distinctive architectural monuments were designed by world-famous architects and are painted in the farm's personalized color schemes.

Rural "palaces" have been designed to provide utmost comfort and care to their occupants... equine or human. Constructed of fireproof materials, carefully sited to pick up the prevailing winds of summer, a barn's ventilation is paramount in preventing disease and discomfort. Most barns aren't heated, except for staff quarters, for the horse's winter coat will provide protection. Good lighting is critical, particularly to a mare's reproductive cycle.

Cupolas, spires, arches, and unique individual stall windows distinguish Bluegrass horse sanctuaries. In addition to sophisticated fire and safety systems, the interior details are often reminiscent of the finest homes, replete with fine polished woods, padded flooring, gleaming brass, and chandeliers. One of the most unusual barns in the region is located on Normandy Farm on Paris Pike. The 12-stall L-shaped barn, built in 1927, is patterned after a barn in Normandy, France, and includes a clock tower, slate roof and ornaments in the forms of bird, cats and other creatures.

The plainer utilitarian tobacco barn is becoming a feature of the area's past. With the changes in tobacco culture eliminating the need for drying barns with their long shutters and ventilators, these stand as a symbol of a heritage that is rapidly changing.

Chicken Talese

SWISS SAUCE

2½	tablespoons butter		1	quart heavy cream
1	teaspoon minced garlic		2	tablespoons grated Parmesan cheese
2½	tablespoons flour		1¼	cups grated Swiss cheese

In a heavy bottom 2-quart saucepan on medium heat, melt butter. Add garlic and lightly sauté for 30 seconds. Whisk in flour to make a roux. Slowly whisk cream in roux to make sauce and reduce heat to medium-low when bubbly. Whisk in Parmesan and Swiss cheeses and a pinch of salt. Simmer on low while preparing chicken.

CHICKEN

	Vegetable oil		1	tablespoon garlic powder
3-4	boneless skinless chicken breasts, cut in 2 pieces		1	tablespoon salt
2	cups flour		1½	teaspoons white pepper
1½	teaspoons paprika		20-24	button mushrooms, sliced
½	teaspoon cumin			Leaf spinach

Fill a 12-inch sauté pan to ¼-inch with vegetable or canola oil. Slowly heat oil to medium heat. While oil is heating, combine in a medium bowl, flour, paprika, cumin, garlic powder, salt and pepper. Dredge cut chicken in spiced flour and place in hot oil. Sauté 4 to 6 minutes on each side until fully cooked and golden brown. Remove and set on paper towels to drain. Add sliced mushrooms to oil and sauté 2 to 3 minutes. Remove to a paper towel to drain.

On a plate, place a bed of fresh leaf spinach. Top with 2 pieces of chicken and mushrooms. Cover all with generous portion of Swiss Sauce.

Recipe was named for poet and writer Gay Talese.

Serves 6-8

Alfalfa Restaurant

Six like-minded vegetarians opened Alfalfa Restaurant on April 7, 1973, featuring an eclectic mix of vegetarian foods, marked by a hearty breakfast. Opening on South Limestone Street in the heart of the University of Kentucky campus, the restaurant moved to its current location on Main Street in downtown Lexington in July 2004. While no longer strictly vegetarian, Alfalfa continues the tradition of using fresh whole foods to prepare unique dishes that satisfy even the most discerning palate. Brunch at Alfalfa has been a staple for thousands of Lexingtonians for decades, and the location provides a perfect setting for a dinner date before seeing a play at the Downtown Arts Center.

Grilled Chicken with Cayenne Spice Rub

2   (4 pound) chickens, quartered, rinsed and patted dry

CAYENNE SPICE RUB AND SEASONED BUTTER

2   tablespoons salt

1   tablespoon coarsely ground black pepper

1   tablespoon firmly packed brown sugar

2   teaspoons garlic powder

1½ teaspoons cornstarch

1½ teaspoons onion powder

1   teaspoon lemon pepper

1   teaspoon chili powder

1   teaspoon cayenne pepper

½   cup unsalted butter, softened

1   sourdough baguette, cut diagonally ¾-inch thick slices

In a small bowl, combine salt, pepper, brown sugar, garlic powder, cornstarch, onion powder, lemon pepper, chili powder and cayenne pepper, whisk to blend well. Transfer 1 tablespoon of spice rub to a medium bowl and add butter; mix well. Reserve 4 tablespoons seasoned butter; set aside.

Sprinkle remainder of spice rub on both sides of chicken pieces. Arrange chicken pieces on waxed paper-lined baking sheets. Cover chicken with more waxed paper and let stand in refrigerator 1 to 2 hours.

Prepare grill on medium-high heat. Place chicken on grill, skin side up. Grill 20 minutes. Turn chicken and grill about 15 minutes, until skin is deep golden brown. Turn chicken again and grill, skin side up, about 5 minutes or until chicken is cooked through. Transfer chicken to platter and brush with 4 tablespoons reserved seasoned butter.

Spread remaining seasoned butter on 1 side of baguette slice. Grill bread about 2 minutes on each side, until golden brown. Arrange grilled toast around chicken on platter and serve.

Cayenne Spice Rub also tastes great on pork!

Serves 8

Herb Chicken in a Shell

¼	cup butter	1	cup milk
½	cup chopped celery	1	cup chicken broth
¼	cup flour	2	cups cooked and cubed chicken
1¼	teaspoons crushed chives	4	Pepperidge Farm pastry shells (baked)
1	teaspoon crushed rosemary		Salt and pepper, to taste
¼	teaspoon tarragon		

In a large saucepan, melt butter and sauté celery over low heat for 10 minutes or until tender. Whisk in flour and stir for 1 to 2 minutes. Add all herbs. Stir in milk and broth; cook, stirring constantly, until sauce is thickened and bubbly. Add chicken and season to taste with salt and pepper. Place in pastry shells and serve.

Serves 4-6

Quail with Blackberry Wine Sauce

BLACKBERRY WINE SAUCE

1	cup blackberry preserves	1	cup white wine

Heat blackberry preserves and wine to a boil; reduce heat and simmer until preserves are melted and mixture is reduced by a third.

QUAIL

	Olive oil	1	Granny Smith apple, cut into 8 wedges
	Kosher salt, to taste	6-8	dressed quail
	Black pepper, to taste	6-8	bacon slices

Preheat oven to 350 degrees. Rub quail with olive oil and season with salt and pepper. Place 1 apple wedge inside each quail and wrap with 1 slice of bacon. Secure with toothpick and place breast side up on a rack in a shallow roasting pan. Roast, uncovered, approximately 30 minutes. Brush generously with Blackberry Sauce and roast until done, about 15 to 20 minutes longer. Serve remaining warm Blackberry Sauce with quail.

Serves 6

Burgoo

'BER-goo' 'Ber-GOO'

"Don't ask, just eat!"

Squire J. Winston Coleman, author and Kentucky historian, claimed that burgoo is to Kentucky what 'Clam Chowder is to New England, Fisherman's stew is to San Francisco, and Gumbo is to New Orleans.' A stew containing any number of meats (at least three), vegetables, seasonings, spirits, all bound by a highly-seasoned gravy and guided by a secret recipe, burgoo's cooking time is listed in days because the concoction improves with age. Many cooks note that if you can recognize any component of the stew...a carrot or piece of okra...it's not burgoo yet!

The etymology of the word remains a subject of conjecture... 'barbecue' combined with 'goo'..the stew's gravy. Some say the term originated with sailors who often ate a gruel of bulgar. There are as many stories and legends as there are cooks and recipes.

One of the more famous burgoo masters was Gus Jaubert, who operated the Magnolia Saloon on North Mill Street and cooked for John Hunt Morgan's army. Modern Burgoo cooks may be secretive about their recipes and flexible with the supply of ingredients...beef, chicken, lamb, pork along with potatoes, cabbage, carrots, peas.

Tradition demands cooking outdoors in an iron kettle, over a wood fire, stirring almost constantly, and serving in a tin cup.

Keeneland's Burgoo

Feeding as many as 30,000 people daily during the Spring and Fall race meets, Turf Catering's Chef Ed Boutilier and his crew prepare 360 gallons of burgoo every morning. The Chef doesn't agree with the old saying, 'if you can recognize anything, it isn't burgoo yet!' He prefers that some of the vegetables 'hold their shape.'

Kentucky Burgoo

3 pounds stew meat (cubed)

1 teaspoon ground thyme

1 teaspoon ground sage

1 teaspoon granulated garlic

1 teaspoon ground oregano

1 cup diced celery

1 cup diced carrot

1 cup diced onion

1 (12 ounce) can diced tomatoes in juice

3 pounds frozen mixed vegetables
(should contain corn, lima beans and green beans)

1 (7 ounce) can tomato puree

1 (7 ounce) can tomato sauce

1 pound sliced frozen okra

1 tablespoon beef base

1 teaspoon Worcestershire sauce

1 teaspoon lemon juice

1 teaspoon Tabasco sauce

1 cup sherry wine

1 cup red wine

3 pounds diced potatoes

In a large stockpot, brown stew meat with thyme, sage, garlic and oregano. Add remaining ingredients and cover with water. Bring to a boil and reduce to simmer for a minimum of 2 hours or until ingredients have been tenderized but do not dissolve. Potatoes should be fork tender but hold their shape. Adjust seasoning to taste and thicken if needed with cornstarch.

Serves 10-12

Fabulous Pot Roast

1	tablespoon chopped fresh thyme or 1 teaspoon dried	4	pounds boneless beef chuck, excess fat trimmed
1	tablespoon chopped fresh rosemary or 1 teaspoon dried	2	tablespoons vegetable oil
1	tablespoon paprika	½	cup water, beef or chicken broth
1	tablespoon kosher salt	5	cups thinly sliced onions (about 3 large)
1	teaspoon freshly ground black pepper	6	garlic cloves, chopped
			Salt and freshly ground pepper, to taste

In a small bowl, combine thyme, rosemary, paprika, salt and pepper. Rub meat thoroughly with spices. Wrap well and store overnight in refrigerator.

Preheat oven to 350 degrees. In a large, heavy casserole or Dutch oven, heat the vegetable oil over medium-high heat, brown meat on all sides, about 5 minutes. Remove and set aside. Pour off any fat from the pan and deglaze the pan with water or broth, scraping up any browned bits with a wooden spoon. Put roast back in pan, cover with sliced onion and garlic, cover and bake 1 hour. Remove cover, turn roast over so that it is on top of onion and continue to cook, uncovered, 1 hour, adding more liquid if needed. Replace cover and continue to cook 1 hour more, or until meat is fork tender. Remove meat from pot and let it rest, covered loosely with foil. Add salt and pepper, to taste. Cut meat into thick slices or separate into chunks. Spoon sauce and onion over each serving.

Serves 6

Hearty Beef Stew

4	pounds bottom round, well trimmed and cut into 2-inch pieces	1	pound potatoes, cut into 2-inch pieces
1	cup all-purpose flour	½	pound baby carrots
⅓	cup olive oil	2	cups beef broth
2	large onions, diced	1	tablespoon kosher salt
1	(6 ounce) can tomato paste	1	teaspoon dried thyme leaves
1	cup dry red wine	1	bay leaf
		1	cup frozen peas, thawed

Coat beef in flour. Heat a few tablespoons of oil in a large skillet over medium-high heat. Brown meat, a few pieces at a time, adding more oil as necessary. Transfer to a 4 to 6-quart crockpot. Add onion to skillet and cook over medium heat until tender, about 10 minutes. Stir in tomato paste and coat onion; transfer to crockpot. Pour wine into skillet and scrape up any browned bits; add to crockpot. Stir in potatoes, carrots, broth, salt, thyme and bay leaf. Cover and cook on low heat for 7 hours, 30 minutes, or on high heat 4 hours. Remove bay leaf. Add peas and heat through.

Serves 8-10

Succulent Pork Tenderloin

½	cup soy sauce	2	tablespoons minced garlic
¼	cup sesame oil	2	tablespoons brown sugar
¼	cup rice wine vinegar	½	cup water
	Fresh ginger, 2-inch piece, sliced	1	(3 pound) pork tenderloin
1	bunch cilantro, minced		

Prepare marinade by mixing soy sauce, sesame oil, rice wine vinegar, ginger, cilantro, garlic, sugar and water. Trim excess fat off pork tenderloin. Place pork and marinade in a zip top bag. Let marinate up to 12 hours in refrigerator.

Prepare grill for cooking. When grill is ready, remove tenderloin from marinade and place on oiled grill. Cook on high 5 minutes on each side. Reduce heat to medium and cook until tenderloin is lightly firm to touch (170 degrees on meat thermometer). Serve with Cranberry Chutney.

Serves 4-6

Cranberry Chutney

1 cup chopped fresh orange sections

1 teaspoon cinnamon

½ cup orange juice

4 cups finely chopped fresh cranberries

2 cups sugar

1 cup chopped Golden Delicious apple

½ cup chopped walnuts

1 tablespoon white vinegar

½ teaspoon ground ginger

In a medium saucepan, combine all ingredients and bring to a boil. Reduce heat and simmer 5 minutes. Chill overnight. Serve with beef, pork or poultry.

Race Day BBQ Pork Sandwich

4   pound shoulder pork roast

DRY RUB

2 tablespoons salt	2 tablespoons paprika
2 tablespoons black pepper	1½ teaspoons cayenne
2 tablespoons dark brown sugar	

MARINADE

2 cups apple juice	1½ teaspoons garlic powder
1 cup apple cider vinegar	1½ teaspoons liquid smoke
2 tablespoons Worcestershire sauce	

6   soft hamburger buns
     Garnish: barbeque sauce and coleslaw

In a small bowl, combine dry rub ingredients. Sprinkle dry rub all over pork roast, pressing into the pork. Cover with plastic and refrigerate at least 2 hours.

Preheat oven to 325 degrees. In a medium bowl, combine apple juice, vinegar, Worcestershire sauce, garlic powder and liquid smoke. Pour into a large Dutch oven. Place pork in Dutch oven and tightly cover with aluminum foil and lid. Place in oven and brush roast with cooking liquid every hour. Roast 4 hours or until fork tender and shreds easily. Remove from oven and let stand until cool enough to handle. Shred pork, with a fork or tongs, into bite-size pieces. Serve on buns. Garnish with extra barbeque sauce and coleslaw, as desired.

Serves 6

Parkette Drive-In

Fed by two nearby drive-in theaters, the Parkette Drive-In opened on Fayette County's Belt-Line Highway in 1952. Joe Smiley's car hops waited on bleacher seats in the parking lot for a cloud of dust to rise from Liberty Road's graveled surface, indicating the next customer was near. Springing into action, they served Poor Boy Double Decker Hamburgers, hand dipped fried chicken, and shakes and malts.

Surviving several years of change and a series of new owners, Parkette Drive-In remains a New Circle Road landmark. Parkette's nostalgic 1950s-era sign promotes modern-day car hops who serve Poor Boys and fried chicken prepared from Joe Smiley's original recipe.

Fish Tacos with Chipotle Cream

FISH

2 tablespoons olive oil

2 tablespoons freshly squeezed lime juice

¼ teaspoon salt

Freshly ground black pepper

1 pound white flaky fish fillets
(tilapia or halibut)

8 (6 inch) corn tortillas

1½ cups shredded green cabbage or lettuce

½ cup corn kernels

¼ cup chopped fresh cilantro leaves

Lime wedges

In a small bowl, whisk together oil, lime juice, salt and pepper. Pour over fish and let marinate 20 minutes.

Preheat and prepare grill or nonstick grill pan. Remove fish from marinade and grill on medium-high heat until cooked through, about 3 minutes per side. Set fish aside on a plate 5 minutes.

Heat tortillas on grill or a grill pan 30 seconds each side. Flake fish with a fork. Top each tortilla with 1 teaspoon Chipotle Cream. Top with fish, cabbage, corn and cilantro. Serve with lime wedges.

CHIPOTLE CREAM

½ cup plain nonfat yogurt

2 tablespoons mayonnaise

2 teaspoons chipotle pepper in
adobo sauce

Place yogurt in a strainer, lined with a paper towel, placed over a bowl to drain and thicken for 20 minutes. In a small bowl, combine thickened yogurt, mayonnaise and chipotle pepper. Set aside.

Sporting Artists

Prominent stockmen were proud of their animals. Alvan Fisher (1792-1863) was said to have painted the first portrait of a great American Thoroughbred in 1823, but it wasn't until Swiss born painter, Edward Troye settled in the Bluegrass that animal portraiture flourished. In the late 1820s Troye spent years painting hundreds of livestock portraits, but many were lost during the Civil War. Troye painted not only horses, but prize sheep and cattle, as well as prominent families. Commanding $60 for a horse, $40 for a bull, and $30 for a cow, Troye was faulted for his inability to portray human hands. In many area homes such livestock portraits can be seen today, demonstrating the importance of the animal in Bluegrass heritage.

Tropical Black Beans and Rice

1	(14 ounce) can chicken broth		1	(15 ounce) can black beans, rinsed and drained
½	cup coconut			
1	tablespoon margarine or butter		½	cup sliced green onions
1	cup uncooked long-grain rice			

In a medium saucepan, combine broth, coconut and margarine. Bring to a boil and stir in rice. Reduce heat, cover and simmer 15 minutes. Stir in beans and onion. Cover and cook an additional 5 minutes or until liquid is absorbed.

May be served as an entrée or as a side.

Serves 4-6

Spanakopita

1	pound frozen spinach		1	cup (approximately 4 ounces) crumbled feta cheese
½	cup finely chopped onion			
2	tablespoons extra virgin olive oil		1	large egg, lightly beaten
1-2	garlic cloves, crushed			Salt and pepper to taste
2	tablespoons chopped fresh cilantro		¼	cup butter, unsalted
½	teaspoon freshly grated nutmeg		4	sheets phyllo pastry

Cook spinach according to package directions. Drain and squeeze out liquid then chop.

Preheat oven to 350 degrees. Butter an 8-inch square pan. Sauté onion in olive oil until almost soft then add garlic and continue to sauté until onion is soft but not brown. Add drained spinach; cook, stirring, 2 minutes. Let cool slightly. Stir in cilantro, nutmeg and cheese. Add beaten egg and mix well. Season with salt and pepper. In a small saucepan, melt butter. Brush one sheet of phyllo pastry with butter. Lay in pan, pressing down into corners. Let excess dough hang over edges of pan. Brush a second sheet of phyllo pastry with butter and lay in pan at a right angle to first sheet. Repeat with phyllo pastry. Spoon spinach mixture into pan. Fold excess dough over the filling to cover. Leave dough in slight folds. Brush with melted butter. Bake in oven 40 minutes or until golden brown and crisp. Cut into 9 squares. Serve hot, warm or cold.

Serves 9

2010 Alltech FEI World Equestrian Games

As the Kentucky Horse Park marked its 30th Anniversary in 2008, it joined Lexington and Fayette County in preparing to host the World Equestrian Games. Held every four years since 1990, and never before outside Europe, the Games are comprised of the world championships in eight equestrian sports—show jumping, dressage, eventing, driving, reining, vaulting, endurance and para-equestrian. The Fédération Equestre Internationale (FEI) is recogized by the Olympic Committee as the international governing body of equestrian sport. Skilled athletes and their equine partners convene at the Kentucky Horse Park's new sate-of-the art indoor and outdoor arenas to compete in the specialized events.

The 2010 Alltech FEI World Equestrian Games bring to Kentucky the world's best horses, riders, drivers, and vaulters, and represent the largest equestrian sporting event ever held in the United States.

Nutty Wild Rice

½	cup wild rice	¼	cup chopped mint or parsley
½	cup brown rice	4	green onions, thinly sliced
5½	cups chicken broth	¼	cup olive oil
1	cup broken pecan pieces	⅓	cup fresh orange juice
1	cup golden raisins	½-¾	teaspoon salt
	Grated zest of 1 large orange		Pepper, to taste

Cook rice in chicken broth according to package directions. Drain. Add remaining ingredients to rice and toss gently. Adjust seasonings to taste. Let mixture stand 2 hours to allow flavors to develop. Serve at room temperature.

Serves 6

Festive Vegetable Risotto

1	(32 ounce) can chicken broth	1	cup Arborio rice
2	tablespoons olive oil	1	cup baby spinach
1	cup sliced mushrooms	2	tablespoons butter
1	cup diced red or yellow bell pepper	¼	cup grated Parmesan cheese
½	cup chopped onions	2	tablespoons heavy cream

Heat broth to boiling; set aside. In a large nonstick saucepan, heat oil and cook mushrooms, bell peppers and onions until tender-crisp. Add rice and cook about 2 minutes until slightly brown.

Add 1 cup broth to rice mixture; cook stirring constantly, until broth is almost absorbed. Repeat, adding 1 cup broth at a time, stirring until broth is almost absorbed, about 15 minutes total. Add spinach. Cook 3 minutes more, stirring constantly, until broth is almost absorbed and rice is tender. Stir in butter, cheese and cream.

Butternut Squash Pudding

3	cups cooked and mashed squash		4	large eggs, beaten
½	cup butter, unsalted		1	teaspoon kosher salt
2	cups firmly packed brown sugar		½	teaspoon coarse black pepper
1	cup milk		¼	teaspoon cinnamon
¼	cup maple syrup or 1 tablespoon maple extract			

Cook squash until tender. Preheat oven to 350 degrees. Mash or puree in food processor while still hot; add butter. Add rest of ingredients and blend well. Pour into a buttered baking dish and bake until set; approximately 30 to 45 minutes.

Serves 8

Harvest Acorn Squash

1	acorn squash		1	tablespoon sugar
½	cup water		1	heaping teaspoon mace
½	cup firmly packed brown sugar		4	teaspoons butter

Preheat oven to 400 degrees. Peel, cut and remove seed from squash. Place in water and simmer about 20 minutes. Drain water and put squash into a baking dish. Add sugars and mace. Dot with butter. Bake until syrupy, about 10 to 15 minutes.

Serves 2

Oh, So Sweet Potato Casserole

3	cups cooked sweet potatoes, mashed	½	cup margarine
1	cup sugar	1	cup firmly packed brown sugar
2	large eggs	½	cup all-purpose flour
1	teaspoon vanilla extract	1	cup finely chopped pecans
½	cup milk	⅓	cup margarine

Preheat oven to 350 degrees. In a large bowl, combine sweet potatoes, sugar, eggs, vanilla, milk and ½ cup margarine. Beat until smooth. Spoon mixture into a greased 2-quart shallow casserole dish. Combine brown sugar, flour, ⅓ cup margarine and pecans. Sprinkle over top of casserole. Bake 30 minutes.

Serves 15

Town Branch Broccoli Casserole

1	(19 ounce) bag frozen chopped broccoli	1	(8 ounce) package cream cheese, room temperature, cubed
2	tablespoons butter	1	medium onion, chopped
2	tablespoons flour	2	cups shredded Parmesan cheese
1	teaspoon salt		Seasoned breadcrumbs
2	cups milk		

Preheat oven to 350 degrees. In a saucepan, cover broccoli with water and bring to a boil. Boil 1 minute and drain.

To make sauce, melt butter in a saucepan over medium heat. Add flour and salt; stir until smooth. Add milk all at once and stir until mixture thickens. Add cream cheese and whisk until smooth.

Layer broccoli, onion, sauce and Parmesan cheese in a deep 2-quart casserole dish. Repeat layers until the broccoli is used ending with sauce, Parmesan cheese and seasoned breadcrumbs. Bake 45 minutes until bubbly.

Serves 8 to 10

Town Branch

'Branch' is a term describing a moving body of water 'branching' from a larger creek or river. Emanating from the south fork of 86-mile-long Elkhorn Creek, Town Branch bears as much influence on Lexington's origin and history as any other natural phenomenon.

On the banks of a creek at the site of a crystal spring, William and Francis McConnell's scouting party first camped in 1775. The creek and spring were later named Town Branch and McConnell Springs. Town Branch, a major supply route for the pioneer city, once flowed through what is now downtown Lexington. In the early 1930s, the water source was redirected into a subsurface conduit running under Vine Street in an effort to eliminate flooding in the region.

Country Scalloped Corn

½	cup margarine, melted	2	(15½ ounce) cans cream style corn
3	large eggs	1	(16 ounce) bag frozen whole kernel corn
1	(16 ounce) container sour cream	1	(8½ ounce) box Jiffy Corn Muffin Mix

Preheat oven to 375 degrees. In a large bowl, combine melted margarine and eggs; stir well. Add sour cream and stir. Add cream style and frozen corn and mix well. Add the corn muffin mix and stir well. Pour mixture into a buttered 9x13-inch casserole dish. Bake 55 to 60 minutes or until lightly brown.

Serves 10 to 12

Corn Pudding

MERRICK INN RESTAURANT

¾	cup flour	8	large eggs, beaten
¾	cup sugar	4	(14¾ ounce) cans cream style corn
	Pinch of salt	4	(15¼ ounce) cans whole kernel corn, drained
1	cup butter, melted	½	cup whole milk

Preheat oven to 350 degrees. In a large bowl, combine flour, sugar and salt. Add melted butter. In a separate bowl beat eggs and add to butter mixture. Add cream style, whole kernel corn and milk. Pour into a well greased 11x13-inch casserole dish. Stir with fork, once, about every 15 to 20 minutes during baking time. Bake until golden brown; approximately 1 hour.

Isaac Murphy

Isaac Burns Murphy (1861-1896), Kentucky's record-setting African-American jockey began his career as an exercise rider at Lexington stables. At age fourteen, Isaac Murphy won his first race as a jockey and from there established numerous records that stand today. He rode 40 percent winners in 1886 and was the first jockey to win three Kentucky Derby races.

Horse owner, trainer, and jockey, Isaac Murphy was posthumously inducted into the National Museum of Racing and Hall of Fame at Saratoga, New York, and in 1977 his body was reinterred at the Kentucky Horse Park.

The Isaac Murphy Memorial Art Garden is an ongoing Lexington project, contributing to the recognition of African Americans' contribution to Lexington's thoroughbred industry.

Early Taverns and Hotels

Lexington's early taverns were meeting places, post offices, and centers of activity reminiscent of old English inns. The first Sheaf of Wheat Tavern (1784), established on West Main Street near Broadway was followed by the second between Upper and Lime. Robert Megowan's two-story log tavern hosted the organizational meeting of government and the 1792 inauguration of Kentucky's first governor, Isaac Shelby. For several years, the Sheaf of Wheat's second floor temporarily housed the Commonwealth Treasurer's office until Frankfort was established as the permanent capital city.

The Phoenix Hotel, 120-122 East Main to the corner of Main and Limestone, maintained the record for being the oldest occupied hotel site in Kentucky for 180 years, from 1797 until 1977. Originating as Postlethwaits in 1797, Wilson's, Keene's, and Brennan's, the "Phoenix" moniker originated from the fact that the Hotel rose twice from its own ashes following a series of disabling fires. A favorite motto was attributed to the bustling Phoenix site: *"If you can't meet a person at Main and Limestone Streets, one of you is dead."*

The Phoenix Hotel's activities paralleled the history of the country throughout its 100 years... Thomas Jefferson's election to the Presidency, Lafayette's visit to the United States in 1825, celebrations to commemorate Lexington's 100th Birthday in 1879. Crowds gathered in 1884 to marvel at the first electric lights in the area. The Phoenix welcomed World War II soldiers in 1942, and a bevy of female coeds in 1966, temporarily housed until the new University of Kentucky dorm complex opened. 1956 brought President and Mrs. Eisenhower to Lexington's Phoenix Hotel, and four years later, Lexington was abuzz with the news that Presidential candidate John F. Kennedy, his mother Rose, and sister-in-law, Mrs. Robert Kennedy had checked into the Main Street hotel.

Only in Kentucky...Tuillerie, a horse owned by Narrow Lane Farm, slept in the Phoenix lobby during the 1972 convention of the Kentucky Hotel and Motel Association. Through no fault of the equine visitor, the Phoenix registered its last guest in 1977 and is today site of Lexington's main Public Library.

The Lafayette Hotel, designed by Northern Kentucky architectural firm of E.A. and C.C. Weber, creators of Kentucky's 1914 Governor's Mansion, hosted its gala grand opening in 1920. 400 people resplendent in evening dress and jewels, before dancing until dawn, enjoyed an elaborate menu of caviar, turtle soup, fresh salmon, sweetbreads, beef tenderloin, and ice cream bombe. Over the years, Lexington youth recall being guided through menu selection and an array of flatware and silver finger bowls by popular head waiter, William Roscoe Drake. In 1982, the hotel site became offices for the Urban County Government.

The Clarendon-Leland Hotel was established in 1875 and the Drake in 1926 at 321-333 West Short Street. Later named the Henry Clay (1950), the hotel operated until 1964.

Yeast Cornbread

1	package yeast	1	teaspoon salt
½	cup yellow cornmeal	2	tablespoons butter
2	cups whole milk, divided	3½	cups all-purpose flour
½	cup sugar	2	large eggs

Dissolve yeast and water according to package directions. Combine cornmeal and ½ cup milk; stir until it makes a paste. Heat remaining milk and add paste. Stir until boiling and forms a "mush." Add sugar, salt and butter. Allow mixture to cool. In a separate bowl, combine flour with cooled milk mixture. Add eggs and dissolved yeast. Knead about 5 minutes (dough will be sticky). Allow to rise until dough doubles in size. Put into 2 greased loaf pans and let rise again. Preheat oven to 350 degrees and bake 35 minutes. When bread is finished baking, brush tops with melted butter. Cool on wire racks.

Makes 2 loaves

Southern Spoon Bread

WEISENBERGER MILL

2½	cups milk	4	large egg yolks, beaten
1	cup Weisenberger cornmeal	1	teaspoon baking powder
1	teaspoon salt	4	large egg whites, stiffly beaten
1½	tablespoons melted butter		

Preheat oven to 325 degrees. Combine milk and cornmeal. Stir until smooth, add salt. Cook over hot water, stirring constantly, until thick. Add melted butter. Cool slightly 10 minutes. Add egg yolks and baking powder; mix well. Fold in egg whites. Turn into a buttered 1½-quart casserole dish. Bake 1 hour or until firm.

Notable Neighbor: Weisenberger Mill

Fayette County's neighbor, Weisenberger Mill is located in scenic Scott County on the south Elkhorn Creek which has been providing water to power the mill's twin turbines since the early 1800s. Today Mac Weisenberger and his son Philip, are the fifth and sixth generations of the family to operate the mill. Utilizing Kentucky-grown white and yellow corn, as well as soft wheat, products are milled on roller or stone mills. Offering more than seventy items in various package sizes, Weisenberger Mill's products provide the basis for many classic Kentucky recipes.

Go Bananas Nut Bread

½	cup butter, softened		2	cups sifted all-purpose flour
1	cup sugar		1	teaspoon baking soda
2	large eggs		½	teaspoon salt
3	large very ripe bananas, mashed		½	cup chopped walnuts

Preheat oven to 350 degrees. In a large bowl, cream butter and sugar thoroughly. Add eggs one at a time, beating after each addition. Add mashed bananas and beat well. Sift flour, soda and salt together; add to banana mixture and mix well. Fold in walnuts. Pour into a greased and floured 9x5x3-inch loaf pan. Bake 1 hour, 10 minutes or until knife inserted in middle comes out clean. Allow to cool completely before serving.

Serves 10-12

Super-Moist Pumpkin Bread

1	cup sugar		1	(3.4 ounce) package instant vanilla pudding
1½	cups all-purpose flour		1	cup cooked pumpkin
½	teaspoon salt		½	cup canola oil
½	teaspoon nutmeg		½	cup applesauce
½	teaspoon cinnamon		4	large egg whites
1	teaspoon baking soda			

Preheat oven to 350 degrees. In a large bowl, mix sugar, flour, salt, nutmeg, cinnamon, baking soda and vanilla pudding. Combine pumpkin, oil, applesauce and egg whites and mix with dry ingredients until well combined. Pour into a greased loaf pan and bake 1 hour or until toothpick inserted comes out clean.

Serves 12

Expression: Upper Crust

In the eighteenth century, bread was portioned according to the diner's status. Workers consumed the burnt bottom of the loaf, the family ate the middle, and guests received the top, or the 'upper crust.'

Notable Neighbor: Kentucky River Palisades

Traveling by boat along a 100-mile stretch of the Kentucky River, the eye rises 300-400 feet through majestic limestone and white marble cliffs to the rimrock. The Kentucky River Palisades area, at the center of the Inner Bluegrass Region, was created as the river channeled through the Commonwealth's oldest rock formations for hundreds of thousands of years.

The picturesque Palisade region, 100 broken miles of it, stretching through Fayette County from Madison to Franklin County, is home to numerous endangered amphibians and mammals. Wet weather springs, limestone outcrops, caves, and deep gorges support a diverse ecosystem containing the largest concentration of rare plant species within the area. Due to the efforts of numerous local, state and national conservation groups, fortunate travelers may catch a glimpse of a great blue heron or the peregrine falcon, gliding and soaring, protected in one of the Commonwealth's most majestic natural landmarks.

Spalding's Doughnut Bread Pudding

JONATHAN AT GRATZ PARK

1 gallon dried glazed doughnuts cut into ½-inch cubes, about 18 to 20 doughnuts	2 cups firmly packed brown sugar
10 large eggs	2 teaspoons vanilla extract
1 quart half-and-half	1 teaspoon salt
	2 tablespoons butter, melted

In a large bowl, combine eggs, half-and-half, brown sugar, vanilla extract and salt. Mix well. Add dried doughnut cubes. Allow the doughnuts to soak in the custard base 45 minutes.

Preheat oven to 350 degrees. Brush insides of a 6x9-inch baking dish with butter. Pour mixture into baking dish and cover with aluminum foil and bake 30 minutes. Remove foil and bake another 15 minutes. Prior to serving, spoon Wild Turkey Honey Liqueur Sauce over bread pudding.

WILD TURKEY HONEY LIQUEUR SAUCE

½ pound butter, melted	½ teaspoon freshly ground nutmeg
4 tablespoons water	¼ teaspoon salt
2 cups sugar	2 large eggs
½ cup Wild Turkey American Honey Liqueur	

In a small saucepan, combine melted butter, water, sugar, Wild Turkey Liqueur, nutmeg and salt. Place saucepan over low heat and stir until sugar has melted into the sauce. Remove from heat and whisk vigorously until sauce becomes light and fluffy. Add eggs to sauce and return to medium heat. Simmer sauce, whisking constantly, until thickened. Remove from heat and keep at room temperature until ready to serve.

Serves 12

Spalding's Bakery

*"Each Spalding's doughnut is a hand-crafted masterpiece.
A box of them is like snowflakes; no two are identical."*

Since Bowman J. Spalding and his wife Zelma sold doughnuts from their home in 1929, the Spalding family has been producing matchless breakfast treats by hand from a secret family recipe, involving birch rising boards. Each Spalding's doughnut is uniquely shaped with crusty ridges.

In previous eras and former locations the daily production was 350 dozen, and when the supply ran out the doors were closed. The Spaldings also began closing on Tuesdays during World War II food rationing and just kept up the tradition.

Located on Winchester Road, Spalding's reopened in March, 2006, after leaving doughnut lovers without their favorite treat for fifteen months. The first day back brought connoisseurs who were willing to wait as long as 3½ hours for an anticipated Spalding doughnut.

The Lexington Bowl

*"1854—presented by the citizens of Lexington to
Dr. Elisha Warfield as a token of their esteem for the immortal horse Lexington."*

Garner and Winchester Silversmiths crafted the Lexington Bowl in honor of Dr. Elisha Warfield, beloved Lexington physician and breeder of fine racing stock. The 15-inch pedestal punch bowl remains one of the finest examples of early silver craftsmanship in racing tradition. Depicting scenes of a full-scale race, the trophy is heavily embellished with filigree flowers and scroll work. The Lexington Bowl, presented to the winning owner of Keeneland's Blue Grass Stakes from 1937 to 1952, is now a part of the Keeneland collection.

Image: Keeneland

183

Green Tea Granita

1¼	cups water, divided		1	cup fresh orange juice
2	tablespoons fresh ginger		½	cup fresh lemon juice
1	green tea bag		½	cup honey

In a saucepan, combine ¾ cup water, ginger and tea bag to a boil. Remove from heat and allow to steep 15 minutes. Strain and pour into a freezer safe container. Stir in juices, remaining ½ cup water and honey. Freeze for at least 2 hours or overnight. Take a fork and rake over frozen Granita (it will look like snow). Keep frozen until ready to serve with your favorite fresh fruit.

Maxwell Springs…Maxwell Place

*"No man can call himself a true Kentuckian
who has not watered his horse at Maxwell Springs."* Henry Clay

John Maxwell, one of Lexington's earliest pioneer settlers, came to Kentucky in 1774 with James Harrod, helped select the town's name, built the first blockhouse, and signed a 1782 petition to the Virginia General Assembly requesting the official establishment of the town of Lexington.

Near one of three large springs fed by the Elkhorn Creek, John and Sarah Maxwell chose a site in 1788 for their cabin and lived there for forty years. John Maxwell, Fayette County's first coroner and an original member of the Presbyterian Church, offered Maxwell Springs to the citizens of Lexington for the annual Fourth of July celebration, political gatherings, picnics, barbecues, and fairs.

During the Civil War, the public grounds were utilized for troop quarters and wagon and artillery storage. After the War, Maxwell Springs became the home of the Agricultural and Mechanical College, and is now the site of the University of Kentucky campus. Maxwell Place, formerly Judge James Mulligan's home, was famous as the center of many Lexington social activities, and continues that tradition today as the home of UK's president.

Caramel Apple Pie

6-8 tart apples (Granny Smith and Jonathan)   1 teaspoon cinnamon
Juice of 1 lemon   ¼ teaspoon salt
2 (9 inch) pie crusts, unbaked   2 tablespoons butter, melted
¼ cup sugar   ⅓ cup dark corn syrup
2 tablespoons flour

Preheat oven to 400 degrees. Peel and pare apples. Mix with lemon juice and place in unbaked pie crusts. Combine sugar, flour, cinnamon, salt, melted butter and corn syrup. Pour over apples. Bake 40 minutes or until apples are soft. Remove from oven and add topping.

TOPPING

¼ cup firmly packed brown sugar   ¼ cup dark corn syrup
2 tablespoons flour   ¼ cup chopped walnuts
2 tablespoons butter, melted

In a small bowl, combine topping ingredients and spread mixture over pie. Return to oven and bake an additional 5 minutes.

Serves 8

Blue Grass Trust for Historic Preservation

The coveted Blue Grass Trust plaque of excellence graces more than 800 historically significant properties in the Inner Bluegrass. The program is administered by the Blue Grass Trust for Historic Preservation, whose administrative offices are located in Gratz Park. Called into action in 1955 when the John Wesley Hunt house was in danger of being demolished, the Trust organized, raised funds, and preserved the historic house, beginning its fifty-year mission of education, advocacy, and service. The Trust owns and operates the Hunt-Morgan House as a public museum and event facility.

Bring on the Chocolate Pie

CRUST

1¼ cups flour
½   teaspoon salt
½   cup shortening

3   tablespoons cold water
    Powdered sugar

In a mixing bowl, combine flour and salt. Cut in shortening until pieces are the size of small peas. Add a small amount of water at a time, toss with a fork. Push to the side of bowl until all is moistened. Form dough into a ball. Refrigerate before rolling.

Preheat oven to 375 degrees. Roll dough out and place in pie pan. Poke holes with a fork throughout dough. Dust crust with powdered sugar to keep crust from getting soggy. Bake until golden brown. Let cool completely.

FILLING

3   tablespoons cocoa
3   tablespoons cornstarch
1½   cups sugar
3   large egg yolks (reserve whites)

2   cups evaporated milk
1   tablespoon butter
1   teaspoon vanilla extract

In a saucepan, combine dry ingredients together and blend. Add egg yolks and milk. Bring to a boil and stir until thick. Remove from heat; add butter and vanilla. Let cool while making meringue.

Preheat oven to 350 degrees. After filling has cooled, pour into cooled crust. Spread meringue over filling. Bake 10 to 15 minutes or until golden brown. Cover and refrigerate leftovers.

MERINGUE

2   tablespoons sugar
1   tablespoon cornstarch
½   cup water
¾   teaspoon vanilla extract, divided

3   egg whites
⅛   teaspoon salt
¼   cup sugar

In a saucepan, combine sugar, cornstarch, water and ½ teaspoon vanilla extract. Cook until thick and clear. Remove from heat and set aside. In a medium bowl, combine egg whites, salt and remaining ¼ teaspoon vanilla extract; beat with a mixer until stiff. Add sugar in small amounts and continue beating until stiff peaks form. Add hot sugar mixture to egg whites and beat until meringue stands stiff.

Serves 8

Racing Silks

The term silks, also colors, refers to the color-specific, geometrically-patterned jackets and caps worn by jockeys during a race. Each stable, farm, or racing organization designs and registers a specific color combination and pattern with the Jockey Club, just as it does each horse's name. Originating in eighteenth century England as a need to distinguish among horses racing in a field, the custom of personalized silks translates to the horse's saddleblanket and other racing and stable identifiers.

Among famous silks are the devil's red and blue of Calumet Farm, worn by the jockeys of Kentucky Derby winners Citation and Ponder, and the blue and green bulls eye of Fayette County's Overbrook Farm, worn by the jockey of 1996 Derby winner, Grindstone.

Photo Finish Pumpkin Pie

1	cup sugar		2	large eggs, beaten
½	cup firmly packed brown sugar		1	(12 ounce) can evaporated milk
½	teaspoon salt		1	teaspoon vanilla extract
½	teaspoon cinnamon		2	cups canned pumpkin
½	teaspoon allspice		1	(9 inch) pie shell, unbaked
½	teaspoon cloves			Garnish: fresh whipped cream
½	teaspoon nutmeg			

Preheat oven to 350 degrees. In a medium mixing bowl, blend sugars, salt, cinnamon, allspice, cloves and nutmeg. In a separate bowl, combine beaten eggs, milk and vanilla extract. Combine egg mixture with sugar mixture and pumpkin. Beat until smooth. Pour filling into unbaked pie shell. Bake 55 to 60 minutes or until knife inserted in pie comes out clean. Cool before slicing. Serve with whipped cream.

Serves 6-8

Frost on the Pumpkin Pie

CRUST

1¼ cups graham cracker crumbs	¼ teaspoon nutmeg
3 tablespoons sugar	⅛ teaspoon ground cloves
1½ teaspoons cinnamon	⅓ cup butter, melted

Preheat oven to 350 degrees. In a small bowl, combine all crust ingredients. Stir until blended. Reserve 2 tablespoons of crust mixture for top of pie. Press crumbs into a 9-inch glass pie pan. Bake 6 minutes. Remove from oven and let cool.

FILLING

1 (16 ounce) can vanilla frosting	1 teaspoon cinnamon
1 cup sour cream	¼ teaspoon cloves
1 cup canned pumpkin	1 (8 ounce) container frozen whipped topping, thawed
½ teaspoon ginger	

In a large bowl, combine all ingredients except whipped topping. Beat 2 minutes. Fold in 1 cup whipped topping; pour into crust. Spread remaining whipped topping on top and sprinkle with the 2 tablespoons of reserved crumbs. Refrigerate at least 4 hours before serving.

Serves 8-10

Bluegrass Land Preservation

In 2006, The World Monuments Fund included seven counties surrounding Lexington on its list of 100 most endangered sites. Despite ambitious land preservation programs, the Bluegrass Region has lost more than 80,000 acres of farmland during the past decade. Fayette County has a history of valuing and protecting farmland including creation of the Urban Services Boundary and Purchase of Development Rights program, which have protected approximately 25,000 acres of Fayette County's rural land. The Bluegrass Conservancy, a private non-profit land trust, holds conservation easements on 10,000 acres of the Region's farmland, preserving it for agriculture and other open-space activities.

Flourless Chocolate Cake

1⅔ cups (10 ounces) bittersweet or semisweet chocolate morsels
1 cup unsalted butter, cut into pieces
¼ cup water
½ teaspoon instant coffee granules
⅓ cup sugar
8 large eggs
Powdered sugar
Sweetened whipped cream

Position a rack on the lower third of oven and preheat to 325 degrees. Grease bottom of a 9-inch spingform pan. Line bottom with parchment or wax paper. Grease paper.

In a medium, heavy-duty saucepan, place morsels, butter, water and coffee granules. Heat over medium-low heat, stirring constantly, until melted and smooth. Add sugar and stir until smooth. Remove from heat. In a large mixing bowl, beat eggs 5 minutes or until it doubles in volume. Fold ⅓ beaten eggs into chocolate mixture. Fold in remaining beaten eggs ⅓ at a time until thoroughly incorporated. Pour batter into prepared pan. Bake 33 to 35 minutes or until cake has risen (center will still move and appear unbaked) and edges start to get firm and shiny. Cool completely in pan or on wire rack (center will sink slightly).

Cover cake and refrigerate 4 hours or overnight. Cake can be made up to 4 days in advance. About 30 minutes before serving, remove side of pan by first running a knife around the edge of cake, invert cake on a sheet of parchment or wax paper. Peel off parchment or wax paper that was used in pan liner. Turn cake right side up on serving platter. Dust with powdered sugar and serve with whipped cream.

Serves 12

Fresh Apple Cake

1 cup canola oil
2 large eggs
2 cups sugar
1 teaspoon vanilla extract
2¼ cups flour
1 teaspoon baking soda
1 teaspoon cinnamon
1 cup chopped walnuts
1 cup raisins
3 cups peeled and chopped apples
1 (6 ounce) package butterscotch chips

Preheat oven to 350 degrees. In a large mixing bowl, combine oil, eggs, sugar and vanilla. Sift flour, baking soda and cinnamon and add to mixture. Stir in walnuts, raisins and apples. Mix well. Spread in a greased 9x13-inch pan. Sprinkle butterscotch chips on top. Bake 45 to 50 minutes. Cool and cut into squares.

Serves 16

Lexington's Theaters

1930s and 40s weekends in the county seat brought thousands of shoppers from surrounding towns to Lexington, drawn by restaurants, vaudeville acts, and movies. The major motion picture houses of the day were:

880-seat State Theatre (constructed in 1929, renovated in 1996)

1,400-seat Strand Theatre (1915-1979)

934-seat Ada Meade Theatre, (the Hippodrome) (1913-1955)

1,500-seat Ben Ali Theatre with its lavish Tiffany Studios interior (1913-1965)

The Kentucky (1922-). Featuring the Mighty Wurlitzer organ that played along with silent films and air conditioning created by blowing air over ice blocks behind the screen, the Kentucky Theatre's timeline progressed through a number of recreations and renovations, until 1991 when it was renovated by the Urban County Government. The theatre and its next door sister, the State, present specialty first-run films, civic events, and live music including the weekly recorded radio show "The Woodsongs Old-Time Radio Hour."

The Lyric, an entertainment center in the African-American community from 1948-1963, hosted first-run films and entertainers such as the Temptations and Duke Ellington. In July 2009, the Urban County Government began a $5.56 million restoration project for the Lyric Theatre and Cultural Arts Center.

Image: University of Kentucky Archives

Coca-Cola Cake

2   cups sugar
2   cups all-purpose flour
½   cup miniature marshmallows
½   cup butter
½   cup canola oil
3   tablespoons cocoa

1   cup Coca-Cola
½   cup buttermilk
1   teaspoon baking soda
2   eggs
1   teaspoon vanilla extract

Preheat oven to 350 degrees. In a mixing bowl, sift sugar and flour; add marshmallows. In a saucepan, combine butter, oil, cocoa and Coca-Cola. Bring to a boil and pour over dry ingredients; blend well. Add buttermilk, baking soda, eggs and vanilla extract. Mix and pour into a well-greased 9x13-inch pan. Bake 45 minutes. Prepare frosting while cake is cooking. Remove from oven and frost immediately.

Image: Tim Terry Collection

FROSTING
½ cup butter
3 tablespoons cocoa
6 tablespoons Coca-Cola
1 (16 ounce) box powdered sugar
1 teaspoon vanilla extract
1 cup chopped pecans

In a saucepan, combine butter, cocoa and Coca Cola. Bring to a boil. In a large mixing bowl, combine powdered sugar with boiling chocolate mixture. Blend well. Fold in vanilla extract and pecans. Spread over hot cake. When cool, cut into squares and serve.

Serves 20

Dixiana and Domino Stud

The address is 1301 Dixiana-Domino Road, near Paris and Ironworks Pike. Stone pillars anchor the shared driveway, the left one inscribed 'Dixiana,' the right 'Domino.' One named in honor of the great nineteenth century mare Dixie and the other for the famous stallion Domino, undefeated Champion Two-Year-Old and 1893 Horse of the Year, these two Bluegrass farms have shared a history since Dixiana's founding in 1877.

Dixiana Farm, established by an early horse breeder and agent, later became part of Elmendorf Farm, was resold and divided over the years, one portion joining Domino Stud in the early 1950s, until today, when the original acreage has been reunited under one owner.

During its history Domino Stud was owned from 1970 until 1988 by W.B. Terry (1918-2009), owner and chairman of the Board of Coca Cola Bottling Company Mideast. The Terrys hosted parties at the farm's stately mansion, Oak Hill, entertaining politicians, movie stars, and industry figures. In addition to a number of notable stallions, the farm produced one of the family's favorite mares, Mr. T's Tune, named in honor of Frances Terry. Becoming an excellent marketing tool for her owner, the mare enjoyed Coca Cola, which she drank from a can at her retirement party.

White Chocolate Cake

1	cup butter, softened		2½	cups all-purpose flour
2	cups sugar		1	teaspoon baking powder
¼	pound white chocolate, softened		1	cup buttermilk
5	large eggs, separated		1	cup chopped pecans
1	teaspoon vanilla extract		1	cup coconut

Preheat oven to 350 degrees. In a large mixing bowl, cream the sugar, butter and white chocolate. Add the egg yolks and vanilla extract; beat well. Add the flour, baking powder and buttermilk; mix well. In a separate bowl, beat egg whites and fold into batter. Fold in pecans and coconut. Butter a 9x13-inch pan and layer bottom with waxed paper. Pour batter into prepared pan and bake 1 hour. Allow cake to cool completely. Remove from pan and frost sides and top of cake.

ICING

2	cups granulated sugar		1	teaspoon vanilla extract
2	sticks margarine			Powdered sugar to thicken icing as needed
⅔	cup evaporated milk			

In a saucepan, combine sugar, margarine, milk and vanilla extract. Place over medium heat and stir until sugar dissolves. Bring mixture to a rapid boil and cook 5 minutes, stirring constantly. Remove from heat. Beat with a mixer adding powdered sugar, 1 tablespoon at a time as needed, to thicken icing to a spreading consistency.

Serves 12-14

Cranberry Crunch

1	cup uncooked rolled oats		½	cup butter
½	cup sifted all-purpose flour		1	(1 pound) can cranberry sauce (jellied or whole)
1	cup firmly packed brown sugar			

Preheat oven to 350 degrees. Grease an 8x8x2-inch pan. Mix oats, flour and sugar. With a pastry cutter or 2 knives (scissor-fashion), cut in butter until crumbly. Place half of mixture in bottom of pan. Cover with cranberry sauce. Top with remaining oat mixture. Bake 45 minutes. Serve hot with vanilla ice cream or whipped topping.

Serves 6 to 8

Pumpkin Oatmeal Cookies

4	cups all-purpose flour		2	cups firmly packed brown sugar
2	cups oatmeal		1	cup sugar
2	teaspoons baking soda		1	large egg
3	teaspoons cinnamon		1	teaspoon vanilla extract
¼	teaspoon nutmeg		1	(16 ounce) can pumpkin
⅛	teaspoon ground cloves		1	cup chocolate chips
1	teaspoon salt		½	cup chopped pecans
1½	cups butter, softened			

Preheat oven to 350 degrees. In a mixing bowl, combine flour, oatmeal, baking soda, cinnamon, nutmeg, cloves and salt. Set mixture aside. Cream butter. Gradually add sugars and mix until light and fluffy. Add egg and vanilla extract; mix well. Alternate adding canned pumpkin and dry mixture. Batter will be thick. Add chocolate chips and pecans. Spoon tablespoons of batter onto baking sheet and bake 18 to 20 minutes or until golden brown.

Makes 4 dozen

Horse Mania

'Horse Mania' rode through Lexington late June to mid-November, 2000 bringing with it 79 life-size fiberglass horses extravagantly decorated by local artists. A collaboration between the Kentucky Thoroughbred Association and the Lexington Arts and Cultural Council, the public art project was sponsored by community businesses, farms, or patrons. The five-month event culminated in an auction profiting local charities dedicated to the public arts. With clever names such as Horse Cents (a lifesize horse completely covered in copper pennies) and Chard-de-neigh (covered with china chards), the city-wide public art project was a winner!

As the Bluegrass Region welcomes visitors from all over the world for the 2010 Alltech FEI World Equestrian Games, LexArts is 'leading the charge' for a 2010 public arts project featuring a new herd of unique horses. "In a tip of the hat to the international flavor of the Games, Horse Mania 2010 will include a horse from each of Lexington's four Sister Cities – Deauville, France; County Kildare, Ireland; Shinhidaka, Japan; and Newmarket, England. The Sister Cities horses will be decorated by artists from each of these countries and then flown back to Lexington, via horse transport, to be displayed with the rest of the horses."

Vegitariat

Kentucky Agriculture Society

In 1838, early Bluegrass leaders banded together to form the Kentucky Agriculture Society, inducting Governor Isaac Shelby as first president. Dedicated to building and improving the livestock industry, the Society hosted fairs and shows during which members exhibited prize bulls, cows, and other livestock. Agriculture societies evolved into agricultural experiment stations, Agricultural and Mechanical Colleges, and publishers of farm journals.

The English tradition of offering fair prizes made of silver beakers, pitchers, and trophies began in 1816 on the Lewis Sanders farm at a "Shew and Cattle Fair." At the 1818 fair, prizes included silver cups, silver goblets, sugar tongs, candlesticks, teaspoons, elaborate bowls, and a cream ladle. Competition for the silver trophies among owners and breeders was so keen that it further encouraged the development of fine blooded stock for which Kentucky is so famous today. The prize winners usually contributed the cost of their silver pieces to the fair promoters so that similar awards could be offered the following year.

Kentucky silver craft was stimulated by the silver prize practice, which continues today, particularly in the Thoroughbred racing culture. Prizes became more elaborate over the years, illustrated by the $2 million Calumet Thoroughbred Trophy collection exhibited at the Kentucky Horse Park.

Asa Blanchard Coin Silver Beaker

WINTER

MENU

Chocolate Eggnog

Brie and Cranberry Pizza

Oyster Bisque

Apple Spinach Salad

Apricot-Rosemary Glazed Chicken

Holiday Potato Casserole

Lexington Corn Pudding

Overnight Crescent Rolls

Blackberry Jam Cake with Caramel Frosting

WINTER

*"It was said that in the old days if you examined the contents
of a Kentuckian's pocket you would have found a sheaf of invitations—
to a ball, a New Year's Day Open House, a formal dinner.... for Kentuckians have
always loved to entertain and have always been over fond of good food."*

~ *Out of Kentucky Kitchens,* Marion Flexner

Travelers and poets wax eloquent when describing the Bluegrass Region of Kentucky, of which Lexington is the heart. Natives remark on the joy of enjoying four distinct seasons…a change of weather, wardrobe, menus, events, and cuisine…and none more distinct than winter, a season of rest for gardens and farm fields. Horse farms plan for next year's crop of foals and livestock farmers utilize the stockpile of hay gathered during summer days.

Following the cold foods of Summer and Autumn's soups and casseroles, winter kitchens produce comfort dishes to ward off the season's chill and holiday fare prepared for festive entertaining. From the early 1800s, Lexington maintained a style of living similar to the finest in the East, featuring a melting pot of cuisines and traditions brought by travelers and natives of many cultures. Of necessity, foodways brought from the English rural system involved preserved foods. Brining, pickling, smoking, and preserving became the traditional basis for many foods enjoyed today: country hams, fruit butters, marmalades, pickled vegetables and fruits.

Modern Bluegrass social life finds expression in events that range from simple, old-fashioned neighborhood gatherings to the activities of hundreds of societies, clubs, and cultural groups. Traditionally, Lexington residents relish any reason to plan a party and celebrate. The sports calendar wraps up the football season and anticipates the next basketball tip-off. Perhaps the teams will play in post season tournaments, affording yet another opportunity for gathering and celebrating…and eating!

Winter holidays offer a succession of prospects for opening homes and welcoming family, friends, and neighbors in Bluegrass style. Lexington's harvest and holiday tables groan with traditional fare handed down from the past, prepared in modern kitchens with contemporary flair. Honoring age-old custom that has characterized Lexington for centuries, elegant homes, gardens, and parks are bedecked with holiday finery in anticipation of another Thanksgiving, Christmas, and New Year's season. The Bluegrass celebrates the holidays in a style befitting the 'Athens of the West.'

Image: Winter Divider Page, Old Bradley Farm

Blanketing the Bluegrass

Snow, which the Bluegrass sees on occasion, presents a pristine backdrop for miles of board fencing on Bluegrass farms. The black plank fence, usually four horizontal planks high, is most often seen in the modern Bluegrass farmscape. Although seemingly identical,

upon closer inspection many variations are noted: oak, red cedar, locust posts; batten boards or not; pasture-side or road-side posts; and the most contentious question of all—white or black paint? Whatever the issue, horsemen plan fencing with the well being of the equine in mind. For example, posts installed on the road side of the pasture reduce the possibility of injury to the animal.

In the late nineteenth century, board fences were whitewashed with lime solution and later nearly all farm fences were painted white. Although some argue that the white fence is easier for the horse to see at night, it requires almost constant maintenance and white paint is considerably more costly than black, therefore, black fences are more prevalent today. Modern horsemen have replaced creosote-based black paint with safer, more environmentally-friendly choices.

The Kentucky Gate

Complementing the fence as a Bluegrass cultural icon, the Kentucky gate graced farm entrances throughout the region during the twentieth century. The Lincoln Automatic Gate, invented at the close of the Civil War, was manufactured in Fayette County for years and sold around the world.

Livestock required containment but horse and carriage riders and later automobile drivers needed an easy method of ingress and egress. The traveler reached from horseback to enter the farm by pulling a rope or leather strap attached to the gate's arms…thus, the lazy gate was christened.

Image: Kentucky Historical Society

Elmendorf Farm, Miss Daisy Procter Dangerfield, Office Manager

Courtsey Betty Hoopes

Chocolate Eggnog

1½	tablespoons instant coffee granules	½	cup chocolate syrup
½	cup hot water	¼	teaspoon cinnamon
1	(32 ounce) carton refrigerated eggnog	½	cup whipping cream, whipped
½	cup brandy		

Dissolve instant coffee granules in hot water; cool. Combine coffee, eggnog and brandy. Add chocolate syrup and cinnamon; cover and chill thoroughly. Fold in whipping cream just before serving.

Makes 1½ quarts

Holiday Punch

3	cups pineapple juice	⅛	teaspoon salt
3	cups cranberry juice	1½	teaspoons whole cloves
1½	cups water	1	cinnamon stick
⅓	cup firmly packed brown sugar		

Combine juices, water, sugar and salt in a clean coffee percolator. Place cloves and cinnamon stick in basket and perk. Serve hot.

Serves 10

Elmendorf

Paris Pike's Elmendorf Farm has stood as a fixture in Fayette County since the nineteenth century when it was bought and named by Daniel Swigert. In 1897, James Ben Ali Haggin, copper baron from California, expanded his Paris Pike purchase to 10,000 acres by buying neighboring farms. Elmendorf resembled a small city, with its own power plant and a model dairy that produced dairy products for years and participated in research credited with revolutionizing 20th century dairy production.

Today, only the marble columns remain from Green Hills, but in its heyday the southern mansion with its surrounding greenhouses was the scene of elegant entertaining. In 1902, the Haggins celebrated Green Hills' completion with a premier party of supper, dancing of the 'cotillion,' a 'receiving party,' and construction of a hardwood floored pavilion behind the main house.

Elmendorf has seen a succession of owners…Widener, Gluck, Cooke, and today the Lampton family. Showcasing miles of famed Bluegrass stone fencing, the original Elmendorf Farm has provided the foundation acreage for modern Normandy Farm, Old Kenney Farm, Clovelly Farm, Green Gates Farm, Spendthrift Farm, Greentree Stud, Gainesway Farm, and others.

Joyous Wassail

8	cups apple juice	1	teaspoon whole allspice
2	cups cranberry juice	1	small orange, heavily studded with cloves
¾	cup sugar		
2	sticks cinnamon		

Combine all ingredients in a slow cooker. Cover and cook on high 1 hour, then on low 4 to 8 hours. Remove cinnamon stick and strain liquid to remove whole allspice. Serve hot.

Serves 10

Coffee Punch

1	quart hot water	1	quart milk
7	tablespoons instant coffee	1	quart vanilla ice cream
1	cup sugar		

Bring water to a boil; add coffee and sugar. Stir until dissolved. Chill in pitcher in refrigerator. When ready to serve, place coffee mixture in punch bowl. Add 1 quart milk and stir. Add 1 quart ice cream one scoop at a time.

Serves 16

Memorable Menus: The Freezer

Main Street and Walton

1929 Menu

Beaten Biscuits 2 for 5 cents   Malted Milks 20 cents

Black Walnut Frappe 15 cents

"A Cup of Splendid Coffee" 5 cents

Menu: Betty Hoopes

Early Lexington Silversmiths

Silver coins from foreign countries constituted the first currency in the Bluegrass. It was this silver that citizens took to the early silversmiths for melting into tableware and silver serving pieces.

Lexington attracted the area's first wave of silversmiths, as Samuel Ayres wrote in 1789, *"I have the greatest turn of business that I ever had in all my life, and I have a journeyman…and yet we do not appear to be able to do half the business that may be had."* He also advertised for a *"quantity of old silver for which I will give five shillings per ounce."* Many early silversmiths also served as clock makers, jewelers, or gunsmiths.

Asa Blanchard, one of Lexington's most renowned silversmiths, opened his shop on the corner of Short and Mill Streets. He and his apprentices created fine tea sets, sugar tongs, watches, and clocks for Bluegrass homes for thirty years (1808-1838). In the August 28, 1818 issue of the Kentucky Gazette, Blanchard advertised that he had for sale *"coffee and tea pots, slop bowls, sugar dishes, cream ewers, pitchers, canns, tumblers, ladles, and spoons of all kinds."*

Other notable craftsmen of the nineteenth century included David Humphreys who made the first seal press for the Commonwealth of Kentucky when it was granted statehood. Antoine Dumesnil, Andrew January, Edward West Jr., George W. Stewart, and the firm of Garner and Winchester contributed to Lexington's popularity as a center of culture and artistry.

The Works Progress Administration, 1942:

"The first quarter of the nineteenth century was the golden age of Kentucky silver, stimulated by the practice of giving prizes made of silver at the local agricultural fairs."

A.A. Blanchard Coin Silver Spoon

Collection of Franklin and Betty Hoopes

Smiley Pete... A Friend To All

Horses aren't the only animals revered in the Bluegrass. On Lexington's new Court House plaza rests a bronze plaque, relocated from its original site at Main and Limestone, bearing the image of a beloved town dog and dedicated, "Smiley Pete, April 1943-August, 1957...Missed by All." He earned the name by baring his teeth into a sort of canine grin.

Downtown resident and neighborhood fixture in the 1950s, Smiley Pete was part spitz, part shepherd, part bird dog, and a few other varieties. Cared for by local merchants and surviving on his panhandling skills, he thrived for years on a daily routine of "hamburger and waffles at Brandy's Kitchen, a bowl of draft beer at the Turf Bar, a Hershey bar at Short and Lime Liquor, a dog biscuit and water at Carter's Supply, and evening popcorn at the old movie theaters." Regular baths and trips to the vet were arranged by his caregivers.

At his death Smiley Pete was buried by friends under a large tree on North Broadway...'A Friend to All and Friend of All.' Continuing a tradition of honoring Lexington's heritage, the Downtown Lexington Corporation each year presents the Smiley Pete Award, recognizing an individual, business, or organization making an impact on downtown Lexington.

Image: University of Kentukcy Archives

Blueberry Scones

2½ cups all-purpose flour

1 tablespoon baking powder

¼ cup sugar

½ teaspoon salt

1 stick cold unsalted butter

⅔ cup heavy cream (have additional cream available due to variances in flour)

1 cup frozen blueberries

Preheat oven to 425 degrees. In a large bowl, mix flour, baking powder, sugar and salt. Cut butter into ½-inch cubes and gently cut them into the dry ingredients (mixture will look like cornmeal when complete). Add cream and stir with a fork until a loose dough comes together. Lightly flour a clean work surface and place dough in the center. Flatten dough with your hands and put frozen blueberries on half of the surface. Pull the other flap over the blueberries and pat down to implant the berries in the dough. Knead dough 10 to 12 times until it comes together.

To make triangles, cut dough in half and make 2 small balls. Flatten each with a rolling pin into ½-inch-thick circle. Cut like a pizza into 6 to 8 pieces. Place on lightly greased baking sheet with ½-inch space on each side. Bake 12 minutes or until they are medium brown on top.

Magee's Bakery

Famous for number one seller transparent or chess pie, as well as iced cookies and birthday cakes, Lexington's family-owned Magee's Bakery has been an East Main Street staple for more than 50 years.

Generations of several Lexington families have celebrated birthdays with Magee's birthday cakes, always topped by the famous butter cream icing. Many mornings at 6:30, Magee's opens its doors to a line of customers, waiting to indulge in a slice of the famous breakfast casserole or a warm doughnut.

Magee's Bakery first created desserts at Berea College in the 1920s, and shortly after moved its headquarters to Maysville, supplying the tobacco markets with delectable treats. In 1956, the Higgins family purchased the Lexington bakery, and has offered Lexingtonians sought-after breakfast pastries, unique deli sandwiches, and famous desserts for the past half century.

Wake Up Coffee Cake

CAKE

1	cup butter	1	teaspoon baking soda
1	cup sugar	1	teaspoon baking powder
2	large eggs	½	teaspoon salt
1	teaspoon vanilla extract	1	cup sour cream
2	cups sifted flour		

TOPPING

⅓	cup firmly packed brown sugar	1	teaspoon cinnamon
¼	cup sugar	1	cup chopped walnuts

Preheat oven to 350 degrees. Mix all topping ingredients together and set aside.

Cream butter and sugar until light and fluffy. Add eggs and vanilla; beat thoroughly. In a separate bowl, mix flour, baking soda, baking powder and salt. Add dry ingredients alternately with sour cream to the butter mixture (beat after each addition). Spread half of batter in a greased and floured 9x13-inch pan. Spread half of topping on batter. Top with remaining batter and other half of topping. Bake 25 minutes.

Serves 24

Valley View Ferry

Image: University of Kentucky Archives

A 1785 "perpetual and irrevocable franchise" ferry privilege granted to Revolutionary War hero and local land owner, John Craig, by the Virginia Assembly today operates as the Commonwealth's oldest recorded commercial business. Linking the banks of the Kentucky River, Valley View Ferry has transported passengers and vehicles between Fayette, Madison, and Jessamine counties for more than two hundred years.

Originally powered by workhorses, the Ferry now operates via a motor and cable system, transporting three vehicles each trip and as many as 250 cars per day.

Sweet Potato Muffins

1¾	cups all-purpose flour		1	(15 ounce) can sweet potatoes (yams), drained and mashed
1½	teaspoons baking powder		½	cup milk
1	teaspoon ground cinnamon		1	teaspoon grated lemon peel
3	tablespoons canola oil		1¾	cups peeled and chopped baking apples
¾	cup firmly packed light brown sugar		⅓	cup chopped walnuts
1	large egg		⅓	cup golden raisins
1	large egg white			

Preheat oven to 400 degrees. Coat 18 muffin tin cups with nonstick cooking spray or line with paper liners. In a bowl, mix together flour, baking powder and cinnamon; set aside. In another bowl, mix together oil, brown sugar, egg, egg white, mashed sweet potatoes and milk until well combined. Make a well in the center of dry ingredients and add potato mixture, stirring until moistened. Do not over mix. Fold in grated lemon peel, apples, walnuts and raisins. Spoon batter into prepared muffin tins, filling about three fourths full. Bake 20 to 25 minutes or until done.

18 muffins

Bluegrass Music

Similar to traditional Bluegrass food, Bluegrass music is rooted in the classic music of England, Ireland and Scotland, with influences from African-American blues and gospel. Bluegrass Music derives its name from Blue Grass Boys, a band formed in 1938 by late Rosine, Kentucky native Bill Monroe. Classic Bluegrass instruments are guitar, banjo, dobro, fiddle, and mandolin, and the music features close harmony and instrumental solos.

Creamy Clam Dip

1   large round loaf bread (about 24 ounces), uncut

2   (8 ounce) packages cream cheese, softened

3   (6½ ounce) cans chopped clams, drained (reserve ¼ cup liquid)

2   tablespoons grated onion

2   tablespoons beer

2   teaspoons Worcestershire sauce

2   teaspoons lemon juice

1   teaspoon hot pepper sauce

½   teaspoon salt

Garnish: parsley

Preheat oven to 250 degrees. With a sharp knife cut top of bread loaf. Hollow loaf, leaving 1½ to 2 inches thick shell. Cut removed bread in cubes; set both aside.

In large bowl, beat cream cheese until smooth. Stir in clams, reserved clam juice, onion, beer, Worcestershire sauce, lemon juice, hot pepper sauce and salt until well blended.

On a baking sheet make a cross with two sheets of foil, each long enough to cover the baking sheet. Center bread shell on baking sheet. Pour clam mixture into shell. Place bread top over mixture. Wrap loaf with foil. Bake 3 hours. When ready to serve, remove top and add parsley for color. Serve with bread cubes or raw vegetables.

Cranberry Delight Spread

1   (8 ounce) package cream cheese

2   tablespoons concentrated orange juice

⅛   teaspoon cinnamon

1   tablespoon sugar

Zest of 1 orange

¼   cup finely chopped dried cranberries

¼   cup finely chopped pecans

Mix cream cheese, orange juice, cinnamon and sugar with electric mixer on medium speed until smooth. Fold in orange zest, cranberries and pecans. Refrigerate several hours or overnight. Spoon into a bowl and garnish with a small mint leaf, slice of cranberry, or zest of orange. Serve with crackers.

Makes 1½ cups

Brie and Cranberry Pizza

1   (8 ounce) can refrigerated crescent dinner rolls

1   (8 ounce) round Brie cheese, rind removed, cut into ½-inch cubes

¾   cup canned whole berry cranberry sauce

½   cup chopped pecans

Preheat oven to 425 degrees. Lightly oil a 12-inch pizza pan, round baking stone or 9x13-inch pan with olive or vegetable oil. Unroll dough, separate into triangles; place on pan with tips toward center. Press out dough with hands until flat and all edges are sealed. Bake 5 to 8 minutes until light golden brown. Remove from oven. Sprinkle partially baked crust with cheese. Place cranberry sauce in small bowl and stir to break up pieces. Spoon cranberry sauce over cheese. Sprinkle pecans over top. Return to oven and bake an additional 10 minutes or until cheese is melted and crust is golden brown. Cool 5 minutes; cut into wedges or squares to serve.

Serves 4-6

Baked Brie

2   tablespoons butter

1   large onion, chopped

2   tablespoons minced garlic

1   (16 ounce) wheel Brie cheese, rind trimmed and cut into pieces

1   (8 ounce) package cream cheese, cut into pieces

¾   cup sour cream

2   tablespoons fresh lemon juice

2   teaspoons brown sugar

1   teaspoon Worcestershire sauce

Salt, to taste

Pepper, to taste

1   round loaf sourdough bread, hollowed out with a bread lid

Preheat oven to 400 degrees. In a large skillet over medium-low heat melt butter; add onion and garlic. Sauté until golden brown (about 10 minutes). Microwave cheeses until melted. Add sour cream, lemon juice, brown sugar, Worcestershire sauce, sautéed onions and garlic to melted cheese. Add salt and pepper, to taste. Spoon mixture into hollowed bread loaf. Top with bread lid. Wrap loaf in foil and bake 1 hour or until bubbly. Serve with raw vegetables and bread squares.

Yuletide Cheese Ball

1   (8 ounce) package cream cheese
1   tablespoon finely diced onion
1   teaspoon Worcestershire sauce

2   teaspoons Accent
1   package pressed beef (sliced)

Mix cream cheese, onion, Worcestershire sauce and Accent. Slice beef into small pieces and add to cream cheese mixture. Mix well and form into ball. Refrigerate at least 2 hours before serving.

Serves 8

University of Kentucky

With origins as early as 1865 when classes at the Agricultural and Mechanical College were offered at Henry Clay's Ashland Farm, the University of Kentucky has evolved through two locations and three names. Beginning with 190 students and a faculty of ten, today the land grant University's student count has exceeded 27,000.

The campus sits on 795 acres in the heart of Lexington, boasts 16 colleges, a graduate school, 14 campus libraries, a University Press, and nationally-recognized medical school/hospital complex. UK continues its tradition of supporting the Commonwealth through the College of Agriculture's Agricultural Experiment Stations, Cooperative Extension Service, and from 1962-1997, 14 community colleges.

The University of Kentucky Alumni roster lists Dr. Thomas Hunt Morgan, scientist and winner of the 1933 Nobel Prize in Medicine, and William Lipscomb, 1976 winner of the Nobel Prize in Chemistry. U.K. has graduated seven governors, U.S. senators and representatives, and numerous leaders of industry, business, and the arts.

The UK sports roster boasts multiple national championships, Olympic medalists, a nationally-ranked cheerleading squad, seven men's basketball NCAA championships, and legions of passionate "Wildcat" fans for whom basketball and football are ways of life.

Memorial Hall

The Lexington Orphan Society

Lexington's Orphan Society, one of the oldest charitable foundations in the United States, had no permanent source of funding during most of its history. Formed in 1833 to assist hundreds of orphans left by the devastating cholera epidemic, the society has been maintained for years by ladies of Lexington's leading families. In the Society's collection is a letter from Henry Clay, thanking the Society for asking him to serve in an advisory capacity for the organization.

In 1833, the Orphan Society purchased the Dr. James Fishback house on Third Street for the Lexington Orphan Asylum to house a 'family' of orphaned children aged four to sixteen. In addition to organizing concerts and other fundraising events, the ladies conducted regular visits to the orphanage, recording their reports in a visiting book. Rules included the 'family' rising at daylight, conducting morning and evening worship, and saying grace before each meal. "Soup shall be had twice a week, at least dessert twice, and cake once a week. Bread, meat and vegetables, such as matron may direct, but always plentiful."

Operating there until 1907, the Society then acquired the John McMurtry property on Short Street, which it maintained until 1972, when the facility became home to the Living Arts and Science Center. In 1972, the Lexington Orphan Society, one of the oldest in the United States, turned its attention to supporting child-oriented organizations in the community.

"The Managers of the Orphan Society
beg leave to announce to the
ladies and gentlemen of Lexington
and vicinity,
that they propose to give a concert
of vocal and instrumental music,
for the benefit of the orphan asylum
at Mr. Brennan's ballroom on
Tuesday evening next, Feb'y 6th
All the members of the musical professions,
and some of the most distinguished Amateurs
in this city, have kindly offered their assistance
in the performances on this occasion." 1843

Oyster Bisque

1	quart oysters	½	teaspoon kosher salt
1	bay leaf	¼	teaspoon white pepper
2	medium onions, chopped and divided	1	teaspoon Worcestershire sauce
2	ribs celery, chopped and divided	1	pint light cream
½	cup butter	¼	cup dry sherry
¼	cup all-purpose flour		Garnish: fresh parsley

Drain and chop oysters; set aside. Add enough water to the drained oyster liquor to make 1 quart. Add bay leaf, 1 onion and ½ of celery; simmer, uncovered, 30 minutes. Remove from heat and allow to ripen at least 1 hour. Strain. In a saucepan, melt butter. Add remaining onion and celery; sauté 5 minutes. Stir in flour but do not brown. Remove from heat and add part of the oyster stock, stirring until smooth. Add salt, pepper and Worcestershire sauce; simmer over low heat 10 minutes. Add oysters and cream; simmer gently 2 to 3 minutes. Add sherry just before serving. Serve in warm bowls and garnish with fresh chopped parsley.

Serves 6

Expression: Below The Salt

'Below the salt,' or 'beneath the salt,' is just one of the many English phrases that refers to salt, for example, 'worth one's salt ', 'take with a grain of salt', 'the salt of the earth.' This is an indication of the long-standing importance given to salt in society.

In medieval England, salt was scarce, expensive and only affordable by the higher ranks of society. At that time the nobility sat at the 'high table' and their commoner servants at lower trestle tables. Salt was placed in the center of the high table. Only those of rank had access to it. Those less favored on the lower tables were below (or beneath) the salt.

White Chicken Chili

8	boneless, skinless chicken breasts	1	tablespoon ground cumin
1	cup diced onion	½	teaspoon chili powder
1	(4½ ounce) can diced green chiles	1½	teaspoons dried oregano
4	cups chicken broth	2	teaspoons dried parsley flakes
3-4	(15 ounce) cans great Northern beans	½	teaspoon dried basil
1	cup salsa	½-1	tablespoon salt
1	tablespoon dried crushed red pepper		Garnish: shredded Monterey Jack cheese, sour cream, tortilla chips, salsa and sliced green onions
2	teaspoons garlic powder		

Place chicken in a large Dutch oven and cover with water; bring to a boil. Boil 45 to 60 minutes or until done. Drain water and cube chicken. Cook chicken, onion, chiles and 4 cups broth in Dutch oven or stock pot over medium heat, stirring often, until warm. Add beans, salsa, red pepper, garlic powder, cumin, chili powder, oregano, parsley, basil and salt. Reduce heat and simmer, stirring often (about 20 minutes). Garnish with shredded cheese, sour cream, tortilla chips, salsa and/or sliced green onions. Serve with cornbread.

Serves 14

Pioneer Beef and Barley Soup

1½	pounds sirloin steak, cubed	½	teaspoon pepper
1	tablespoon oil	1	teaspoon celery flakes
3	medium carrots, 1-inch thick slices	1	teaspoon dried oregano
1	cup chopped onions	¾	cup pearl barley
½	teaspoon dried basil	2	(14½ ounce) cans beef broth
½	teaspoon dried thyme	1	(14 ounce) can seasoned diced tomatoes
2	teaspoons dried rosemary		

In a large skillet, brown steak strips in oil; place in crockpot. Add the remaining ingredients to crockpot and cook on low 8 to 10 hours.

Serves 6

1½   pounds lean ground beef

2   tablespoons vegetable oil

1   large onion, chopped

1   tablespoon minced garlic

1   (15 ounce) can diced tomatoes

2   (15 ounce) cans tomato sauce

2   (15 ounce) cans dark red kidney beans, drained

    Worcestershire sauce, to taste

1   teaspoon salt

1   tablespoon chili powder

1   teaspoon pepper

    Tabasco sauce, to taste

1   teaspoon cayenne pepper

1   teaspoon cumin powder

    Garnish: oyster crackers and shredded cheese

In a large pot, brown beef and drain. In a large skillet, heat oil and sauté onion and garlic on medium heat, stirring occasionally. Once onion mixture is done, add to beef in pot. Add diced tomatoes, tomato sauce, beans, 4 shakes of Worcestershire sauce, salt and chili powder to pot. Bring to a boil, reduce heat and simmer, covered, 15 minutes. After 15 minutes, add pepper, Tabasco sauce to taste, cayenne pepper and cumin powder. Cover and let simmer for another 15 minutes. Serve with oyster crackers and shredded cheese.

Serves 4

Memorable Menus: Brookings

Harold Brooking was known as Lexington's Chili King for 53 years. Brookings Restaurant on Euclid Avenue was the haunt of UK sports figures, most notably basketball coach, Adolph Rupp, who claimed his own booth. Regulars enjoyed the Rock-Ola jukebox and pinball machine.

Tobacco Heritage

The production and manufacture of Hemp provided the foundation for many Lexington fortunes from 1790-1860. After the Civil War, the manufacture of hemp ceased, to be replaced by burley tobacco.

Native Americans were growing tobacco long before the first settlers arrived in the new world, and gradually the leaf became accepted as payment of taxes and was in demand for export. History records that as early as 1787 General James Wilkinson transported hogsheads or barrels of tobacco down the Mississippi River by flatboat and established a trade outlet for the state's leaf.

The early 1900s ushered in the era of Burley Tobacco to Lexington. The American Tobacco Company established its headquarters in Lexington and the Burley Loose Leaf Tobacco Company constructed a large warehouse for the manufacture of twist and plug tobacco. Holding its first sale in 1905, the loose leaf burley market, with numerous warehouses, was among the world's largest by the 1940s.

The Works Progress Administration: "In 1938, Lexington was the greatest loose-leaf burley tobacco market in the world, and over its 26 auction sales floors, the crop passes from the ownership of the farmer into the hands of the processor and manufacturer…upon the results of the sales turns the prosperity of the Bluegrass. Sales have run as high as 70 million pounds in a single year. The 1936 acreage, yielded 55 million pounds and commanded $20,000,000. The city prospered on this foundation."

Image: Kentucky Historical Society

The 2004 growing season saw the last of the farmer-supported, federal tobacco quota and price support system, resulting in a dramatic change in tobacco culture in the Bluegrass.

Apple Spinach Salad

SALAD
1 pound fresh spinach

1 apple, unpeeled, cored and cut into thin slices

2 tablespoons lemon juice

4 green onions, sliced

1-2 ounce package sliced almonds, toasted

2 slices bacon, cooked and crumbled

Remove spinach stems and wash well. To prevent apple slices from turning brown, toss in lemon juice and drain. Combine spinach, green onion, apple slices and almonds. Toss with bacon.

DRESSING
⅓ cup olive oil

⅓ cup red wine vinegar

3 tablespoons sugar

¾ teaspoon dry mustard

¼ teaspoon coarse black pepper

¼ teaspoon kosher salt

Combine olive oil and remaining ingredients in a jar and shake well. Pour desired amount of salad dressing over spinach salad and toss.

Serves 6

First Newspaper: Kentucke Gazette

John Bradford, pioneer printer and journalist, worked by candlelight and set type by hand in order to establish Kentucky's first newspaper, the Kentucke Gazette in 1787. The Gazette was the only paper published within 500 miles of Lexington and gave readers foreign, national, and local news, including the first meetings in Lexington that led to Kentucky's statehood in 1792. In publication for more than sixty-five years, the Gazette was delivered to subscribers by post boys on horseback, representing the first effort to provide mail delivery to Lexington.

In the early days, it was considered improper to mention women in the newspaper...only names of those of ill repute or wives who had been divorced by their husbands were listed.

Cranberry Fluff Salad

2	cups coarsely ground raw cranberries
¾	cup sugar
2	cups unpeeled, chopped apples
2	cups seedless grapes
3	cups miniature marshmallows
½	cup English walnuts
¼	teaspoon salt
1	cup frozen whipped topping, thawed

In a medium bowl, mix cranberries and sugar. Let stand overnight. Combine apples, grapes, marshmallows, walnuts and salt; add to cranberries. Fold in whipped topping.

Serves 12

Double Berry Salad

1	(3 ounce) package raspberry flavored gelatin
1	cup boiling water
1	(16 ounce) can whole berry cranberry sauce
¾	cup finely chopped celery
½	cup chopped pecans
	Lettuce leaves
	Garnish: celery leaves and fresh cranberries

Combine gelatin and boiling water, stirring 2 minutes or until gelatin dissolves. Chill until mixture is the consistency of unbeaten egg whites. Stir in cranberry sauce, celery and pecans. Spoon mixture into lightly oiled individual molds or a 4 cup bowl. Cover and chill until firm. If using molds, unmold onto a lettuce-lined plate. Garnish, if desired.

Serves 8

Expression: Salad Days

This phrase was uttered by Cleopatra in Shakespeare's Antony and Cleopatra. Regretting her youthful dalliances with Julius Caesar as foolish: "My salad days, when I was green in judgment, cold in blood."

Ribbon Salad

1	(3 ounce) box lime gelatin	2	cups milk
1	(3 ounce) box lemon gelatin	1	cup sugar
1	(3 ounce) box orange gelatin	1	teaspoon vanilla extract
1	(3 ounce) box cherry gelatin	2	envelopes Knox plain gelatin
4	cups boiling water, divided	2	cups sour cream
2	cups cold water, divided		

Combine each box of flavored gelatin with 1 cup of boiling water and ½ cup cold water as you are ready to use it. Mix the lime gelatin first, cool to room temperature and place in a 9x13-inch dish. Place in the refrigerator to set.

In a saucepan, heat milk, sugar and vanilla extract to a boiling point; add plain gelatin. (Whisk well as you are adding plain gelatin solution to prevent clumps from forming.) Add sour cream and set aside to cool.

When the lime gelatin layer has gelled, remove from refrigerator and place 1½ cups of the cooked mixture over the lime gelatin layer. Set back into the refrigerator until the layer is solid.

Next, mix the lemon gelatin; cool to room temperature and place over the sour cream layer. Set in refrigerator until set. Remove from refrigerator and place 1½ cups of the cooked mixture over the lemon gelatin. Return to refrigerator until the layer is solid.

Repeat layers with orange gelatin and cooked mixture; end with a layer of cherry gelatin.

Bing Cherry Salad

1	(20 ounce) can crushed pineapple	2	(3 ounce) packages cherry gelatin
1	(16½ ounce) can pitted Bing cherries	1	cup chopped pecans, toasted
1	(12 ounce) can cola soda		

Drain pineapple and cherries; reserve juice. In a saucepan, combine juices and cola; bring to a boil over medium heat. Stir in gelatin. Remove from heat and stir 2 minutes. Add pineapple, cherries and pecans. Pour into a mold. Cover and chill 8 hours. Unmold onto a serving dish.

Serves 12

Hot Curried Fruit

⅓ cup butter

1 cup firmly packed light brown sugar

1-4 teaspoons curry powder

1 (16 ounce) can sliced peaches, drained well

1 (16 ounce) can pear slices, drained

1 (20 ounce) can pineapple chunks in heavy syrup, drained

1 (16 ounce) can apricot halves, drained and cut into slices

Preheat oven to 325 degrees. In a small saucepan, melt butter with sugar and curry powder. In a 7x11x2-inch ovenproof glass dish, combine all the fruits with the butter mixture. Bake 1 hour or until the sauce has cooked down. May be served immediately or cooled and refrigerated in a tightly closed container for up to 1 week. Serve hot.

Serves 12

Old Morrison, Transylvania University

Transylvania University

Kentucky University, The Agricultural and Mechanical College of Kentucky, University of Kentucky, Transylvania University, Lexington Theological Seminary, and Danville's Centre College all have roots in one educational institution. After being established in 1780 by an act of the Virginia General Assembly, Transylvania Seminary, the sixteenth college in the United States and first west of the Allegheny Mountains, relocated from Danville to the rapidly growing community of Lexington. Undergoing numerous affiliations, leadership and name changes, and plagued by sectarian controversies over the years, the school opened as Transylvania University in January, 1799 in historic Gratz Park.

After 1818, under the direction of President Reverend Horace Holley (1818-1827), the university established a medical school, law school, divinity school, and a college of arts and sciences, bringing additional students from all over the South, giving Lexington its reputation as the first educational center in the West...and contributing to Lexington's designation as 'The Athens of the West.' Trustees moved the school to its present location north of Third Street after a fire destroyed the single campus building. Old Morrison, designed by architect Gideon Shryock and completed in 1833 under the supervision of Henry Clay, board member and law instructor, serves today as the campus centerpiece.

Transylvania, meaning "across the woods" in Latin, has moved far from its origins in the heavily-forested region of then western Virginia, and today is a distinguished liberal arts school of approximately 1,100 students. A strong athletics program involves one-fourth of Transy students with the Pioneer Hall of Fame including the names of notable coaches and players.

Transylvania is linked with famous names in American history, as George Washington, Thomas Jefferson, John Adams, and Aaron Burr were early supporters. Among distinguished alumni are Texas hero, Stephen Austin, famed abolitionist Cassius M. Clay; U.S. vice presidents John C. Breckinridge and Richard M. Johnson; Supreme Court Justice John Marshall Harlan; 50 U.S. senators, 101 U.S. representatives, 36 governors, and 34 ambassadors.

Apricot-Rosemary Glazed Chicken

1	(8 ounce) jar apricot preserves		4	sprigs fresh rosemary, finely chopped
½	cup apricot nectar		6	boneless, skinless chicken breasts
3	tablespoons white wine vinegar			Salt and pepper, to taste
6	garlic cloves, minced		1	cup chicken broth

Preheat oven to 450 degrees. In a saucepan, over low heat, combine preserves, nectar, vinegar, garlic and rosemary. Heat until preserves melt. Transfer ½ cup glaze to a bowl and reserve.

Arrange chicken breasts in a 9x13-inch glass dish. Brush chicken with 1 cup glaze; sprinkle with salt and pepper. Roast until chicken is thoroughly cooked and glaze forms a sticky coat, approximately 45 minutes. Brush chicken twice during the cooking process with remaining glaze.

Increase temperature to 500 degrees and roast until chicken begins to brown, about 10 minutes longer. Transfer to a platter. Scrape the pan juices and any browned bits from the pan into a glass measuring cup. Add enough chicken broth to the juices to measure 1¾ cups sauce. Bring sauce to a boil over medium-high heat, whisking in enough reserved glaze to flavor and thicken sauce, as desired. Serve sauce over chicken.

Serves 6

Cranberry Chicken

3	pounds boneless chicken breasts		1	(10 to 12 ounce) bottle catalina salad dressing
1	(14 ounce) can whole berry cranberry sauce		1	packet dry onion soup mix
			5	cups cooked white or brown rice

Preheat oven to 350 degrees. Place chicken in a 9x13-inch greased baking dish. Combine cranberry sauce, salad dressing and dry onion soup mix. Pour mixture over chicken. Cover and bake 1 hour. Uncover and bake 30 minutes more or until bubbly. Prepare rice according to package directions. Serve chicken with sauce mixture over rice.

Apricot preserves may be substituted for the can of cranberry sauce.

Serves 6

Down Home Chicken and Dumplings

CHICKEN BROTH

5	pound whole chicken		2	bay leaves
2	cups carrots		6	chicken bouillon cubes
16	cups water		½	teaspoon whole peppercorns
3	celery stalks		1	teaspoon salt

Remove innards from chicken and discard. Place all chicken broth ingredients in a 9-quart pot and bring to a boil. Boil about 35 minutes until chicken is fully cooked. Remove chicken; debone, shred meat and set aside. Discard carrots, peppercorns and celery. Reduce heat to low.

DUMPLINGS

4	cups flour		3	tablespoons shortening
½	cup buttermilk		1	large egg
½	cup water		1	teaspoon salt

In a large mixing bowl, combine all dumpling ingredients until well mixed and forms a ball. Roll ball out thin and cut into 2x2-inch squares to form dumplings.

Bring chicken broth back to a boil, drop each dumpling in broth and reduce heat to low. Cover and simmer on low 20 minutes. Add chicken back into broth and dumpling mixture.

Memorable Menus: The Saratoga

The Saratoga, a Chevy Chase landmark known for good food and eclectic clientele, opened in 1953 and became famous for its steaks and pies. Other popular 'Toga' menu items were

Mrs. McKinney's Snappy Beer Cheese $2.95

Fried Bologna $2.50

Cold Meatloaf on White $4.95

Chicken and Dumplings $6.95

Menu: Betty Hoopes

Italian Chicken Roll

8	(3 to 4 ounce) boneless, skinless chicken breasts	2	medium onions
	Butter	3	green bell peppers
8	slices Swiss cheese		Basil, to taste
8	slices ham	1	(26 ounce) jar marinara sauce

Preheat oven to 350 degrees. Pound each chicken breast flat. Roll each breast tight and stick a toothpick through to hold in place. Simmer chicken rolls in butter until white in color. Remove from pan and wrap each chicken roll with 1 slice of cheese and 1 slice of ham, then install toothpick again to hold in place. Sauté diced onion, bell pepper and basil in butter from cooked chicken. Add marinara sauce and simmer 15 minutes. Place chicken rolls in casserole dish. Pour marinara sauce over rolls and bake 30 minutes.

Serves 8

Cheapside Duck Enchiladas

CHEAPSIDE BAR AND GRILL

3¼	pound smoked duck	8	tomato-basil tortillas
12	ounces cream cheese, softened	2	cups heavy cream
1	(5¾ ounce) can green chilies, diced	2	cups grated Monterey Jack cheese
¾	teaspoon ground coriander	1	tablespoon Cajun seasoning

Preheat oven to 350 degrees. Remove skin from duck. Shred meat. In a mixing bowl, combine cream cheese, green chilies and coriander. Mix well with a rubber spatula.

Divide cream cheese mixture and shredded duck among tortillas. Roll up burrito style and place in a 9x13-inch baking dish.

Pour heavy cream over enchiladas and sprinkle Monterey Jack cheese evenly over enchiladas. Sprinkle Cajun seasoning over enchiladas. Bake 30 minutes or until golden and bubbly.

Serves 8

DUXELLES

3	pints white button mushrooms		2	tablespoons unsalted butter
2	shallots, chopped		2	tablespoons extra virgin olive oil
4	cloves garlic, chopped			Salt and pepper, to taste
2	sprigs fresh thyme, leaves only			

Add mushrooms, shallots, garlic and thyme to a food processor and pulse until finely chopped. Sauté mixture in butter and olive oil 8 to 10 minutes until most of liquid has evaporated. Season with salt and pepper.

BEEF

1	(3 pound) center cut beef tenderloin		6	sprigs thyme, leaves only
	Extra virgin olive oil		2	tablespoons Dijon mustard
	Salt and pepper, to taste		1	pound puff pastry, thawed
12	thin slices prosciutto		2	large eggs, beaten

Tie tenderloin in 4 places. Drizzle with olive oil, salt and pepper; sear all over in a heavy skillet coated with olive oil. Meanwhile, set prosciutto on a sheet of plastic wrap. Shingle prosciutto so it forms a rectangle big enough to encompass the beef. Cover prosciutto with a layer of duxelles. Season with salt, pepper and thyme. When beef is seared remove twine and cover with Dijon mustard. Roll beef up in prosciutto and duxelles using plastic wrap to tie it up tight. Tuck in ends of prosciutto as you roll the beef. Seal in plastic wrap and refrigerate 30 minutes. Preheat oven to 425 degrees. Roll puff pastry to ¼-inch thickness on a floured surface. Remove beef from plastic and wrap in puff pastry, brushing with egg wash to seal. Top with salt and place seam side down on a baking sheet. Brush top of pastry with egg wash, then make a couple of slits in pastry with a knife. Bake 40 to 45 minutes until pastry is golden brown and beef registers 125 degrees.

Memorable Menus: Little Inn

The Little Inn opened in 1930 as a Prohibition-era roadhouse just outside Lexington's city limits. The Winchester Road establishment operated for the next 60 years, often referred to as one of the few restaurants between Lexington and Eastern Kentucky. The Little Inn was known for its prime rib, great steaks, frog legs, lamb fries, and 'the best bleu cheese dressing.' In fact, a large painting of a prime rib was painted on one side of the Winchester Road building.

'Great Steaks and the BEST Bleu Cheese Dressing'

Elegant Beef Tenderloin

1	(2 pound) tenderloin	2	tablespoons soy sauce
½	cup softened butter, divided	1	teaspoon Dijon mustard
¼	cup chopped green onions	¾	cup dry sherry or dry white wine

Preheat oven to 400 degrees. Rub tenderloin with butter. Place tenderloin on rack in a shallow pan and bake 20 minutes. In a small saucepan, cook green onions in remaining butter until tender. Add soy sauce and mustard. Stir in sherry. Heat just to boiling. Pour sauce over tenderloin. Return tenderloin to oven and bake 25 to 30 minutes for medium-rare (internal temperature 170 degrees), basting frequently.

Serves 4-6

The Jockey Club

Lexington is home to The Jockey Club, holder of the official breed registry for Thoroughbred horses in the United States, Canada, and Puerto Rico. Each registered horse's DNA must be categorized and its pedigree lines traced to horses recorded in The American Stud Book, the official listing of all horses registered and imported into North America. Jockey Club rules dictate the naming of Thoroughbreds: 18 letters or less, many more technical taboos, and no overlap with the 550,000 registered names or 100,000 permanently retired champions' names. After all requirements are satisfied, the animal is officially 'registered.'

The name for the 1973 Triple Crown winner, Secretariat, was chosen by a secretary at Meadow Stables after five other choices were rejected. There will never be another Secretariat or Seabiscuit. The names of all Hall of Fame inductees, major award winners, and horses with cumulative earnings above $2 million are permanently retired.

Mini Meat Loaves

1½	pounds ground sirloin	1½	teaspoons salt
¾	cup old-fashioned oats, uncooked	¼	teaspoon pepper
¼	cup chopped onion	1	tablespoon Worcestershire sauce
¼	cup chopped celery	1	large egg, beaten
¼	cup chopped green pepper	1	cup tomato sauce

Preheat oven to 325 degrees. In a large bowl, combine all ingredients. Form balls and place in regular size greased muffin tins. Cook 25 minutes. Let stand 5 minutes before removing from muffin tin.

Serves 6-8

Reuben Casserole

1	(16 ounce) jar sauerkraut, well drained	1	small onion, chopped
1	pound cooked corned beef, cut into cubes	½	teaspoon minced garlic
		1	cup shredded mozzarella cheese
½	cup sour cream	1	cup shredded Cheddar cheese
½	cup mayonnaise	2	tablespoons butter, melted

Preheat oven to 350 degrees. In a bowl, combine sauerkraut, corned beef, sour cream, mayonnaise, onion and garlic. Transfer to a greased 7x11x2-inch baking dish. Sprinkle with cheese and drizzle with butter. Bake, uncovered, 25 to 30 minutes or until heated through. Serve over rye bread or with rye crackers.

Serves 6-8

Country Ham

Noted Kentucky food editor and columnist, Marion Flexner, noted: "Hickory-smoked old country ham is perhaps Kentucky's most distinctive entry for the Culinary Hall of Fame."

A fresh ham is salt or sugar cured and aged and smoked for six months to three years, depending on desired dryness and flavor. Straight from the smokehouse, the hams aren't visually appealing, but must be scrubbed, trimmed and soaked in preparation for cooking. The cured ham is then baked, steamed, or boiled and sliced the Kentucky way...tissue paper thin. If to be fried, the ham is sliced a bit thicker and accompanied by another Kentucky specialty, red eye gravy, made from the ham drippings and water or coffee.

No Bluegrass holiday or derby celebration would be complete without old Kentucky ham. It is easily in a class by itself. "In the Bluegrass, it was either an insult to a dinner guest or a confession that you were tottering on the verge of poverty if you failed to serve a slice of ham with your fried chicken." Kentucky epicurean Alvin Harlow

Country Ham

1 (12 to 15 pound) country ham, scrubbed and trimmed
1 gallon buttermilk
1¼ cups firmly packed brown sugar, divided
½ cup cornmeal
Crosse and Blackwell Ham Glaze

Place ham in a large bucket or other container. Cover with buttermilk and top with enough water to cover. Soak 24 to 48 hours. Remove from liquid mixture; discard liquid. Clean top of ham with scrub brush. Place in roasting pan and cover with water. Boil on top of stove 20 minutes per pound. The last hour of boiling, add ¾ cup brown sugar.

Preheat oven to 425 degrees. Remove ham from water. Remove skin leaving fat. Combine remaining ½ cup brown sugar and cornmeal. Pat with cornmeal mixture and top with Crosse and Blackwell Ham Glaze. Bake 25 minutes to set glaze. Slice and serve.

Serves 10-12

4	teaspoons prepared mustard	1	cup mayonnaise
1	tablespoon curry powder	6	ounces lump crabmeat
½	teaspoon salt		Freshly grated Parmesan cheese
2	teaspoons lemon juice	½	cup cooked wild rice

Preheat oven to 350 degrees. Mix the mustard, curry, salt and lemon juice with mayonnaise. Divide rice into 2 baking sea shells or small ovenproof casseroles. Cover with crabmeat. Spread curry sauce over crabmeat and sprinkle with Parmesan cheese. Bake about 20 minutes or place under the broiler until bubbling.

Stanley Demos' signature dish that is sure to bring back memories from The Coach House Restaurant!

Serves 2

Memorable Menus: Coach House

Founded in 1969 by Stanley Demos, the Coach House on Broadway, at one time a five-star restaurant, bottled and distributed its famous Coach House Champagne Salad Dressing for decades.

COMPLETE LUNCHEON
$1.15

Fricasee of Chicken over Hot Biscuits

Escalloped Potatoes   Green String Beans

Fresh Apple Pie

Coach House Rolls

Coffee or Tea

(No Substitutions)

Menu: Jerome and Virginia Redfearn

231

Salmon Wellington with Dill Sauce

1½ pounds fresh salmon fillets
    (four 6 ounce pieces)
½   teaspoon dried dill weed
1¼ pounds frozen chopped spinach
    (2 packages)

4   ounces crumbled feta cheese
8   phyllo dough sheets
    Butter flavored cooking spray

Preheat oven to 350 degrees. Sprinkle salmon pieces with dill weed. Microwave spinach according to package directions. Drain well, divide and spread over salmon. Top with feta cheese.

Thaw phyllo sheets according to package directions. Spray half of each sheet with cooking spray one at a time. Fold each half and spray top. Place 2 sheets together and place salmon, feta side up into center of phyllo. Fold phyllo around salmon covering completely. Fold phyllo ends under to seal and place seam side down on baking sheet. Bake 25 to 30 minutes or until golden brown. Top with Dill Sauce.

DILL SAUCE
⅓   cup non-fat plain yogurt
⅓   cup mayonnaise
2   tablespoons chopped fresh parsley

1   tablespoon chopped green onions
1   teaspoon lemon juice
¼   teaspoon dried dill weed

In a small bowl, combine yogurt, mayonnaise, parsley, green onion, lemon juice and dill weed. Chill. Pour sauce over salmon before serving.

Serves 4

Spicy Baked Shrimp

1   cup butter, melted
3   cloves garlic, minced
3   teaspoons Tabasco sauce
½   teaspoon salt
    Juice of 1 lemon

¾   cup chili sauce
⅓   cup white wine
1   pound uncooked shrimp, peeled and
    deveined
2   cups uncooked rice

Preheat oven to 300 degrees. Lay shrimp in a 9x13-inch glass pan. In a small bowl, combine butter, garlic, Tabasco sauce, salt, lemon juice, chili sauce and wine; pour over shrimp. Bake 30 minutes or 1 hour for large shrimp.

Cook rice according to package directions. Lay rice on a plate and spoon shrimp and accompanying sauce onto rice.

Serves 3-4

Fettuccine Alfredo

10	tablespoons butter		Dash of salt
3	teaspoons chopped parsley		Dash of white pepper
16	ounces heavy cream	1	pound fettuccine
4	tablespoons grated Romano cheese		

In a medium saucepan, melt butter until it begins to bubble (approximately 2 minutes). Add parsley and simmer. Add cream and simmer 1 minute. Add Romano cheese, salt and white pepper; simmer 90 seconds, until sauce starts to thicken. If prefer a thinner sauce, add a little more cream.

Cook fettuccine in a pot of boiling water seasoned with salt. Cook until firm but not over done; drain. Toss fettuccine and sauce together and simmer 7 minutes. Serve immediately.

Make fettuccine at the same time you are preparing the sauce. Vegetables, chicken or shrimp may be added for variety. Add extra cheese for a stronger taste.

Serves 4

Furniture Makers

In 1806, Lexington boasted more than three hundred houses and numerous shops. This cultured center, influenced by "European elegance" attracted many early furniture makers. Fortescue Cuming, in his 1808 travelogue: "There are found cabinet-maker's shops here where household furniture is manufactured in as handsome a style as in any part of America, and where the high finish given to the native walnut and cherry timber, precluded the regret that mahogany is not to be had at an immense expense."

In 1805, Porter Clay advertised: "Furniture of the newest and most elegant fashions may be had on the shortest notice." Porter, Henry Clay's brother, and others crafted corner cupboards, chests of drawers, sugar chests, chairs, dining and cart tables. These early works of art grace many Bluegrass homes and have been highly prized by collectors over the years.

Hemp in Lexington

In **Lewis Collins'** *Kentucky History Review* is a listing of 1817 Lexington's manufacturers:

12 cotton manufacturers, 3 woolen mills

3 paper mills, 3 steam grist mills

gunpowder mill, a lead factory

iron and brass foundries

4 hat factories, 4 coach factories, 5 tanners and curriers

12 hemp factories for making cotton, bagging and hempen yarn

6 cabinet makers

3 tobacco factories

Many of the names associated with Lexington business are connected with nineteenth century hemp production…Hunt, Gratz, Anderson, Clay. Hemp is the fiber extracted from the inner bark of the plant *Cannabis sativa,* and was introduced to the Bluegrass at an early date. The area's high-nitrogen soil produced a fine crop and Fayette County became a hub of hemp production. By 1817 Lexington factories were manufacturing one million yards of bagging for cotton bales, rope, cloth sheeting, and floor covering annually, and in 1838, eighteen rope walks (hemp factories or processing houses) in Lexington and Fayette County employed 1,000 workers.

Before the mechanization of the industry, rope making was done in a long, narrow building called a ropewalk, some hundreds of feet long, in which the rope was spun and twisted by hand utilizing horse power at one end of the walk. Hemp was in great demand by farmers in the cotton belt, and until the duty-free importation of jute from the Philippines began in 1898, it continued to be one of the principal cash crops marketed in Lexington.

Image: Kentucky Historical Society

234

Wild Rice with Cranberries

RICE

1	(7 ounce) box wild rice	½	cup diced yellow bell pepper
½	cup diced celery	½	cup chopped pecans, toasted
½	cup diced red bell pepper	¾	cup dried cranberries

Cook rice as directed on package. Drain and cool. In a large metal bowl, combine rice with celery, peppers, pecans and cranberries. Add dressing and refrigerate. Serve cold.

DRESSING

5	tablespoons balsamic vinegar	1	tablespoon vegetable oil
½	teaspoon salt	1	tablespoon olive oil
1½	tablespoons brown sugar		Salt and pepper, to taste
¾	teaspoon Dijon mustard		

In a small bowl, whisk vinegar, salt, brown sugar and mustard. Slowly whisk in the oils until well emulsified.

Memorable Menus:
KEITH'S

1941
BAR AND CHOP HOUSE

Air Conditioned for the Comfort of our Patrons

GOOD FOOD IS NOT CHEAP
CHEAP FOOD IS NOT GOOD

129 E. Main St. Phone 2052

Menu: Betty Hoopes

Southern Cornbread Stuffing

CORNBREAD

1	cup self-rising cornmeal	2	large eggs
½	cup self-rising flour	2	tablespoons vegetable oil
¾	cup buttermilk		

Preheat oven to 350 degrees. In a mixing bowl, combine all ingredients and mix well. Pour batter into an 8x8-inch baking dish. Bake 20 to 25 minutes and allow to cool completely.

STUFFING

1	recipe cornbread, crumbled	7	cups chicken broth
7	slices dried white bread	1	teaspoon salt
1	sleeve saltine crackers		Pepper, to taste
2	cups chopped celery	1	teaspoon sage
1	large onion, chopped	1	tablespoon poultry seasoning
½	cup butter	5	large eggs, beaten

Preheat oven to 350 degrees. In a large bowl, combine crumbled cornbread, bread slices and saltines; set aside. In a saucepan, sauté celery and onion in butter until transparent. Pour over cornbread mixture. Add broth and mix well. Add salt, pepper, sage and poultry seasoning; mix well. Add beaten eggs and mix well. Pour mixture into a greased 2½-quart baking pan and bake 45 minutes until done.

Squash Dressing

3	cups cooked and mashed yellow squash, drained (3 to 4 squash)	3	large whole eggs
		2	cups cooked, crumbled cornbread
1	white onion, chopped	½	cup oil
1	(10¾ ounce) can cream of chicken soup		Salt and pepper, to taste

Preheat oven to 350 degrees. To cook squash, cut unpeeled squash into slices and boil in a small amount of water 10 minutes; drain. Cook onion slightly in a small amount of oil. In a mixing bowl, combine onion with drained squash. Add remaining ingredients and stir. Pour into a greased 2-quart casserole dish and bake 30 minutes.

Serves 8

Creamy Mashed Potatoes

5	pounds potatoes	1	teaspoon salt, or to taste
1	(8 ounce) package cream cheese		Dash of pepper
1	cup sour cream		

Peel potatoes, quarter and boil in salted water 25 minutes or until tender. Drain thoroughly. Return to heat to dry for a few minutes, tossing potatoes in the pan until potatoes become mealy on the outside. Mash potatoes. Combine cream cheese and sour cream together. Add to mashed potatoes. Add salt and pepper, to taste. Place in greased casserole dish. Cover and refrigerate overnight. Remove from refrigerator and allow potatoes to reach room temperature before baking. Preheat oven to 350 degrees and bake 45 minutes.

Serves 10

Holiday Potato Casserole

3	pounds potatoes, peeled and quartered	½	cup finely chopped green bell pepper
½	cup butter	½	cup finely chopped red bell pepper
2	(3 ounce) packages cream cheese, softened	1	bunch green onions, finely chopped
1½	cups (6 ounces) shredded Cheddar cheese, divided	1	cup grated Parmesan cheese
		¼	cup whole milk
1	(2 ounce) jar diced pimento, drained	1	teaspoon kosher salt

Preheat oven to 350 degrees. Cook potatoes in boiling water, covered, until tender. Drain and mash. Add butter and cream cheese; beat at medium speed with an electric mixer until smooth. Stir in 1 cup Cheddar cheese, pimentos, green and red bell pepper, onion, Parmesan cheese, milk and salt. Spoon into a lightly greased /x11x1½-inch baking dish. Bake 30 minutes or until thoroughly heated. Sprinkle with remaining ½ cup Cheddar cheese and bake an additional 5 minutes or until cheese melts.

Serves 8

Baked Macaroni and Cheese

1	(8 ounce) package dried elbow macaroni (about 2¼ cups, uncooked)	½	teaspoon ground black pepper
¼	cup butter	¼	teaspoon hot sauce
¼	cup all-purpose flour	2	cups shredded sharp Cheddar cheese
2	cups whole milk	6	tablespoons grated Parmigiano-Reggiano cheese
1	tablespoon whole-grain Dijon mustard	½	cup fresh breadcrumbs
½	teaspoon salt	2	tablespoons butter, melted

Preheat oven to 350 degrees. Cook macaroni according to package directions. Drain and set aside. Melt ¼ cup butter in a large heavy saucepan over low heat; add flour and stir constantly until smooth, about 3 to 5 minutes. Turn heat to medium and gradually whisk in milk; stirring or whisking constantly until thickened, about 10 minutes. Stir in pasta, mustard, salt, pepper, hot sauce and Cheddar cheese; stirring just until cheese begins to melt. Pour pasta mixture into a lightly greased 9x13-inch baking dish. Sprinkle with Parmigiano-Reggiano cheese. Top with breadcrumbs and drizzle 2 tablespoons melted butter evenly on top of casserole. Bake, uncovered, 25 minutes or until bubbly and golden brown. Let stand 5 minutes before serving.

Memorable Menus:
Rogers Restaurant

"A Castle where everyday food is King."

Reputed to be among Lexington's oldest establishments (1923-2004), Rogers Restaurant operated in several Lexington locations over the years, as well as in Carlisle. Owner and founder George Rogers cured country hams from his Woodford County hogs, and created his famous chili. Eventually, the restaurant moved to Broadway, and was owned by the Ellinger family until it closed in 2004. Rogers on Broadway became a favorite with Angliana Avenue tobacco warehousemen and cattlemen. Over the years, staff reported that they prepared everything from scratch, peeled potatoes every day, fried chicken in iron skillets, putting the drippings into the gravy. The menu also featured a Bluegrass specialty, lamb fries.

Menu: Betty Hoopes

Lexington Corn Pudding

6	large whole eggs	1	teaspoon kosher salt
3	cups whipping cream	¼	teaspoon freshly ground black pepper
3	cups partially thawed white shoepeg corn or fresh corn cut from cob (about 4-6 ears)	1	teaspoon flour
		½	teaspoon baking powder
½	cup sugar	1	tablespoon butter, melted

Preheat oven to 350 degrees. In a large mixing bowl, combine eggs and whipping cream, beating until smooth; add corn to mixture. Combine dry ingredients and add to corn mixture. Add melted butter and stir. Pour into a 2-quart greased baking dish. Bake until set and slightly golden brown on top, approximately 50 minutes.

Serves 8

Green Bean Bundles

2	(16 ounce) cans whole green beans	½	cup butter
8	slices uncooked bacon	1	cup firmly packed brown sugar
8	toothpicks	2	teaspoons garlic powder

Preheat oven to 350 degrees. Drain beans and divide each can into 4 bundles (8 bundles total). Wrap each bundle with a strip of uncooked bacon and secure with a toothpick. Lay bundles in an ungreased 9x13-inch pan.

In a saucepan, melt butter, brown sugar and garlic powder. Cook on low heat until butter is melted and mixture is smooth. Pour over bundles. Bake 30 minutes, uncovered.

Serves 4

WinStar Farm

On Fayette County's western border, just inside neighboring Woodford County, lies the Pisgah Historic District. In this area surrounded by the most historic farms in the state, Texans Bill Casner and Kenny Troutt began acquiring acreage in 2000. Today, WinStar Farm LLC has amassed more than 1,500 carefully preserved and improved acres and boasts of "good soil, good horses, and good people."

WinStar has realized success as a breeding and racing Thoroughbred farm, but 2010 proved to be a banner year, with victories by Super Saver in the Kentucky Derby and a few weeks later, Drosselmeyer in the Belmont Stakes.

Tomato Pudding

ANNE EVANS, *Executive Director Governor's Mansion*

4	cups dried bread, cubed	1	cup melted butter
2	cups (4 to 5 large) fresh tomatoes, seeded, slightly puréed with chunks left in	1	teaspoon curry powder
		1	cup firmly packed brown sugar
		1	small onion, grated

Preheat oven to 350 degrees. Grease a 3-quart soufflé dish with butter and spread bread cubes on bottom. In a saucepan, combine tomatoes, butter, curry powder, brown sugar and onion. When mixture becomes good and hot, pour over bread cubes. Bake 40 minutes or until set.

Serves 6

Spinach Oyster Casserole

2	packages frozen spinach	1	teaspoon anise seed
1	quart oysters	1	garlic clove, crushed
6	tablespoons butter, melted		Salt and pepper, to taste
1	cup dry breadcrumbs		Dash of Tabasco
½	medium onion, grated		Parmesan cheese, to taste

Preheat oven to 350 degrees. In a large mixing bowl, combine spinach, oysters, butter, breadcrumbs, onion, anise, garlic, salt, pepper and Tabasco sauce; pour into a casserole dish. Sprinkle with Parmesan cheese. Bake, covered, 20 minutes.

Bluegrass Superstition:

A silver coin placed in the shoe will bring good luck.

Madam Belle Brezing

"the most orderly of disorderly houses"

Belle Brezing (aka: Belle Breezing, Belle Breazing)

One of few Lexington legends to have her obituary printed in Time magazine, widely renowned to have purportedly been the model for the infamous Belle Watling in Margaret Mitchell's *Gone With the Wind,* Mary Belle Cox was born on June 16, 1860, the second illegitimate daughter of Sarah Ann Cox, dressmaker and occasional prostitute.

During the next decades, surviving hardships and following family tradition, Brezing worked for a local madam in the house that is currently the Mary Todd Lincoln House and later opened three brothels, two on North Upper Street and the most famous on Megowan Street. Among the houses in the area referred to as "the hill," Belle Brezing's brothel was the most lavishly decorated, the most expensive, and the most popular.

Belle Brezing, reportedly one of the wealthiest women in the area, attracted clientele from all over the nation. During the Spanish-American War in 1898, soldiers billeted in Lexington visited Brezing's house and spread her reputation even further around the country.

After the temperance movement swept the nation, the brothels on the hill were closed in 1915, with Brezing's never to reopen. After Belle Brezing's death, two estate and salvage auctions attracted huge crowds and the auctioneer's chant continued for days as the contents and architectural elements of 59 Megowan Street (now 153 N. Eastern Avenue) were sold to the highest bidder.

Notable Neighbors: The Shakers

"... the world came to them for their food. .."

Located thirty minutes from Lexington, Shaker Village at Pleasant Hill, a recreated Shaker community, specializes in a heritage of hospitality and agriculture. America's oldest communal religious society, the nineteenth-century Pleasant Hill sect lived and worked on 4,000 acres of prime farmland in neighboring Mercer County. Expert stockmen and cropsmen, the Shakers grew extensive fruit orchards and vegetable gardens and marketed garden seeds as well as award-winning fruit preserves (55,500 jars from 1858-1860). Known for their homemade products, the Shakers were among the first in the country to grow and classify herbs for the pharmaceutical market.

Numerous 'dependencies' were clustered around each dwelling house: butter house, fruit drying house, chicken house, woodhouse, and the round bee house. The Shakers of Pleasant Hill were pleased with their 500-tree apple orchards and were willing to experiment with imported bees and beehives. From a Shaker diary: "the same week some of the brethren took 212 pounds of honey."

During the Civil War, both Union and Confederate soldiers experienced Shaker hospitality. Entry from a Shaker diary, October, 1862: "The roar of artillery at intervals between Harrodsburg and Danville announced that the work of death and destruction was going on within 8 or 10 miles of this sacred spot. We have fed more than a thousand persons today..."

Today the 3,000-acre restored Shaker Village offers an Inn, 14 restored buildings, and food that is reminiscent of the original Shaker hospitality.

Behold in Spring See Everything:
Alive and Clot'hd in beauty
Shall I Alone, an idle drone
Be slothful in my duty
To gather honey see the Bee Fly,
Around from flower to flower
A good example there for me
To well improve each hour.

Isaac Watts 1655 English Hymn sung by the Shakers

Angel Biscuits

5 cups self-rising flour	¾ cup canola oil
⅓ cup sugar	2½ cups warm buttermilk
2 packages dry yeast	

In a plastic container with a cover, combine flour, sugar and yeast. Add oil and warm buttermilk; mix thoroughly. Cover and refrigerate for 24 hours.

Preheat oven to 450 degrees. Grease a 9x13-inch pan with canola oil; set aside. Punch down dough. Roll dough out onto a floured surface to ½-inch thickness. Cut with a small biscuit cutter and place biscuits in oiled pan; turning over once. Bake 10 to 12 minutes.

Makes 20 biscuits

Honey Lovers' Butter Spread

½ cup butter, softened
⅔ cup honey
½ teaspoon grated lemon rind

In a mixing bowl, beat butter at medium speed with an electric mixer until creamy; gradually add honey and beat well. Add lemon rind; beat well. Cover and chill for at least 3 hours. Butter should be a creamy spreadable consistency. Serve in a bowl.

Makes 1 cup

Shaker Landing

243

Beaten Biscuits

Traditional Southern canapés… tiny dense biscuits, no larger than 1½-inches in diameter, beaten biscuits usually cushion paper-thin shards of Country Ham, often basted with mustard or other sauce.

Legend associates the origin of Beaten Biscuits with sailors' 'sea biscuits' or chuck wagon 'hardtack.' The beaten biscuit came to Kentucky from the Virginia tea table and has been traditionally associated with special entertaining due to the amount of labor involved.

Sometimes referred to as a 'biscuit beaten into submission' the 'flinty biscuit' is a Southern Bluegrass delicacy…so to speak. Most cooks strive to make bread light and fluffy, but beaten biscuits are hard, crisp, and almost cracker-like. The classic recipe calls for flour, lard, salt, and milk, and the dough must be worked one hundred and fifty times or until it is blistered, elastic, and smooth. Until the biscuits became popular, the desired texture was achieved by beating the dough with a mallet, rolling pin, or heavy object. In later days, special marble or granite-topped tables with a handled roller, reminiscent of a washing machine wringer, were designed to accomplish the desired effect. The dough is flattened, cut with a small round cutter, and pricked with a fork before being baked in a hot oven.

Miss Susie Jackson of Woodford County, famous caterer, intoned that if you didn't have beaten biscuits and country ham, you had no party at all! Miss Susie's biscuits contained a secret ingredient and a secret process that made them crunchy… all hundreds of thousands of them.

Beaten Biscuits

3½ cups sifted, all-purpose,
    low-protein soft wheat flour
½ teaspoon baking powder
½ teaspoon salt
2 tablespoons sugar
½ cup chilled lard
¾ cup chilled half-and-half

Sift dry ingredients. In a food processor, add dry ingredients and cut in lard pulsing until mixture resembles fine crumbs. Add the cold half-and-half into dry ingredients until dough forms into a ball. Place in plastic bag and leave on counter several hours.

Divide dough in half. Place each portion in food processor with plastic blade and process for 2 minutes. Press both portions together on floured surface. Roll dough to ¼-inch thickness. Fold from edges into center and roll again; repeat 6-8 times until dough is silky. Fold last time but do not roll.

Preheat oven to 325 degrees. Cut with 1½-inch round cutter. Place on ungreased baking pan sheet and prick with fork. Bake 5 minutes on lower rack, move to center rack and bake for 20 to 25 minutes. Biscuits should not brown but should be dry and flaky inside. Place in a tightly covered tin; will keep for one week.

18-20 biscuits

Overnight Crescent Rolls

1 package dry yeast
¼ cup warm water
¾ cup milk
½ cup sugar
2 large eggs, well beaten
½ cup butter, melted
½ teaspoon salt
4¾ cups all-purpose flour

Dissolve yeast in warm water 5 minutes. Add milk and sugar; stir until blended. Add eggs and melted butter; blend. Add salt to flour and add to dough 1 cup at a time. Mix with hands until dough forms a smooth ball. Place in greased bowl. Turn dough over so all of the dough is greased evenly. Cover with cloth or plastic wrap. Set on counter overnight.

The next morning, divide dough into 3 balls. Roll each ball out onto a floured surface to the size of a 9-inch pie pan; cut into 8 to 10 pie shaped wedges. Roll up each wedge from large end into shape of crescent roll. Place rolls on greased cookie sheet. Allow rolls to rise until double in size, approximately 45 minutes to 1 hour. Preheat oven to 350 degrees and bake 10 minutes. Brush with melted butter after rolls are baked.

Serves 30

Stuffed Baguettes

2   pre-baked French baguettes
1   (8 ounce) package cream cheese
1   (10 ounce) package frozen creamed
       spinach, thawed
½   teaspoon garlic salt
1½   cups shredded Swiss cheese

Preheat oven to 350 degrees. Dig out the top and middle of the French baguettes to create a ditch. Combine cream cheese, creamed spinach and garlic salt until well mixed. Stir Swiss cheese into cream mixture. Evenly spoon mixture into ditch of each loaf of bread. Wrap each loaf in foil and bake 30 to 35 minutes. Cut into 2-inch pieces and serve warm.

Serves 24

Vinery – Spurr Road

Kentucky Colonels

In the nineteenth century, Kentucky Colonels served a military function. After the War of 1812, Governor Isaac Shelby commissioned one of his officers as an aid-de-camp with the rank and grade of Colonel. Thereafter, Colonels in uniform served a ceremonial function as they stood as symbolic guards during state events.

The Honorable Order of Kentucky Colonels held its inaugural meeting in 1931. Today, thousands of Kentucky Colonels, commissioned because of their service to and pride in Kentucky, live in every state and 35 foreign countries. The official list includes celebrities, politicians, businessmen, and 'proud Kentuckians.' Since 1951, the Honorable Order has distributed thousands of grants to charitable and educational agencies across Kentucky, surpassing more than one million dollars donated each year.

The Kentucky Sugar Chest

A unique Bluegrass furniture form evolved from the sweet tooth! From early days, dessert was an anticipated course at lunch and dinner, pastries and puddings were prized, coffee and tea were sweetened with sugar, and fruits were preserved with the treasured commodity. Many Kentuckians utilized less costly maple sugar, also known as "Kentucky sugar," (12 cents per pound), but white (50 cents per pound) and brown sugar (20 cents) became symbols of power, wealth, and status. During the early nineteenth century a pound of sugar might cost more than an acre of Bluegrass land.

Brought from the West Indies via New Orleans upriver on barges and keelboats once a year, sugar stock was precious and expensive. Until supplies became more readily available due to the advent of the steamboat in 1818, Kentucky housewives purchased a year's supply, rationed and guarded the 'white gold.'

Sugar was manufactured and shipped in hard cones, or sugar loafs. Depending on the quality, the cones ranged from 5-14 inches in diameter,11-30 inches in height, and weighed from 5 to 35 pounds. An average cone could cost in excess of $27.00. Sugar nips, heavy pliers with sharp blades at the end, were used to nip the hard cones into chunks that were ground or dissolved in water before being added to the pudding or pie.

During the late eighteenth century, furniture makers responded to the need of Lexington households to store large amounts of the precious commodity under lock and key. The most common form of sugar chest resembled a box with legs, with a divided interior...one for white sugar and one for brown. At the top or bottom of the sugar receptacle, cabinetmakers constructed a long drawer for storage of the sugar nips, and perhaps a ledger drawer, because the good wife recorded to the teaspoon how much sugar was on hand.

The sugar chest appears to have been popular almost exclusively in Kentucky, particularly the Inner Bluegrass region, although a few have been found in Tennessee. Often camouflaged as a desk or cupboard, the chest was usually displayed in the dining room or parlor as a symbol of status and wealth. Constructed of the finest hardwoods, most often cherry or walnut, many were embellished with intricately detailed inlay and carvings. Kentucky Sugar Chests are prized by collectors for their scarcity and quality of craftsmanship, and remain a symbol of all that is uniquely the Bluegrass.

Apple Bread Pudding

1	Granny Smith apple, peeled and chopped		3	large eggs
½	teaspoon ground cinnamon, divided		1½	cups 2% milk
½	(16 ounce) Italian bread loaf, cut into bite-size pieces		1	cup apple cider
	Vegetable cooking spray		¼	cup firmly packed brown sugar
			1	teaspoon vanilla extract
			¼	teaspoon ground nutmeg

Sauté apple and ¼ teaspoon cinnamon in a lightly greased skillet over medium-high heat 2 minutes or until tender.

In a 7x11-inch baking dish coated with cooking spray, combine bread and apple. In a separate bowl, whisk together eggs, milk, apple cider, brown sugar, vanilla, nutmeg and remaining ¼ teaspoon cinnamon; pour over bread mixture in baking dish. Cover and chill 1 hour.

Preheat oven to 350 degrees. Bake 45 to 50 minutes or until top is crisp and golden brown. Serve warm with a scoop of vanilla ice cream.

Serves 8

Memorable Menus:
George Schange's Fruit Store and Confectionery

George Schange's Fruit Store and Confectionery offered milk shakes for 5 cents on the Southeast corner of Mill and Main. The Confectionery later became Schange's Candy Kitchen in the late 1800s, offering soda water and ice cream.

Warm Me Up Banana Pudding

1⅓ cups sugar
3½ tablespoons flour
Dash of salt
3 large eggs, separated
3 cups whole milk

1¼ teaspoons vanilla extract
1 (12 ounce) package vanilla wafers
6 medium bananas
¼ cup plus 2 tablespoons sugar
1 teaspoon vanilla extract

Preheat oven to 325 degrees. In a heavy saucepan, combine sugar, flour and salt. Beat egg yolks until thick; add milk and mix well. Add to dry ingredients and stir well. Cook over medium heat, stirring constantly, until smooth and thickened. Remove from heat; stir in 1¼ teaspoons vanilla extract.

Arrange ⅓ vanilla wafers in the bottom of a 3-quart baking dish. Slice 2 bananas and layer over wafers. Pour ⅓ pudding mixture over bananas. Repeat layers twice.

Beat egg whites with electric mixer at high speed until foamy. Gradually add ¼ cup plus 2 tablespoons sugar, 1 tablespoon at a time beating until stiff peaks form. Add 1 teaspoon vanilla extract and beat until blended. Spread meringue evenly over pudding, sealing to edge of dish. Bake 25 to 28 minutes or until meringue is golden brown. Serve warm.

Serves 8-10

Memorable Menus: Dutch Mill Restaurant

Operating from 1950 to 1995, The Dutch Mill on Limestone was noted for chili, cube steak, fried chicken, yeast rolls, cornbread, and fruit cobblers...all from 'scratch'. Chocolate, coconut, and banana pies were so popular that patrons called a day ahead to reserve a slice for the next day's dessert! The Dutch Mill's owners, the Parsons family, also developed Velvet's Ice Cream, one of the area's first ice cream companies.

Grandma's Boiled Custard

1 gallon whole milk
16 large whole eggs
2 cups sugar

2 teaspoons vanilla extract
Freshly grated nutmeg, to taste

In a double boiler, heat milk until warm. In a mixing bowl, beat eggs and sugar together until light in color. Beat 1 cup of warm milk into egg mixture. Slowly add back into hot milk, stirring as you add. Cook over double boiler for approximately 30 minutes until thick, stirring constantly. Do not boil custard. Add vanilla extract and grated fresh nutmeg, to taste. Chill. Custard will thicken as it cools.

Serve custard over ice cream or with whipped cream. Sprinkle nutmeg on top, just before serving.

In Kentucky, we think our own Bourbon enhances the flavor of boiled custard.

Serves 20

Pecan Tarts

TART SHELLS
1 (3 ounce) package cream cheese, softened

½ cup butter, softened
1 cup flour

Combine cream cheese, butter and flour. Mix well. Chill overnight.

TARTS
¾ cup firmly packed brown sugar
1 tablespoon butter, softened
1 large egg

1 teaspoon vanilla extract
Pinch of salt
⅔ cup chopped pecans

Preheat oven to 350 degrees. Shape chilled tart shell dough into 24 small balls. Press each ball into mini tart pan and flatten until bottom and sides of the well are covered evenly.

In a mixing bowl, combine brown sugar and butter. Add egg and vanilla. Add salt and pecans; stir well. Spoon mixture into tart shells. Bake approximately 25 minutes.

Serves 24

Chess Pie

5	large eggs, lightly beaten	2	tablespoons flour
2	cups sugar	½	teaspoon cinnamon
⅔	cup buttermilk	1	teaspoon vanilla extract
½	cup butter, melted	1	(9 inch) pastry shell, unbaked

Preheat oven to 350 degrees. In a large mixing bowl, combine eggs, sugar, buttermilk, melted butter, flour, cinnamon and vanilla extract; stir well. Pour filling into pie shell. Bake 45 minutes or until set. Cool on a wire rack.

Serves 8

Gingerbread Cake

1	cup molasses	½	teaspoon ground cloves
1½	cups boiling water	1½	teaspoons ginger
1	teaspoon baking soda	½	teaspoon allspice
½	cup shortening	2	large eggs, well-beaten
1	cup sugar	2½	cups sifted all-purpose flour
½	teaspoon salt	3	teaspoons baking powder
2	teaspoons cinnamon		

Preheat oven to 375 degrees. In a large mixing bowl, combine molasses with boiling water; add baking soda. Let cool. In a separate bowl, cream shortening and sugar; add to cooled molasses mixture. Add salt, cinnamon, cloves, ginger and allspice; beat well. Add eggs.

In a separate bowl, sift flour with baking powder and add to batter (batter will be thin). Pour batter into a well-buttered 9x13-inch pan and bake 15 minutes. Reduce heat to 350 degrees and bake an additional 15 minutes. Cool slightly on rack. Serve warm with whipped cream or dairy topping.

Bluegrass Superstition:

To kill a cricket in the horse stall is considered bad luck.

Hunt-Morgan House

Hopemont, home of the Hunt and Morgan families, built in 1814 for the first millionaire west of the Alleghenies, is today a restored museum house. Hemp merchant, John Wesley Hunt was the grandfather of General John Hunt Morgan and great grandfather of Dr. Thomas Hunt Morgan, the first Kentuckian to win a Nobel Prize. The Bluegrass Trust restored The Hunt-Morgan House in 1955 and operates it as a public event museum.

Known for her hospitality, Henrietta Hunt Morgan prepared this Black Cake on special occasions. Local legend has General Morgan riding his mare Black Bess up the front steps of the Hunt Morgan House, stopping to kiss his mother in the hall, (perhaps pocketing a slice of Black Cake) and galloping out the back door with Union troops in hot pursuit!

Henrietta Hunt Morgan's Black Cake

12	large eggs	1	pound candied fruit
1	pound sugar	1	pound preserved ginger (Chinese)
1	pound flour	1	pound almonds, blanched and split
1	pound butter		
1	pound currants	½	coffee cup of cinnamon
4	pounds raisins, seeded and split	½	coffee cup of grated nutmeg
¾	pound citron	½	coffee cup golden syrup

Stir 1 level teaspoon of soda with one tumbler of good whiskey. First dredge the fruit with the flour, there will be left only a handful. Cream the butter and sugar, add the yolks then the well whipped whites. Stir in the fruit a handful or so, then a little liquor until the fruit is all used. Lastly the spice and syrup. Bake at least 8 hours in a slow fire.

Recipe Courtesy: Bluegrass Trust/Hunt-Morgan House

Red Velvet Cake

CAKE

½ cup shortening	1 cup buttermilk
1½ cups sugar	1 teaspoon vanilla extract
2 large eggs	1 ounce red food coloring
1 tablespoon cocoa	1 teaspoon baking soda
2 cups flour	1 tablespoon vinegar
½ teaspoon salt	

Preheat oven to 350 degrees. In a large mixing bowl, cream together shortening and sugar; add eggs. Sift together cocoa, flour and salt. Add sifted dry ingredients alternately with buttermilk. Add vanilla extract and food coloring; beat well. In a separate bowl, stir soda into vinegar; fold into cake batter. Pour into 2 (9 inch) greased and floured cake pans. Bake 30 to 35 minutes. Allow cake to cool completely before frosting.

CREAM CHEESE FROSTING

1 (3 ounce) package cream cheese	2 cups sifted powdered sugar
¼ cup butter	½ cup chopped walnuts
1 teaspoon vanilla extract	

In a mixing bowl, beat together cream cheese, butter and vanilla extract until light and fluffy. Gradually add powdered sugar, beating until smooth. Spread frosting between cake layers and over cooled cake; sprinkle with chopped walnuts. If not eaten immediately, cover and store in refrigerator.

Serves 12

Gluck Equine Research Center

Located on the campus of the University of Kentucky, The Maxwell H. Gluck Equine Research Center is one of the leading research facilities in the world. Established in 1987, the Center is dedicated to scientific discovery, education, and dissemination of knowledge for the health and welfare of horses.

Blackberry Jam Cake with Caramel Icing

CAKE

1	cup butter, softened	2	teaspoons baking soda
2	cups sugar	1½	teaspoons cinnamon
6	large whole eggs	1½	teaspoons allspice
1	cup blackberry jam	1½	teaspoons cloves
1	cup apple butter	1½	teaspoons nutmeg
3	cups all-purpose flour	1	cup buttermilk
2	teaspoons cocoa		

Preheat oven to 350 degrees. In a large mixing bowl, cream butter and sugar until light and fluffy. Add eggs, one at a time, beating after each addition. Add blackberry jam and mix well. Add apple butter and mix. Combine flour, cocoa, baking soda, cinnamon, allspice, cloves and nutmeg. Add flour mixture alternately with milk, ending with flour mixture. Batter may be baked in either 3 (8-inch) greased and floured cake pans or a tube pan. Bake 45 minutes. When completely cooled, ice with Caramel Icing.

CARAMEL ICING

2 cups firmly packed brown sugar
1 cup butter
½ cup milk
2 teaspoons vanilla extract
1 pound box powdered sugar

In a saucepan, combine brown sugar, butter and milk. Cook over medium heat until sugar is dissolved and butter melted. Bring to a full boil for about 2 minutes. Remove from heat and add vanilla extract. Pour mixture in a large mixing bowl; add 3 cups powdered sugar and beat. Continue to add the remaining powdered sugar as needed until icing becomes spreading consistency.

Pumpkin Roll

PUMPKIN CAKE

⅔	cup pumpkin		½	teaspoon baking soda
1	cup sugar		¼	teaspoon salt
¾	cup flour		½	teaspoon cinnamon
3	large eggs		½	cup chopped nuts, optional
½	teaspoon baking powder			Powdered sugar

Preheat oven to 375 degrees. Grease a 15-inch cookie sheet generously, including sides, using a butter flavor shortening. Cover with wax paper, leaving enough hanging over ends to hold onto; generously grease wax paper. In a medium bowl, combine all ingredients except nuts, and mix by hand until smooth. Pour onto the cookie sheet and spread evenly so that batter will be a little thicker on the edges. Sprinkle with chopped nuts, as desired. Bake 15 minutes on middle rack of oven.

While cakes cool, prepare a towel for cooling the cake. Using a lint free kitchen towel, lay towel out on a flat surface and cover it with powdered sugar to prevent the cake from sticking to the towel. Take the cake out of the oven, grip the edge with wax paper and carefully flip the cake onto the towel. Very carefully remove wax paper from cake. Sprinkle hot cake with powdered sugar, so the towel doesn't stick to the cake. Roll the cake up tightly with towel and shape until smooth. Set aside and let it cool about 45 minutes.

FILLING

1	(8 ounce) package cream cheese		2	teaspoons butter, softened
1	cup powdered sugar		1	teaspoon vanilla extract

In a medium bowl, combine all the ingredients and mix with a hand mixer on high until smooth. Unroll cooled cake, spoon the filling on cake and spread so that most of the filling is in the center (spread thin on the edges).

Roll the cake up, tightly; cut off the ends, then cut in half down the center of the roll to make 2 rows. Sprinkle with powdered sugar. Wrap in wax paper, then wrap in foil. Place in freezer until 20 minutes prior to serving time. When ready to serve, remove from freezer and cut into slices (cake slices best when frozen) and allow to thaw at least 20 minutes prior to serving.

Serves 14

Cherry Berry on a Cloud

CRUST

6	large egg whites	½	teaspoon cream of tartar
¼	teaspoon salt	1¾	cups sugar

Preheat oven to 275 degrees. Grease a 9x13-inch baking dish. Beat egg whites until foamy. Add salt, cream of tartar and sugar; beat until stiff and glossy, about 15 minutes. Spread in dish. Bake 1 hour. Do not open oven door. Leave baking dish in oven overnight.

FILLING

1	(8 ounce) package cream cheese	2	cups heavy whipping cream, whipped
1	cup sugar	2	cups miniature marshmallows
1	teaspoon vanilla extract		

The next morning, beat cream cheese, sugar and vanilla extract until smooth. Gently fold in whipped cream and marshmallows. Remove crust from oven. Spread mixture over crust. Chill 4 hours.

TOPPING

1	(20 ounce) can cherry pie filling	1	teaspoon lemon juice
1	(10 ounce) package frozen sliced strawberries or 1 (16 ounce) container fresh strawberries, sliced		

Combine topping ingredients and pour over filling.

Serves 10

Expression: Dead Ringer

A ringer was a better horse entered into the race in place of a nag. These horses would have to resemble each other well enough to fool the naked eye, hence the term came to mean an exact double. Dead ringer was first used in the late 19th century, with ringer referring to someone's physical double and dead meaning "absolute" (as in dead heat and dead right).

Baklava

2	cups chopped walnuts	1	pound phyllo dough
½	cup sugar	1	pound drawn butter
1	tablespoon rosewater		

Preheat oven to 300 degrees. In a mixing bowl, combine nuts, sugar and rosewater. Butter a 10x14-inch baking dish. Separate phyllo dough sheets and individually brush drawn butter over each sheet as you layer them in baking dish. Halfway through the layering process, spread nut mixture in a ½-inch layer over the buttered phyllo dough sheets.

Continue layering and brushing melted butter over the remaining phyllo dough sheets. Cut the layered phyllo dough sheets in diamond-shaped pieces. Bake 1 hour or until baklava turns golden brown on top. Remove from oven and immediately pour cool syrup over the baklava, being sure the baklava is well saturated.

SYRUP

| 2 | cups sugar | | Juice of ½ fresh lemon |
| 1 | cup water | 1 | teaspoon rosewater |

In a saucepan, combine sugar, water and lemon juice. Boil over medium heat about 10 to 15 minutes. Before removing from heat, add rosewater. Remove from heat and let cool.

24 pieces

Chocolate Chip Cookies

½	cup butter	2	teaspoons water
½	cup shortening	3	cups all-purpose flour
¾	cup firmly packed brown sugar	1	teaspoon baking soda
¾	cup sugar	¾	teaspoon salt
2	large eggs	1	(12 ounce) package semisweet chocolate chips
1	teaspoon vanilla extract		

Preheat oven to 350 degrees. In a mixing bowl, cream butter and shortening. Add brown sugar and sugar; cream. Add eggs and mix until smooth. Add vanilla extract and water; beat until creamy. Add baking soda and salt to flour; add gradually to batter. Fold in chocolate chips and chill 30 minutes. Drop by teaspoons onto cookie sheet. Grease cookie sheet if it is not a nonstick cookie sheet. Bake 8 to 10 minutes. Cool and place in an airtight container.

Makes 3 dozen

Bourbon

"Nose, "white dog", "angel's share," "finish," "oak char,"....all term associated with one of Kentucky's signature industries. What beverage is regulated by the federal government, can legally only be made in the United States, and is primarily manufactured in Kentucky? The Kentucky Distillers Association claims Kentucky as home to 95% of bourbon's manufacturers, bourbon being America's only native spirit. Among several, the regulations require that bourbon must be made from a mash containing at least 51 percent corn, and must be aged at least two years (most producers age it from four to twelve years.)

By the early 1780s Fayette countians were converting corn, wheat, and rye into whiskey in homemade farm-based facilities. Early commercial distilleries in the area included the Ashland Distillery, Henry Clay Distillery, later the Pepper Distillery, and at least five others. Is it the Bluegrass limestone water that gives the beverage its 'smooth' taste? By the beginning of the nineteenth century bourbon distilling was already a flourishing industry in Kentucky. As early as 1810, approximately 2,000 distilleries were operating in the state, and approximately 140 were located in and around Lexington.

Only Lexington's James E. Pepper Distillery, 1865-1958, survived Prohibition, through the sale of medicinal whiskey. By the 1920s, the distillery was placing advertisements with drug stores for medicinal whiskey that could treat malaria, consumption, influenza, and other maladies. In 1923 the company marketed to pharmacists and "James E. Pepper" whiskey was endorsed and prescribed by over 40,000 physicians throughout the United States. Today, the James E. Pepper Distillery, Manchester Street and Old Frankfort Pike is listed on the National Register of Historic Places. The Pepper family of distillers provided the ancestry for several modern distilleries, including some of those listed on the official Bourbon Trail®, an affiliation of the Region's major distillers.

Kentucky Bourbon Balls

½	cup chopped pecans		5	cups powdered sugar, sifted
¼	cup Kentucky bourbon		6	ounces semi-sweet chocolate chips
6	tablespoons butter, melted		½	block paraffin wax, shaved

Spread nuts evenly in a shallow bowl and pour bourbon over nuts. Let soak overnight. The following day, in a separate bowl, combine butter, 4 cups sugar and soaked nuts. Mix thoroughly until mixture is consistent. Add remaining 1 cup sugar and mix well by hand. Using a 1 tablespoon scoop, evenly scoop balls, rolling each ball in hand with each scoop. Lay rolled balls on wax paper. Chill balls for 10 minutes in refrigerator. In the meantime, prepare chocolate mixture. Melt chocolate and wax in a double boiler. Stir until melted and consistent throughout. Dip each ball into chocolate with a toothpick. Allow excess chocolate to drip off prior to returning balls to wax

paper. Place a pecan half on top of each ball. When all balls have been coated with the chocolate, allow chocolate to harden. Store in airtight containers in a cool place.

48 (1 tablespoon) balls

Old Kentucky Chocolates

Lexington's Old Kentucky Chocolates creates the quintessential bourbon ball—an acorn-sized, creamy fondant center laced with chopped pecans and bourbon, enrobed in rich semisweet chocolate...a Bluegrass tradition.

Old Kentucky Chocolates produces more than 200,000 pounds of candy annually, including pulled cream candy, the second best seller...until Valentine's Day when the local confectionary sells more than 6,000 pounds of chocolate-covered strawberries!

Toffee

1½ cups chopped and toasted pecans, divided
1 cup sugar
1 cup butter

1 tablespoon light corn syrup
¼ cup water
1 cup semisweet chocolate chips

To toast pecans, preheat oven to 350 degrees. Lightly spritz baking sheet with cooking spray. Place pecans on baking sheet and toast until they become aromatic, about 5 minutes. (Watch carefully as they are easily scorched.)

Spread 1 cup pecans into a 9-inch circle on a baking sheet that has been covered with parchment paper. In a heavy saucepan over medium heat, combine sugar, butter, corn syrup and water; bring to a boil, stirring constantly. Cook until mixture is golden brown and candy thermometer registers 290 to 310 degrees, approximately 15 minutes. Pour mixture over pecans on baking sheet.

Sprinkle with chocolate chips and let stand 30 seconds. Spread melted morsels evenly over top and sprinkle with remaining ½ cup pecans. Chill 1 hour. Break into bite-size pieces and store in airtight containers.

For Bourbon Pecan Toffee use ¼ cup bourbon instead of ¼ cup water.

Makes 1½ pounds

Peanut Butter Buckeyes

⅓   pound butter, room temperature
⅓   pound creamy peanut butter
1   pound powdered sugar

8   ounces chocolate chips
¼   bar of paraffin wax

In a large bowl, combine butter and peanut butter with sugar until smooth. Chill the mixture. Once firm, form into small balls. Chill balls until firm.

Melt chocolate chips and paraffin together slowly in the top of a double boiler and mix to combine. Using a toothpick, dip the cold peanut butter balls into the chocolate to coat. Let dry on waxed paper.

Makes approximately 50 balls

Peanut Brittle

2   cups sugar
1   cup light corn syrup
⅓   cup water

1-1½   cups dry roasted peanuts
1   tablespoon butter
1   tablespoon baking soda

Line 2 (15½x12-inch) cookie sheets with aluminum foil. Keep warm. In a 3-quart microwave safe casserole dish, combine sugar, corn syrup and water. Microwave 8 to 10 minutes, stirring occasionally, on full power or until soft-ball stage is reached. Add peanuts; stir and cook 10 to 12 minutes on 80% power level or until hard-crack stage (the mixture will be a light amber color). Remove from microwave and stir in butter and baking soda. Pour onto the cookie sheets. Spread mixture with fork to make a thin surface. Let cool and break apart. Store in a cool, dry place in an airtight container.

Best if made on a cold, dry day.

Makes 1½ quarts

Notable Neighbors: Rebecca Ruth Candy Factory

In 1919, two substitute teachers decided that candy making suited their talents better than teaching. One year before women in the U.S. earned the right to vote, Ruth Hanley Booe and Rebecca Gooch co-founded Frankfort's Rebecca Ruth Candies. Adding to their repertoire of fine candies, the two created Rebecca Ruth Bourbon Balls after a friend mentioned that the two best tastes in the world were a sip of bourbon whiskey and a piece of Ruth's Kentucky Colonel mint candy.

Today, Rebecca Ruth's Candy Factory continues to be family owned and produces candy in the same clapboard house with the red and white striped awning.

Peanut Butter Roll

2	cups sugar		1	large egg white, room temperature
½	cup light corn syrup (with vanilla)		½	teaspoon vanilla extract
	Dash of salt			Powdered sugar
½	cup filtered tap water		1	cup creamy peanut butter

In a heavy 1½-quart saucepan, combine sugar, syrup, salt and water. Mix completely and stir until mixture boils. Simmer at a light boil on medium heat until mixture reaches a firm soft-ball stage on candy thermometer (245 degrees), approximately 20 minutes.

As syrup is cooking, beat egg white and vanilla extract to stiff peak stage. With mixer running, pour hot syrup in a slow stream into beaten egg white and continue to beat until the hot mixture is pliable enough to work with hands, 15 minutes, or until mixture loses sheen and is consistency of firm peanut butter.

Sprinkle powdered sugar onto wax paper or cutting board. Scoop a fourth of mixture onto paper or board and pat to rectangle approximately ¼-inch thick. Spread with ¼ cup peanut butter and shape into a jelly-roll. (May use scraper while rolling, as mixture sticks.) Repeat with fourths of candy and peanut butter, working quickly before mixture cools. Cool rolls completely in refrigerator. Wrap each roll in parchment or waxed paper and store in tin. Slice before serving; serve at room temperature.

Serves 30

Chocolate Fantasy Fudge

3	cups sugar		1	(7 ounce) jar marshmallow creme
¾	cup margarine		1	cup chopped nuts
⅔	cup undiluted evaporated milk		1	teaspoon vanilla extract
1	(12 ounce) package semisweet chocolate chips			

In a heavy 2½-quart saucepan, combine sugar, margarine and milk. Bring to a full, rolling boil, stirring constantly. Continue boiling 5 minutes over medium heat, stirring constantly to prevent scorching. Remove from heat. Stir in chocolate pieces until melted. Add marshmallow creme, nuts and vanilla extract; beat until well blended. Pour into a greased 9x13-inch pan. Cool to room temperature. Cut into squares and store in airtight container in refrigerator.

Makes approximately 3 pounds

Bourbon Caramel Sauce

1½ cups sugar
⅔   cup water
2   teaspoons light corn syrup
¼   cup evaporated milk

¼   cup fat-free half-and-half
1   tablespoon butter
3   tablespoons bourbon

Sprinkle sugar in an even layer in a large, heavy saucepan. Combine water and syrup; pour over sugar. Cook over medium-high heat, stirring gently, until sugar is dissolved, about 4 minutes. Cook an additional 20 minutes or until golden brown (do not stir). Remove from heat. Using a long-handed wooden spoon, gradually stir in milk, half-and-half and butter (mixture will bubble). Cook over low heat until mixture is smooth, stirring constantly. Remove from heat. Stir in bourbon. Serve warm over vanilla ice cream or plain pound cake.

Serves 6-8

Peanut Butter Ice Cream Topping

½   cup sugar
½   cup water
1   (7 ounce) jar marshmallow creme

2   teaspoons chocolate syrup
2   teaspoons butterscotch topping
⅔   cup peanut butter

Bring sugar and water to a boil. Boil for 2 minutes; cool. Add marshmallow crème, chocolate syrup, butterscotch topping and peanut butter and beat until smooth. Serve over vanilla ice cream. Refrigerate remaining topping. If sauce becomes too thick, thin with light corn syrup.

Serves 10

Spiced Pecans

1   large egg white
1   teaspoon water
2   cups pecan halves
½   cup sugar

1   teaspoon ground cinnamon
¼   teaspoon ground allspice
⅛   teaspoon freshly ground black pepper
    Cooking spray

Preheat oven to 250 degrees. Combine egg white and 1 teaspoon water in a small bowl, stirring with a whisk until frothy. Stir in pecans. Add sugar, cinnamon, allspice and black pepper, tossing to coat. Spread nut mixture on a jelly-roll pan coated with cooking spray. Bake for 45 minutes or until dry, stirring once. Cool completely.

Beyond the Fence Committee

CHAIR
Betty Gifford Simms

CO-CHAIRS
Kay Ross
Susan Germann Yackzan

RECIPE CHAIR
Jodi Bloom-Hadaway

RECIPE TESTING CO-CHAIRS
Laura Ashley Dennis
Jenny Bishop

PUBLIC RELATIONS
Geneva Donaldson
Dr. Marta Stone Hayne
Patricia A. Mohrhusen

FINANCE
Donna P. Ghobadi

MARKETING
Ruth Ann Childers

SPONSORSHIP
Ted Collins
Tim Terry

HISTORICAL EDITOR
Margaret Adams Lane

ASSISTANT HISTORICAL EDITOR
Elizabeth Whitney Simms

PHOTOGRAPHY
Marc Manning

Biographical Sketches

After spending twenty years as a graphic arts professional, native Kentuckian **Marc Manning** created a full time business from his lifelong hobby of photography. Inspired by the natural grandeur of Kentucky and a love of the grace and beauty of the horse, Mr. Manning maintains an ongoing commitment to capturing and showcasing the Bluegrass Region for others. Manning's photographs have appeared on the cover and within the pages of national and international publications, including the cover of *Magnificent Stables,* which was published in Paris, France and distributed worldwide. Producer of a series of fine art photography featuring the beauty of the Bluegrass, Mr. Manning lives in Versailles.

Beyond the Fence organizers commissioned Marc Manning to capture Bluegrass Region landscapes and culinary scenes. Other than specifically-credited images, photography was created exclusively for this project or chosen from Mr. Manning's stock portfolio.

"Within a few months, our family lost both my mother and my wife's mother to cancer. It is a personal privilege to participate with the Central Baptist Cancer Program in a project that supports its mission." Marc Manning

Native Kentuckian, **Margaret Lane,** a professional educator, served three gubernatorial terms as Executive Director of Kentucky's Lieutenant Governor's Mansion and the 1914 Governor's Mansion. In 2002, Mrs. Lane coauthored *The People's House, Governor's Mansions of Kentucky* with Kentucky's Historian Laureate Dr. Thomas D. Clark. After directing Visitor Services at the Clark Center for Kentucky History, Mrs. Lane served as Anniversary Historian for the Kentucky Community & Technical College System in 2008, editing *Metamorphosis, KCTCS 10th Anniversary*. Publication of *Anderson's Legacy, Fifty Years of Belcan Corporation* followed in 2008. Inductee into the University of Kentucky Human and Development Sciences Hall of Fame, Mrs. Lane lives in Woodford County.

Serving as Historical Editor for *Beyond the Fence,* Margaret Lane coordinated research and text for historical and cultural entries.

"As an eighth-generation Kentuckian, I am proud and honored to participate in a project that not only supports a very worthy cause, but showcases our beloved Bluegrass."
Margaret Lane

Native Lexingtonian, **Whitney Simms,** graduate of Sayre School, received her degree from the University of Mississippi in 2009 with majors in History and Anthropology. Serving as assistant historical editor, Miss Simms participated in research and text preparation for the cultural entries in *Beyond the Fence.*

Special Acknowledgements

Beyond the Fence: A Culinary View of Historic Lexington represents the generous contribution of countless individuals, organizations and businesses who shared their cherished recipes, time, expertise and support. Our deepest gratitude goes to those listed and to anyone we may have inadvertently failed to mention.

Bluegrass Trust for Historical Preservation

Central Baptist Hospital
    Cardiac Rehabilitation
    Food & Nutrition Department
    Medical Auxiliary

Keeneland
    Ted Bassett
    Chef Ed Boutilier, Turf Catering
    Amy Petit
    Phyllis Rogers
    Fran Taylor

Kentucky Historical Society Research Division

Kentucky Horse Park

Lexington Farmers' Market

Lexington History Museum

Research Staff, Kentucky Room at the
    Lexington Public Library

Kelly Anderson

Kathy Barlow

Ted Barnes

Missy Bartley

Mary Buckles

Montell Buckles

Victor Buenrostro

Ted Collins

Melissa and Daniel Doss

Laura Dicks

Doug Drewes

Jason Flahardy, University of Kentucky Archives

Tammy Flora

B.J. Gooch, Transylvania University Library

Sonne Graham

Brad Hadaway

Betty and Franklin Hoopes

Lori Hudson

Barb Johnson

Brenda Kocher

Steve Kries

Erin Lykins

Lisa Manning

Pam Miller

Jamie Morgan

Nancy Potter

Edward Receski

Virginia and Jerome Redfearn

Warren Rosenthal

David Saier

Veronica Shepherd

Denise Simpson

Tim Terry

John Walker

Sharon Wallace

Vanessa White

Becky Witt

Barb Zangari

Recipe Contributors

Gayle Abbott

Jean Abner

Mary M. Adams

Greg Adams

Karen Arnold

Leslie B. Baldwin

Diane Barnett

Missy Bartley

Betty Bartley

Denise Baugh

Joy Benedict

Governor and Mrs. Steve Beshear
– The Kentucky Governor's
Mansion

Todd Best

Jenny Bishop

Shirley Bishop

Ruby Miriam Bissett

Linda Bloom

Lacey Bloom

Helen Bloom (deceased)

Bluegrass Hospitality Group –
Malone's / Sal's Chophouse

Michele Boggs

Charlene Boggs

Willena Boggs (deceased)

Joe Bologna – Joe Bologna's
Restaurant and Pizzeria

Chef Ed Boutilier – Keeneland's
Turf Catering

Michael Bradley

Nancy Barkley Brannen

Montell Buckles

Victor Buenrostro

Gene C. Bunnell

Anne T. Campbell

Robin Campbell –
Cheapside Bar and Grill

Liz Carnal

Marilyn Caswell

Central Baptist Hospital Clinical
Nutrition Service

Joyce Christopher

Melanie B. Collins

Laura Colliver

Ellen Cornett

Dr. Hope Cottrill

Chef Chris Cox – The Mousetrap

Caroline Cramer

Mary Ann Davis

Nancy DeLetto

Phyllis Dennis

Laura Ashley Dennis

Mary Davis Dicken

Julie Stone Dickie

Lois Dixon

Geneva Donaldson

Shirley S. Dougherty

Cassie Downing

Chef Phil Dunn

Ann Evans – Executive Director
Kentucky Governor's Mansion

Mariann Falco

Karen Famularo

Rhonda Fister

Andrea French

S. J. Garner

Gloria R. Germann

Donna Ghobadi

Debbie Gibson

Mary Lee Goff

Patty Good

Sonne Graham

Ann Griesinger

Wendy Doyle Griffin

Dolores Guiler

Jodi Bloom Hadaway

Eleri Hadaway

Hannah Hadaway

Mary Wis Haggin

Marta Hayne

Annabelle Hensley

Greg Higgins – Magee's Bakery

Karen S. Hill

Genelle Wager Hix

Judy Holmes

Mary Lou Horning

Tina Howard

Cynthia Williams Insko

Diane Irvin

Mollie Jameson

Kendra Jarnagin

Frankie Johnson

Continued on next page

Barbara Johnson

Eleanor Fox Kelly

Cathy Kennedy

Penny Knight

Sharon Koser

Margaret Lane

Lynne Santen Lewis

Ken Lewis

Beth Liette

Kathy Long

Debbie Long, Chef Jonathan
    Gossett — Dudley's on Short

Brittany Lucci

Chef Jonathan Lundy –
    Jonathan at Gratz Park

Beth Clayton Luthye

Heather Lynn

Patricia T. Mason

Mae C. Mason (deceased)

Teresa Kennedy McReynolds

Merrick Inn Restaurant

Victoria Meyer

Jan Miller

Pat Mohrhusen

Annette Mohrhusen

Diane Monahan

Kathleen Mook

Shannon Morrill-Cornelius

Jason Mouser

Jessica Mullins

Teresa Snipes Myers

Marie Neal

Tootsie Nelson – The Coach House

Douglas M. Neuman

Paul Nowacki – Alfalfa Restaurant

Dr. Mehmet Oz

Betty Sue Palmer

Tammy Patsey

Nancy Peggs

Joy Pennington

Ann Peppard

Amy Peppard

Lynne Marie Popela

Barbara K. Potts

Kinch Query

Georgia Rachelson

Marilyn Raider

Rob Ramsey-Ramsey's Diners

Gay Reading, Chef John Martin –
    Ginkgo Tree Café and
    Greentree Tearoom

Martha Reed

Gretchen Rice

Sharon Adams Richter

Amanda Robbins

Kay Ross

Diana Ross

Debbie Rossell

Jill Sawyer

Carrie Sewell

Iman Shalash

Lola Shellenberger

Cindy Shryock

Betty Gifford Simms

Dorothy Smith (deceased)

Julie Smith

Julia T. Smith

Pat Soister

Colbey Penton Sparkman

Wilma L. Spicer

Melba Stambaugh

Kathleen Stanley

Sonya Sullivan

Sue Thomas

Rose Thomas

Sharon Thompson – Lexington
    Herald Leader Food Editor

Rebekah Meador Tilley

Estine Tipton

Audrey Magee Vasher

Amy Vittitow

Lyn Voige

Feather L. Wafford

Mary Lynn Walsh

Elaine Ward

Brenda Watts

Philip Weisenberger –
    Weisenberger Mills

Heather Wetzel

Frances Whitman

Betty R. Williams

Pat Wilson

Deanna Wolfinbarger

Rebecca Wolfinbarger

Max Wolfinbarger

Karen Lewis Woodrum

Susan Yackzan

Morwenna Yackzan (deceased)

Laura Yost

Patty Zutt

Recipe Testers

Gayle Abbott
Mary Margaret Adams
Kelly Anderson
Pamela K. Anderson
Vonda Arvin
Barbara Asbury
Jennifer Baker
Kathy Barlow
Diane Barnett
Missy Bartley
Joy Benedict
Jenny Bishop
Janisse Bishop
Linda Bloom
Lacey Bloom
Charlene Boggs
Pam Bracken
Michael Bradley
Mary Buckles
Quincy Chamberlain
Ruth Ann Childers
Joyce Christopher
Shawna Clifton
Laura Colliver
Liz Combs
Chris Corkins
Lauren Craig
Caroline Cramer
Nancy DeLetto
Phyllis Dennis
Laura Ashley Dennis
Lois Dixon

Geneva Donaldson
Shirley Dougherty
Brenda Draft
Lelia Elam
Kathy Gates
Gloria Germann
Donna Ghobadi
Alena Glass
Patty Good
Sonne Graham
Larry Gray
Mary Ida Gray
Kim Green
Eleri Hadaway
Bradford Hadaway
Jodi Bloom Hadaway
Patti Hafner
Stephanie Hallman
Mary Ann Harlan
Judy Hatch
Rob Hayne
Dr. Marta Hayne
Erin Hayne
Karen Hill
Genelle Hix
Judy Holmes
Penny Howell
Wilma Howell
Cynthia Insko
Mollie Jameson
Barbara Johnson
Penny Knight

Lynn Rikhoff Kolokowsky
Margaret Lane
Becky Lewis
Wendy Lisanby
Regan Lookadoo
Angie Malone
Fred Malone
Denise McCowan
Victoria Meyer
Betsy Miller
Pat Mohrhusen
Shannon Morrill-
    Cornelius
Monica Mosley
Jessica Mullins
Elouise Mullins
Sharon Niece
Heather Noe
Betty Nolan
Julie Northrop
Elizabeth Payton
Nancy Peggs
Ann Peppard
Amy Peppard
Carolyn Perkins
Della Piersall
Martha Proctor
Michelle Purdom
Judy Purdom
Darlene Reed
Gretchen Rice
Sharon Richter

Jane Rogers
Diana Ross
Kay Ross
Julie Rutland
Iman Shalash
Mariam Shalash
Veronica Shepherd
Betty Simms
Julie Smith
Annetta Speaks
Patricia Spragne
Kathleen Stanley
Micheal Stephens
Daniel Stinnett
April Stone
Rose Thomas
Kathy Thurston
Estine Tipton
Marilyn Tyree
Amy Vittitow
Debra Wagner
Amanda Walker
Elbert Walters
Heather Wetzel
Peggy Wheeler
Ann White
Fran Williams
Rebecca Woltinbarger
Susan Yackzan
Laura Yost
Patty Zutt

Seasonal Recipe Index

Sides

Sides (continued)

Breads

Desserts

Desserts (continued)

Recipe Index

Desserts

Entrées

Poultry

Salads

Sides

Soups

Historical Index

Bibliography

2010 ALLTECH FEI WORLD EQUESTRIAN GAMES — *2008 Kentucky Horse Park Magazine, Alltech FEI Brochure, southernlightsky.org*

AGRICULTURE — *fayettealliance.com, visitlex.com 2006*

ALE — *A Pint of History: Lexington Brewing Company, kentuckyale.com*

ALFALFA RESTAURANT — *Simms Interview: Paul Nowacki, Alfalfa Restaurant*

ARBORETUM — *uky.edu/arboretum*

ARTISTRY IN MARBLE — *Lexington, A Century in Photographs–Bettie Kerr and John D. Wright*

ASHLAND: THE HENRY CLAY ESTATE — *Lexington Legacies, Milward, Ashland website,
    Southern United States: An Environmental History, Davis*

BARNS OF THE BLUEGRASS — *Kentucky Bluegrass Country, R. Gerald Alvey, Stable Environment, Sharon Reynolds, Keeneland
    Magazine July, 2008*

BEATEN BISCUITS — *www.dianasdesserts.com, Alvey*

BEER CHEESE — *hallsontheriver.com*

BIBB LETTUCE — *Alvey, Kentucky Encyclopedia*

BLUEGRASS LAND PRESERVATION — *wmf.org/USA_Ken_bluegrass, Bluegrass Conservancy, Lexington Herald 9-30-09*

BLUEGRASS SUPERSTITIONS — *Alvey, Good luck, Bad luck…by Ed Madary Keeneland Magazine – March, 2008*

BLUE GRASS TRUST FOR HISTORIC PRESERVATION — *volunteer.united-e-way.org*

BODLEY-BULLOCK HOUSE — *Gratz Park, Blue Grass Trust, Historic Lexington Tours*

BOURBON — *National Register of Historic Places webstie: nps.gov, Lexington and the Bluegrass Country…
    Workers of the Federal Writers' Project*

BURGOO — *KY Hospitality, a 200-Year Tradition, The Kentucky, Thomas D. Clark, Alvey*

CALUMET — *Lexington Dreamer Driving Tour, Lexington Tourism Map*

CALUMET BAKING POWDER — *Wikipedia, Calumet Baking Powder*

CATTLE — *Kentucky Encyclopedia, A New History of Kentucky, James Klotter, fayettealliance.com*

COOKING WITH BOURBON — *Bourbon Review Summer 2001*

COUNTRY HAM — *Alvey*

DIXIANA AND DOMINO STUD — *Lane interview/Tim Terry, www.dixianafarms.com, www.ntra.com*

DUNCAN HINES — *www.wku.edu/Library, Duncan Hines, The Man behind the Cake Mix, Louis Hatchett*

EARLY SCHOOLS — *Works Progress Administration, 1938*

EARLY TAVERNS AND HOTELS — *Historic Photos of Lexington, W. Gay Reading, Herald Leader…Betty Lee Mastin,
    The Phoenix 1797-1981, 6-15-92*

ELMENDORF — *James Ben Ali Haggin, a Biography, Lexington, Heart of the Bluegrass, John D. Wright, Jr.*

EQUINE BILL OF FARE — *extension.com/horses diet, Lane interviews: Libby Jones, Tim Terry*

EXPRESSIONS: BELOW THE SALT, BRING HOME THE BACON, CHEW THE FAT, COOKING FROM SCRATCH, GET YOUR GOAT, SALAD DAYS — *Food Safety Association, International Food Safety Network, Alvey*

FASIG-TIPTON — *fasigtipton.com*

FAYETTE COUNTY'S COURTHOUSES — *Lexington Herald-Leader, 10-2-2009, KHS Historical Marker Series*

FAYETTE COUNTY'S EARLY CHURCHES — *Lexington and the Bluegrass Country, The American Gudie Series 1938*

FIRST NEWSPAPER: KENTUCKE GAZETTE — *Works Progress Administration*

FURNITURE MAKERS — *Antiques in Kentucky, James Cogar, Lexington Herald, 12-28-1974, Wright*

GAINESWAY AND STONESTREET — *stonestreetfarms.com, Kentucky General Assembly Resolution, 2005, Kentucky Encyclopedia, gainesway.com*

GENERAL MARQUIS DE LAFAYETTE — *Wright*

GIRON'S CONFECTIONARY — *Wright, Lex Walking Tour Brochure*

GRATZ PARK — *Antiques in Kentucky Historic Preservation: Gratz Park in Lexington, Works Progress Administration*

HEADLEY-WHITNEY MUSEUM — *headley-whitney.com, Ladies Home Journal, 11-67*

HEMP IN LEXINGTON — *Kentucky Encyclopedia, A New History of Kentucky, James Klotter, Wright*

HENRY CLAY'S 19TH CENTURY MINT JULEP RECIPE — *Ashland, The Henry Clay Estate*

HORSE MANIA — *horseracing.about.com, www.americantowns.com/ky/lexington*

HUNT-MORGAN HOUSE — *Hunt-Morgan House, Gratz Park, Blue Grass Trust, Historic Lexington Tours*

IROQUOIS HUNT CLUB — *www.iroquoishunt.com, Grimes Mill – Kentucky Landmark on Boone Creek Fayette County – Harry G. Enoch*

ISAAC MURPHY — *KY Horse Park the National Horse Center, V. Lynn Reynolds, 2000, the wellwroughturn.wordpress. com/2009/07/18*

JERRICO — *Fast Food Magazine, July 1972, Lane Interview: Warren Rosenthal*

JOCKEY CLUB — *jockeyclub.com, Name Game Coleman Larkin, Keeneland Magazine, July, 2008*

JOE BOLOGNA'S RESTAURANT & PIZZERIA — *joebologna's.com*

JOYLAND PARK AND DANCE CASINO — *www.redb.com, Wright*

KEENELAND — *Kentucky Encyclopedia, Keeneland.com*

KEENELAND'S TRACK KITCHEN…BLUEGRASS BREAKFAST SECRET — *Simms/Lane interview: Ed Boutilier, Chef, Turf Catering*

KENTUCKY AGRICULTURE SOCIETY — *Silver in Kentucky Life 1780-1870, 1980, Antiques: Ante-bellum Kentucky Silver, Henry H. Harned*

KENTUCKY ASSOCIATION — *WPA: 1938: RACING, Wright, Alvey*

KENTUCKY COLONELS — *kycolonels.org*

KENTUCKY FRIED CHICKEN — *kfc.com*

KENTUCKY GATE — *"Gates," Alvey, city directory, 1941*

KENTUCKY HORSE PARK — *2008 Kentucky Horse Park Magazine, southernlightsky.org*

KENTUCKY HOT BROWN — *Brownhotel.com*

LEXINGTON CEMETERY — *A History of The Lexington Cemetery, Burton Milward*

LEXINGTON FARMERS MARKETS — *Works Progress Administration Publication, 1930, lexingtonfarmersmarket.com*

LEXINGTON OPERA HOUSE — *Wright, Lexington A Century in Photographs, Kerr and Wright*

LEXINGTON ORPHAN SOCIETY — *Music in Lexington before 1840, Joy Carden, Lexington Herald-Leader, 2-4-1973*

LEXINGTON PUBLIC LIBRARY — *Lexington Legacies, Milward, Lexington Tourism Brochure*

LEXINGTON SILVERSMITHS — *Silver in Kentucky Life 1780-1870, 1980, Antiques: Ante-bellum Kentucky Silver, Henry H. Harned*

LEXINGTON'S THEATERS — *kywurlitzer.netfirms.com/kyth.htm, Reading, Herald Leader, October 1, 1922*

LUCRETIA CLAY'S ICE CREAM — *American Heritage Magazine, October, 1956, Everybody Liked Henry Clay*

MADAM BELLE BREZING — *Madam Belle Brezing, E.I. "Buddy" Thompson, Belle Brezing Photographic Collection, 1868-1983 UK Special Collections*

MAGEE'S BAKERY — *www.mageesbakery, Simms/Higgins Interview*

MALONE'S — *bluegrasshospitality.com*

MAN O' WAR — *Kentucky Encyclopedia, Alvey*   .

MARY TODD LINCOLN HOUSE — *Historic Houses of Lexington: 1996, www.mtlhouse.org, White Cake Recipe: Notecard Series*

MAXWELL SPRINGS…MAXWELL PLACE — *Kentucky Encyclopedia*

MCCONNELL SPRINGS — *National Parks Service website, WPA*

MEMORABLE MENUS:
   BROOKINGS, CANARY COTTAGE, COACH HOUSE, GOLDEN HORSESHOE, KEITH'S, (1941 CITY DIRECTORY), LITTLE INN, WINGS TEA HOUSE — *Menus Courtesy Bettye and Franklin Hoopes, Jerome and Virginia Redfearn, Bob Shaw*
   DUTCH MILL RESTAURANT — *October 31, 1970 Herald Leader, KY Historical Society Vertical Files, Hoopes*
   HUTCHINSON DRUG — *The Freezer, October 31, 1970 Herald Leader, KHS*
   NAVARRE CAFÉ — *Wright*
   ROGERS RESTAURANT, THE SARATOGA — *March 30, 2008, Herald Leader, Old Menus, Sharon Thompson*

MERRICK INN — *Merrick Inn Menu*

MINT JULEP — *Kentucky Encyclopedia, Irvin S. Cobb's Own Recipe Book, 1936*

MOCK MINT JULEP — *ale8one.com*

MONTICULE — *monticule.com, www.monticule.com/keeneland-2007*

MUSIC AND CHARITY IN "THE ATHENS OF THE WEST" — *Carden, www.lexsing.org, History of Lexington Kentucky, George W. Ranck*

NOTABLE NEIGHBOR: ALE-8-ONE — *winchester.com*

NOTABLE NEIGHBOR: CASTLEPOST — *thecastlepost.com, Lexington Landmark, The Castle, 2008 Kentucky Horse Park Magazine*

NOTABLE NEIGHBOR: HIGHBRIDGE SPRING WATER — *www.highbridgesprings.com, Kentucky Encyclopedia*

NOTABLE NEIGHBOR: KENTUCKY RIVER PALISADES — *Kentucky River Palisades, Taylor, www.nature.org*

NOTABLE NEIGHBORS: KENTUCKY EXECUTIVE MANSIONS — *The People's House, Governor's Mansions of Kentucky, Thomas D. Clark and Margaret A. Lane*

NOTABLE NEIGHBOR: REBECCA RUTH CANDY FACTORY — *rebecca-ruth-candies.com, atasteofkentucky.com*

NOTABLE NEIGHBORS: THE SHAKERS — *Kentucky Hospitality, a 200-Year Tradition, Bees in America, Tammy Horn, The Kentucky Shakers, Julia Neal*

NOTABLE NEIGHBOR: WEISENBERGER MILL — *Philip Weisenberger*

OLD FAIR GROUNDS AND FLORAL HALL — *www.theredmile.com, Lexington Herald-Leader 4-19-1964, Kentucky Encyclopedia*

OLD KENTUCKY CHOCOLATES — *oldkycandy.com*

OVERBROOK FARM — *www.foodreference.com, overbrookfarm.com, Kentucky Encyclopedia*

PARIS PIKE — *Dreamer Tour…Paris Pike, appaloosa.ktc.engr.uky.edu, www.drystone.org*

PARKETTE DRIVE-IN — *Lexington Herald-Leader, March 30, 2008, Old Menus…Sharon Thompson*

PEDDLERS AND PROVISIONS — *Wright, Reading*

PHOENIX HANDICAP — *Alvey*

POLO IN THE PARK — *2008 Kentucky Horse Park Magazine*

PORTRAIT ARTISTS — *William P. Welsh, Painter and Patriot, William P. Welsh Society, Kentucky Encyclopedia*

PURSE TO THE VICTOR — *sarahmarr.com, Works Progress Administration: 1938*

RACING SILKS — *sarahmarr.com, Works Progress Administration: 1938*

RED MILE STANDARDBREDS — *www.theredmile.com*

ROLEX KENTUCKY THREE-DAY EVENT — *Rolex: 2008 Kentucky Horse Park Magazine*

SADDLEBREDS AND LEXINGTON JUNIOR LEAGUE — *Kentucky Encyclopedia, Alvey, www.tsetattersalls.com/www.tattersalls.com*

SAL'S CHOPHOUSE — *Bluegrasshospitality.com*

SMILEY PETE… A FRIEND TO ALL — *lexingtonkentuckyhistory.blogspot.com, askus.bloginky.com, LuAnn Farrar*

SOUTHERN SWEET TEA — *whatscookingamerica.net*

SPALDING'S BAKERY — *Lexington Herald, The Wait is Over, 3-31-2006*

SPINDLETOP — *Lexington Herald .8-8-1974, spindletophall.org*

SPORTING ARTISTS — *Alvey, Antiques in Kentucky, Edward Troye, Sporting Artist*

THREE CHIMNEYS — *threechimneys.com*

THE POTATO CHIP — *Snack Food Association of America, The Potato Chip Cookbook, Mrs. C.V. Whitney, Keeneland Library*

TOBACCO HERITAGE — *Kentucky Encyclopedia, Handbook of Kentucky, Works Progress Administration*

TRANSYLVANIA UNIVERSITY — *Kentucky Encyclopedia, transy.edu*

UNIVERSITY OF KENTUCKY — *www.uky.edu, Kentucky Encyclopedia, www.ukathletics.com/athletic*

VALLEY VIEW FERRY — *www.lexingtonky.gov, Kentucky Encyclopedia*

WAVELAND — *Lexington Herald-Leader 4-2-1961, Historic Houses of Lexington, Lexington Convention Bureau Brochure*

WHITE THOROUGHBRED — *Jockey Club of America, Thewhitefox.com*

WHITNEY FARM — *Ladies Home Journal 11-67, Lexington Herald 1-20-62*

WINE — *Kentucky Winery Brochure*

WINSTAR FARM — *www.winstarfarm.com*

In Closing...

Sometimes we are bound by fences...sometimes the gate has been left open for us to venture through. Events in everyday life shape who we are and where we are going...sometimes we get to choose the journey and at other times, we don't. It is too often the struggle and challenge of this timeline that makes us look at life differently along the way and reconsider what is important.

The inspiration for *Beyond the Fence: A Culinary View of Historic Lexington* was shaped by personal journeys; passion for "comfort foods" that reflect family life and traditions; the seasonal beauty and history of the Bluegrass region and expressions of fear, anxiety and struggle by patients and their families as they face the realities of a cancer diagnosis.

My sincere gratitude is given to each person who shared a mutual belief in this project so that those who confront cancer are gently touched when they need it the most...

In memory of my husband, Scott, who courageously
confronted a nine month cancer diagnosis and died in 2001.

In honor of our children, Hunter and Whitney, whose journey through life will
forever be shaped by the untimely loss of their father. Thank you for embracing the
vision of this project and providing support along the way, even if it meant I didn't have
time to cook dinner when you were home or return your phone call!!

To the administration, medical staff, employees and volunteers of Central Baptist Hospital,
your commitment and wholehearted support to this book made it tangible.

We will be forever grateful to those individuals and organizations who
sustained our endeavor with their generous financial contributions. Through the
spearheading efforts of Ted Collins and his enthusiasm and support for Beyond the Fence,
we were able to underwrite this project in its entirety.

Each member of our committee served as a pivotal structure, bringing to the table an
abundance of professional talent, enthusiasm and finesse. A very special thank you to each
of you for sharing your time and talents as this book took on its own identity.

continued on next page

*The scope of this project would not have been fulfilled without
Marc Manning or Margaret Lane. I will always be grateful for the countless hours you
devoted to make sure that we showcased the beauty and history of Lexington and our notable
neighbors. You graciously accepted every request…your professional talent, friendship and
commitment over the past year brought this book to fruition.*

*To the recipe contributors and testers, thank you for sharing your timeless recipes,
family traditions and culinary skills that reflect generations of good food!*

*To my family and friends, I have missed you over the past 18 months…
thank you for your continuous support and encouragement. To Ed, thank you for all
of the hours you devoted to this project and for lending a listening ear, allowing the
evolution of "the cookbook" to be the topic of conversation on most days.*

Proceeds from *Beyond the Fence* will be earmarked as a means to meet the needs of cancer patients diagnosed and treated at Central Baptist Hospital. The needs are endless…it might be an attractive gown or robe for a woman to wear during treatment to preserve her femininity after she has just undergone a double mastectomy…to the husband or father who can not purchase the medication that he needs because he must feed his family… genetics…participation in a research trial…an elderly man or woman who has no family nearby or limited income that prohibits affordable transportation for medical care… education initiatives…the list goes on!!

"Janet" ~ Central Baptist Hospital Gardens

It is our commitment to sustain our patients with a power of knowledge, dignity, compassion and quality of life as they confront cancer. To each of you, I will forever be grateful of the overwhelming support you have provided to the fulfillment of this vision and the difference that it will make to the patients that we commit our lives to each day…thanks so much!!

Betty Gifford Simms
Beyond the Fence Chair

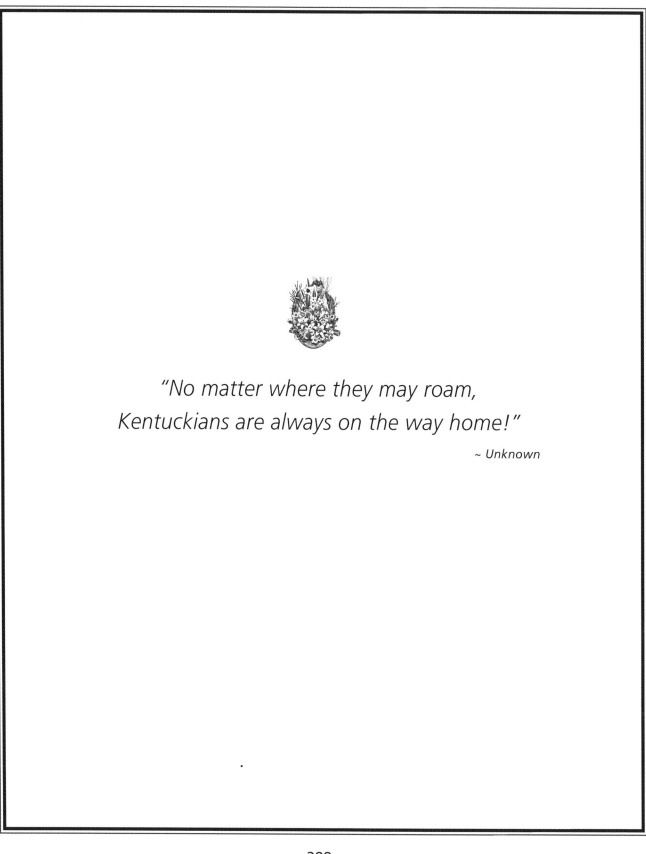

"No matter where they may roam,
Kentuckians are always on the way home!"

~ Unknown